SPREADSHEET PUBLISHING WITH
Quattro Pro

VENTANA

PRESS

SPREADSHEET PUBLISHING WITH
Quattro Pro

Producing effective, attractive charts, graphs, tables & presentations

For Versions 2.0 & 3.0

Christopher Van Buren

Spreadsheet Publishing With Quattro Pro
For Versions 2.0 and 3.0

Library of Congress Cataloging-in-Publication Data

Van Buren, Chris.
      Spreadsheet publishing with Quattro pro : for versions 2.0 and 3.0 / Christopher Van Buren. — 2nd ed.
        p.   cm.
      Includes bibliographical references and index.
      ISBN 0-940087-64-2
      1. Quattro pro (Computer program) 2. Electronic spreadsheets. 3. Business presentations—Graphic methods—Computer programs.
      I. Title.
      HF5548.4.Q39V36 1991
      650'.0285'5369—dc20   91-14986
                                CIP

Cover design: Nancy Frame, Durham, NC
Cover illustration: Gary Palmer, 1991
Book design: Karen Wysocki, Ventana Press
Editorial staff: Robert Bixby, Diana Cooper, Marion Laird, Jeff Qualls, Pam Richardson
Production staff: Rhonda Angel, Alex Taylor, Karen Wysocki
Technical reviewer: Stacy Eggimann, Borland International Product Support, Scotts Valley, CA

Clip-art images provided from the PicturePak™ clip-art libraries by Islandview/MGI.

Islandview/MGI, P.O. Box 11087, Richmond, VA 23230
800/368-3773; 804/673-5601; (fax) 804/285-7822

First Edition, First Printing
Printed in the United States of America

Ventana Press Inc.
P.O. Box 2468
Chapel Hill, NC 27515
919/942-0220
FAX 919/942-1140

LIMITS OF LIABILITY
AND DISCLAIMER OF WARRANTY

DEDICATION

For Trudy and our lives together

ACKNOWLEDGMENTS

Many people helped me with this book, and I would like to extend my gratitude to them: Thanks to Elizabeth, Joe, Marion, Pam, Robert, Diana, Karen, Rhonda, Alex, Jeff and all the great people at Ventana Press for their editing, art, proofing and other contributions—and for making this book a pleasure to work on. Thanks to Nan Borreson at Borland for excellent author support.

I would also like to thank Marketing Graphics Inc. (MGI) and Bitstream Inc. for supplying the excellent clip art and fonts (respectively) used throughout this book. Impact Graphics of San Carlos and Brilliant Image of New York supplied color slide imprint services. My friend and fellow author, Gordon McComb, helped with a needed hardware upgrade and CompuServe advice. Morris Wartenberger provided some useful ideas. Thanks to my agents, Bill Gladstone and Matt Wagner, for managing my career.

I am especially indebted to my wife, Trudy, for helping me organize this book and keeping me relatively sane throughout the past few years.

ABOUT THE AUTHOR

Veteran computer book author Christopher Van Buren has more than a dozen books to his credit, including *Using Excel 3 Macintosh Version, Quattro Pro in Business* and *The First Book of Excel 3 for Windows*. He has written and designed several computer newsletters and has consulted with firms on marketing communications and publication design. He's also been a product marketing manager for a San Diego-based software company.

The author can be reached at

P.O. Box 117144
Burlingame, CA 94010

TRADEMARKS

Trademarked names appear throughout this book. Rather than list the names and entities that own the trademarks or insert a trademark symbol with each mention of the trademarked name, the publisher states that it is using the names only for editorial purposes and to the benefit of the trademark owner with no intention of infringing upon that trademark.

Contents

Introduction

First it was computer graphics. Then desktop publishing. Now . . . spreadsheet publishing? Obviously, a newsletter or product brochure has to look good and communicate quickly. But do we really have to *design* spreadsheets, too? In case you think this is carrying things too far, you have only to look around, and think about your own responses to what you read and what you see on TV. Good design enhances any kind of presentation. And things are often bought and sold based on the way they're presented. A presentation can make you and your message look stupid, smart, unprepared, organized, detailed, aggressive or—you name it. If you present that message well, you'll make your point more convincingly and accomplish what you set out to do. That's the bottom line. Design and presentation can have a direct effect on your success (and your income).

People who work with numbers are beginning to understand that today's spreadsheets should do more than calculate numbers and produce ponderous tables of values. And you can bet that your competitors are thinking about this, too.

Spreadsheet Publishing With Quattro Pro shows you how to use this program's sophisticated features to follow the trend toward design excellence. You'll find the tools you need to make your documents present a more powerful message. And you'll learn how and when to apply these tools. Chances are, you'll find that it takes as much work to design poorly as it does to design well.

I hope some of the examples will provide ideas you can use to increase the effectiveness of your reports, forms, tables, graphs, organization chharts and slide presentations.

WHO NEEDS THIS BOOK?

If you communicate numerical or graphical information, you should be using spreadsheet publishing concepts. Any time you prepare a document that includes a spreadsheet—a document that will be seen by others—you should "spreadsheet publish" it. This applies to financial reports, graphs of sales activity or any other type of business analysis. And if you plan to use Quattro Pro to do this, you'll find all the help you need in this book.

HOW TO USE THIS BOOK

You don't need to know much about Quattro Pro to start using this book. All the steps required for a procedure are provided alongside the explanations. These steps are concise and will serve as an excellent reference later on. You can skip over these steps if you already know them.

On the other hand, this is not a basic guide to Quattro Pro. It's not an advanced guide to Quattro Pro. It contains some basic, some intermediate and some advanced techniques to choose from. And you'll probably learn about things you never knew you could do with Quattro Pro. But the main purpose of this book is to help you use Quattro Pro's features to design your spreadsheets and presentations.

The first section, "Quattro Pro's Publishing Powers," gives you an overview on spreadsheet publishing and introduces you to formatting spreadsheets, creating graphs and using fonts, printers and the Annotator's graphics tools.

The next section of the book, "Putting It All Together," focuses on print media—from design planning to producing the printed pages—and on designing and producing slides, overhead transparencies and screen shows.

The last section, "Design in Action," offers a treasury of "right" and "wrong" design examples and a summary of design do's and don'ts.

A Resources section at the end of the book contains product listings and additional sources of information on Quattro Pro and design.

You may also want to have the book's companion diskette, which contains examples used in this book, spreadsheet templates, graph templates, clip-art images, fonts, slide backgrounds, special utilities and more. Look for a complete description and ordering information in the back of the book.

—Christopher Van Buren

SECTION

QUATTRO PRO'S PUBLISHING POWER

Spreadsheet Publishing Power 1

Welcome to spreadsheet publishing. This is where dull, life-less spreadsheets full of numbers become exciting and appealing presentations. You'll find that spreadsheet publishing concepts apply to anything you can produce with a spreadsheet program—graphs, tables, presentation overheads, financial reports to name a few. With the help of *Spreadsheet Publishing With Quattro Pro*, you'll be able to make your presentations do more and say more.

But before creating those power presentations, let's take a moment to review some basics about spreadsheet publishing, Quattro Pro and your computer system. Many of the topics covered in this chapter are discussed in greater detail later in the book.

PUBLISHING REDEFINED

Spreadsheet publishing is the hot new computer lingo. But what does it mean? The phrase generally describes the process of designing and printing presentation materials with a spreadsheet program. Although most of these materials will never be published in the strict sense of the word, you don't have to be printing camera-ready pages for your annual report or preparing a slide show for an important client to be using spreadsheet publishing. Anything you produce from a spreadsheet that will be shown to another person (or people) qualifies as spreadsheet publishing.

Spreadsheet publishing generally refers to documents and reports that include

- Financial reports
- Budgets
- Expense reports
- Forms
- Graphs
- Databases
- Tables of figures
- Comparison charts

These documents and graphics are produced for the following media:

- Printed pages
- Slides
- Overhead transparencies
- On-screen images

You'll find that the medium you use to communicate information has as much influence on design and format as the message itself. Each of these media has its advantages and design specifications, which you should weigh carefully as you create your project. Let's look at the media and the special design and production considerations that will affect your spreadsheet publishing projects.

THE UBIQUITOUS PRINTED PAGE

Besides being the most common form of communication (next to jabbering), printed pages can be the most effective medium for your presentations. Throughout this book, you'll learn to construct better reports by considering some of the following basic questions.

- Are you using good page composition, including effective use of white space?

- Have you chosen the appropriate fonts to communicate your message? Are you getting the most from your printer and its fonts?

- Are your graphs communicating effectively?

- Will your printouts use color, shades of gray, or black and white?

- Are you using good basic design sense for your graphs, tables, financial reports and forms?

Because people look at printed matter all the time, they may be fairly indifferent to another piece of paper. So your printed reports have to grab their attention. If your spreadsheet published pages appear with word processed pages, make sure the entire report maintains design consistency and the same level of sophistication.

You probably already have a printer capable of giving you effective spreadsheet output. Many inexpensive printers can produce attractive pages from Quattro Pro. Your particular printer may dictate some of the features you can use in Quattro Pro. This is discussed in Chapter 4, "Fonts and Printers," and Chapter 7, "Printing Reports."

SLIDES: COLORFUL MESSENGERS

A slide is generally used as part of a slide show. Typically, each slide is viewed for only a few seconds. Therefore, it must communicate quickly. Each slide should be designed to convey a simple message without a lot of clutter or extra material. If you need to pack information onto a slide presentation, then you need more than one slide.

Slides always use color, and the nature of projection can make them bright and impressive. They're displayed "larger than life" to a captive audience. So use color and graphics to your advantage. (Chapter 8, "Designing Slides, Overheads and Screen Shows," will give you a lot of tips and examples.)

People are used to seeing exciting, colorful projected images in films and on television and billboards. Your slide presentation must strive for the same level of appeal.

But slides must also be believable. Slides should come across as information, not as hype. Audiences are pretty sophisticated; underestimating them can kill your presentation.

Here are some basic considerations about slide production.

- Do your slides use compatible colors and avoid bad color combinations? Do the colors communicate what you want them to?
- Do your slides have too much information on them, or is the information too small to be read?
- Do all the slides in your presentation use the same basic color and design schemes?
- Do the headlines and lists in your slides communicate effectively?
- Are the graphics in your slides appropriate and well designed?

Many of these questions are discussed in Chapter 9, "Creating Slides, Overheads and Screen Shows." But the information in Chapter 3, "Creating Effective Graphs," and Chapter 5, "Using the Annotator," will also be helpful.

To create a color slide with Quattro Pro, you'll need to work with a service bureau that has slide-making capability. Be sure to ask which formats they can accept. Quattro Pro can save your graphs in EPS, Slide EPS, PIC and PCX formats. (Details about creating and saving slides appear in Chapter 9.)

PROJECTING WITH OVERHEADS

Overhead transparencies are similar to slides in that they're projected in a darkened room. But there the similarities end. Overhead presentations usually involve more speaker interaction with the media. The narrator is often changing the transparencies as he or she gives the presentation. Presenters commonly point to the screen to emphasize information.

Transparency presentations generally require fewer images than slide shows, and each overhead is displayed for a longer time. Overheads are often vertically oriented, with dimensions similar to a printed page. Therefore, your transparencies can be designed more like a page than a slide.

Often, transparencies are created in black and white, because they're produced from a black-and-white page on a photocopier. Here are some things we will be considering about overheads:

* If your overheads are in color, do they use color effectively?

* Are you using good page composition, including effective use of white space?

* Are your font choices appropriate and readable?

* Are graphics used appropriately?

Many of these issues are equally important to the printed medium. You'll be able to apply many of the concepts from Chapter 6, "Designing Effective Pages," to your overhead transparencies. Additional information about overheads is covered in Chapters 8 and 9.

DYNAMIC ON-SCREEN IMAGES

On-screen images are dependent upon the hardware being used. Color, black and white, VGA, EGA—all of these are considerations. For best results, create the show using the machine (or equivalent hardware) on which it will be displayed. A black-and-white VGA monitor is treated as a color monitor by Quattro Pro, but it displays color as shades of gray. Analog and digital monitors behave differently also. Hardware considerations are addressed beginning on page 10.

Screen shows are usually viewed by one person at a time. Often, they're interactive, meaning the viewer controls the flow and order of images. Because the viewer can pause at any time, and is relatively close to the monitor, screen images can contain more information than slides. But in some aspects, screen shows are very much like slide shows.

- Both use the same basic dimensions for the image.
- Both are usually given in color.
- Both are progressive and use many images to communicate the message.

But there are also many differences between these two media.

- Slide shows are not interactive, whereas screen shows can involve audience interaction.
- Screens can remain in view for several minutes, whereas slides are usually changed quickly.
- Screens are closer to the viewer's eyes and can contain more information and smaller type than slides.
- Interactive screen shows do not have narration, but must provide all the information right on the screens.

Chapter 8 gives details about designing effective screen shows.

QUATTRO PRO'S SPREADSHEET FEATURES

Of the various spreadsheet programs on the market, Quattro Pro is especially well adapted to spreadsheet publishing tasks. Its printing capabilities take full advantage of laser printers with 300 dots-per-inch (dpi) resolution. And you can access the built-in fonts of your PostScript or LaserJet printer. In fact, output quality is one of Quattro Pro's strongest suits.

Following is a summary of some of the spreadsheet publishing features offered in Quattro Pro Versions 2.0 and 3.0.

SPREADSHEET PUBLISHING WITH VERSION 2.0:

Number Formats
Automatic number formats make your numeric information more attractive. They control decimal places and special numeric symbols, such as dollar signs, commas and percent signs. Quattro Pro doesn't let you create your own custom

formats; but you can produce some interesting results using formulas. (See Chapter 2, "Formatting Spreadsheets," for some ideas.)

Date Formats

Date formats are an extension of number formats, since dates are really just numbers. Quattro Pro offers the basic array of formats for dates and you can add to these with formulas.

Fonts

Quattro Pro gives you up to eight fonts per spreadsheet, and provides high-quality Bitstream fonts. Quattro Pro also gives you access to your printer's built-in fonts. Using the screen preview feature, you can see what these fonts will look like on the final printout. You can also use fonts on your graphs— not just the eight fonts available for the spreadsheet, but as many as you like.

Column Widths

Column widths have an effect on alignment and printing. By changing column widths, you can change the amount of information that fits on a page. Column width also affects the white space on a page, which controls the lightness or darkness of a page. Column widths can be used for indenting listed items.

Lines and Borders

Adding graphic lines and borders to your spreadsheets helps you organize information into sections and blocks. Available in various thicknesses and styles, those elements can also be used to add visual interest to your documents. You can also use them to create forms and tables.

Shades

Quattro Pro gives you gray and black shades for your spreadsheets. Blocks of black shading automatically reverse the type contained in them. Reversed type is an effective way to draw attention to certain information. Gray shades are useful for highlighting information in a report or form.

Graphs

You can communicate numeric data by using various types of graphs, such as several 3D graphs. You can also control individual aspects of these graphs, such as the color and pattern of the data series and the values along the X- and Y-axis.

Text Graphs

A text graph is just an empty graph screen. This is useful for creating simple graphic images using Quattro Pro's annotation tools. You can add these drawings to the spreadsheet or to other graphs. You can also incorporate them into a slide show as information slides, lists or titles.

Graph Annotation

The Annotator provides drawing and editing tools for enhancing graphs or for creating drawings. You can add text, lines, boxes, buttons and more. The results can be used on your spreadsheets to enhance your printed presentation, or they can be used as slides for a slide show.

Printing

Quattro Pro lets you select from numerous printers and keep two settings active for repeated use. You can access your printer's various modes for different print resolutions and can print using draft- or final-quality fonts. Print layout options affect the orientation of the report, its margins and other aspects.

Screen Shows

You can display a sequence of graphs or graphic images as a sort of on-screen slide show. Using macros and graph buttons, you can make this show interactive so the viewer can change directions, pause slides and branch to more detailed information.

Slide Printing

By saving your images as EPS files, you can send them to a slide printing service for color slide output. You can save images in numerous other formats as well.

SPREADSHEET PUBLISHING WITH VERSION 3.0:

WYSIWYG Display

The new WYSIWYG (What You See Is What You Get) display shows your spreadsheets on the screen as they will appear on the printer. All formatting options appear in the spreadsheet, including fonts, cell widths and heights, shading and so on.

Row Heights

Row heights affect the spacing between lines. Usually, Quattro Pro adjusts the row height to match the largest font used in the row. But you can adjust the row height manually to achieve various effects, which can be particularly useful for forms.

Spreadsheet Zoom

You can enlarge and reduce the basic spreadsheet display so that you can see more or less of your spreadsheet on the screen. This has no effect on the printout.

Annotator Grid

A "snap to" grid has been added to the Annotator so you can align objects along a common grid. However, you can use the grid with or without the automatic Snap To feature.

Annotator Drop Shadows

Text created in the Annotator can be formatted with drop shadows, which are useful for slide text and headlines. You can also customize the shadow.

Print to Fit

"Print to fit" automatically makes a print block fit onto a single page. Fonts and other elements are reduced accordingly. This can be a time-saver for simple printouts from large spreadsheets.

Banner Printing

Banner printing lets you eliminate the left and right margins on continuous-feed paper. This is useful for printing reports sideways across two or more pages without margins being inserted between them.

Slide-Show Effects

On-screen slide shows can now include special transition effects between slides. You can choose from fades, dissolves, wipes and more. These effects are discussed in Chapter 8, "Designing Slides, Overheads and Screen Shows."

Sound Effects

On-screen slide shows can also access special sound effects between slides and when interactive buttons are used. These sound effects are also available to your spreadsheet macros.

ProView PowerPack

Version 3.0 offers the special ProView PowerPack, a collection of tools that supplement Quattro Pro's slide presentation and production features. The pack comes with two additional fonts, time-saving macros, extra clip-art, pre-designed slide templates and a color booklet that introduces you to slide shows and the PowerPack supplements. ProView PowerPack is an extended version of the ProShow PowerPack that was included with Version 2.0.

SPREADSHEET PUBLISHING HARDWARE

The better your hardware, the more enjoyable your software will be. Speed, of course, is the primary consideration. So while your 286 machine will run Quattro Pro without problems, a 386 will run it without frustrations.

But with Quattro Pro, graphics capabilities should also be considered, especially with the new WYSIWYG features of Version 3.0. Your display type (EGA or VGA, for example) does not directly affect your printouts, but it determines how you see data on the screen. So indirectly, it affects the final product.

DISPLAY MODES

Quattro Pro has probably already determined what type of graphics you have and has selected the appropriate mode accordingly. However, if you have color VGA graphics, you can switch among the various display modes using the Options-Display Mode command.

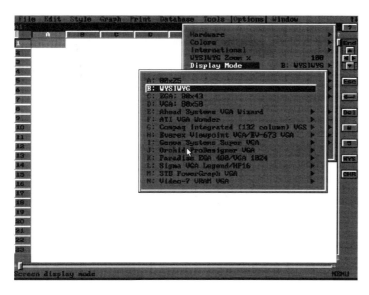

Figure 1-1: Quattro Pro offers four different display modes (Versions 2.0 and 3.0 differ slightly).

NOTE: Version 2.0 offers the Graphics mode in place of the WYSIWYG mode.

Generally, Quattro Pro makes a correct assessment of your graphics display and chooses the mode for you. You generally want the most powerful mode available for your hardware.

The special WYSIWYG mode, available only in Version 3.0, displays all spreadsheet formatting on the screen just as it will appear on the printout. This is one of Version 3.0's primary enhancements; but it requires an EGA or better graphics capability. In Version 2.0, you get the Graphics mode instead. This lets you see Annotator graphs and print preview screens in full WYSIWYG style, but everything else (the spreadsheet) remains in character or text mode. For example, if you created a graph and inserted it into your spreadsheet, this is how it would look in the WYSIWYG and Graphics modes.

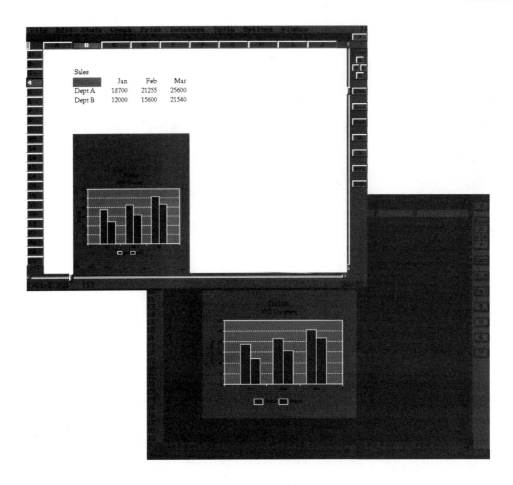

Figure 1-2: Inserting a graph into a spreadsheet has different results in WYSIWYG mode (left) and Graphics mode (right).

The other three modes shown in the figure are text-based modes. They display the spreadsheet and data in text characters. Each offers a different resolution. Here's what the example would look like in one of these modes.

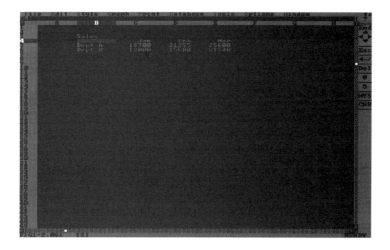

Figure 1-3: Text or CHR mode shows the inserted graph as a high-lighted block representing the graph.

Why would you ever want to switch modes when some modes are obviously more attractive than others? Most often, you would switch from the Graphics or WYSIWYG mode to one of the text-based modes in order to speed up the program. In WYSIWYG mode, Quattro Pro needs more time to update the screen when you make changes. This is especially true when you manipulate large spreadsheets.

So you can switch to your favorite text mode during complex operations or when manipulating spreadsheets, then switch back to WYSIWYG (or Graphics) for formatting and previewing. Although Graphics mode in Version 2.0 doesn't offer the detailed graphics of WYSIWYG, it can still slow down the program when graphs are included in the spreadsheet.

NOTE: If you have a mouse, Version 3.0 gives you buttons for switching between WYSIWYG and text (CHR) mode. These are located on the right edge of the screen and are labeled CHR and WYS.

A POTPOURRI OF PALETTES

In addition to display modes, Quattro Pro offers four different palettes that control the colors available for the program and your spreadsheets. Once you select a palette, you can use it to set various color elements of Quattro Pro via the following commands:

Menus—Choose the Options-Colors-Menu command to change the colors or shades used in menus.

Desktop—Choose the Options-Colors-Desktop command to change the colors or shades used for the desktop. This includes the background colors in Quattro Pro's messages and other elements of the program.

Spreadsheet—Choose the Options-Colors-Spreadsheet command to change the colors or shades used for spreadsheet elements. This includes column headings, highlighted data, protected cells and other elements. You can also change the colors of the WYSIWYG display with this command.

Conditional—Choose the Options-Colors-Conditional command to change the colors or shades used under certain conditions. For example, you can display all negative values in red.

Help—Choose the Options-Colors-Help command to change the colors or shades of the help screens.

File Manager—Choose the Options-Colors-File Manager command to change the colors or shades of the file manager screen.

The palettes are shown in Figure 1-4. Each palette and its colors (or shades) are described in the following sections. Your hardware may dictate which palette you use, but you might find reasons for switching them, such as to view color data in black and white before printing on a black-and-white printer.

Once you choose a palette, Quattro Pro will change to reflect the selection. For example, if you switch from the Black-and-White palette to the Color palette, Quattro Pro will suddenly appear in full color. Plus you can choose from the various

SWITCHING MODES

1. Select Options-Display Mode.
2. Select the desired mode from the list.
3. Press Q to return to the spreadsheet.

Options-Colors commands (listed above) to further change the colors. Selecting one of these commands brings up the palette you've chosen.

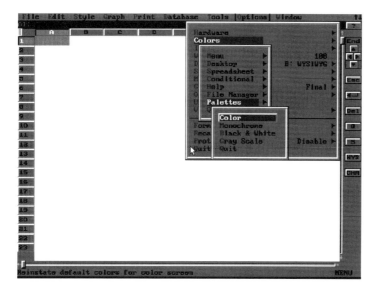

Figure 1-4:   Quattro Pro offers four different palettes for colors and shades. After selecting the palette, you can change the colors of screen and spreadsheet elements.

The Color Palette

The Color palette is useful if you have any type of color system—text or graphics. It offers several colors for the various elements listed under "Palettes." Quattro Pro's colors are shown in Chapter 8, "Designing Slides, Overheads and Screen Shows." As an example, you can display menu options in white on a red background by choosing the Options-Colors-Menu command. The combination "white on red" appears in this palette.

If you have a black-and-white monitor connected to a color video adaptor, Quattro Pro will probably offer you the color option. Go ahead and use it. EGA and VGA systems will translate the colors into 4, 8 or 16 shades of gray (depending on the hardware). And you will be able to create color slides and printouts. The Color palette will look like the palette shown on page 16 in Figure 1-6 for the Black-and-White palette.

The Monochrome Palette

The Monochrome palette for monochrome systems offers five different types of highlighting for the settings in the Options-Colors menu.

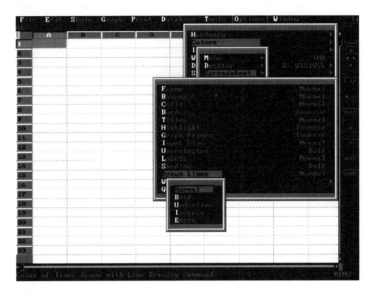

Figure 1-5: The Monochrome palette provides five types of highlighting for monochrome systems.

Generally, this is used on systems without EGA, VGA or a graphics card at all. It offers the fewest choices for controlling the appearance of your data.

The Black-and-White Palette

Use the Black-and-White palette when you have a color system but want to display everything in black and white. This can be useful for previewing black-and-white images on color monitors to see how they will print. The Black-and-White palette converts colors into 4, 8 or 16 shades of gray (depending on your hardware). The palette offers numerous combinations of shades for the menus, desktop and other elements listed above. (Figure 1-6 shows this palette and its combinations.)

CHANGING PALETTES

1. Select Options-Colors-Palettes.
2. Choose the desired palette.
3. Change colors using the new choices available.

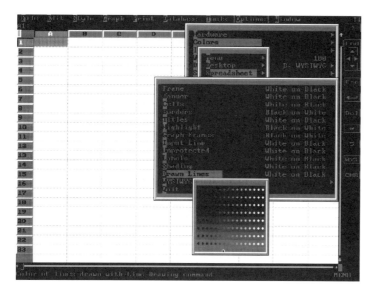

Figure 1-6: The Black-and-White palette shows colors as shades of gray. The dots inside the shaded squares represent the color of text and the shade represents the background.

The Gray-Scale Palette

The Gray-Scale palette is intended for black-and-white monitors connected to color EGA or VGA adapters. But with these systems, you're often better off using the Color palette and choosing colors that have desirable gray shades. (Refer to Figure 1-6 for details about these shades.)

PRINTERS—THE FINAL DESTINATION

Another important link in your system chain is the printer. It's almost this simple: a poor printer results in poor output; a good printer results in good output. Actually, Quattro Pro can even make a poor printer look pretty good. If it supports the printer, Quattro Pro pushes it to the limits of its capabilities. You may be surprised at how nice the output from some inexpensive printers can look.

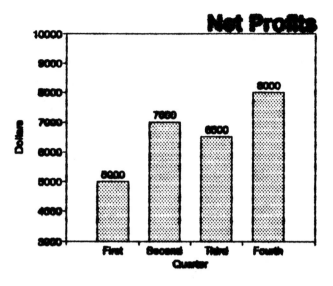

Figure 1-7: Quattro Pro can print to various types of printers. Some low-end printer output can look pretty good.

There are basically three types of printers you can use with Quattro Pro: PostScript printers, HP LaserJet and compatible printers, and everything else. The primary difference among these printers is in the way each handles type styles, or fonts.

PostScript printers require PostScript-compatible fonts. And although Quattro Pro does not use PostScript fonts, it can print spreadsheets to a PostScript printer by using the built-in (or resident) fonts inside the printer itself.

LaserJet printers can use numerous types of fonts and Quattro Pro includes some high-quality fonts for these printers. Plus, Quattro Pro can print spreadsheets using the built-in or cartridge fonts inside the printer.

All other printers in Quattro Pro's printer list are fully supported by Quattro Pro. They will accept any of Quattro Pro's high-quality fonts. Their results will, of course, vary depending on the quality of the printer. (For information about fonts, see Chapter 4, "Fonts and Printers." Details about manipulating printers is covered in Chapter 7, "Printing Reports.")

SIMPLE COMPOSITION
EQUALS GOOD DESIGN

At what point is your spreadsheet adequately designed? What makes one layout better than another? Is the presentation making the same point to every member of the audience? These are subjective questions. You might as well ask yourself, "How much ink is not on the page?" or "What is this presentation not saying?" In other words, good design is difficult to quantify.

But everyone has an innate sense of good design and composition. Some pages look comfortable; others are confusing and uninviting. However, spreadsheet-publishing design has a few basic rules, which will be expanded upon throughout this book.

READ YOUR AUDIENCE

Most messages are aimed at a specific audience. The more you know about them, the better. Your use of fonts and graphics, in particular, should be targeted to the audience. You may think that serious and sober issues, such as financial reporting, require serious and sober design. That may be true. But consider whether your audience has become desensitized to this approach. Maybe a lively design would command more attention.

This isn't to say that the audience dictates the design. Certainly, the message you are giving should do that. But the message should be appropriate to the audience.

How do you determine an appropriate audience approach? Ideally, you would like to test the presentation on several people who will be attending. But, sometimes, just sitting and thinking about your audience can produce good ideas.

COMMUNICATE WITH TYPE

Fonts are possibly the single most influential part of your spreadsheet presentation. Use them appropriately and stick to the basic design concepts you'll read about in Chapter 4,

"Fonts and Printers." If you want to communicate a bold, powerful message, use a bold, powerful font. A friendly, casual font conveys a correspondingly casual message.

We'll Beat Any Price!

	Full	Queen	King
Simmons	$349.95	$489.95	$549.95
Serta	$369.95	$499.95	$569.95

Enjoy Our Hospitality

	Single	Double	Suite
Daily	$89.95	$129.95	$189.95
Weekend	$69.95	$99.95	$189.95

Figure 1-8: Fonts influence the tone of your message. Select fonts to communicate the tone you want.

If you're serious about your spreadsheet presentations, add some extra fonts to your system. You might want to collect some useful clip-art images as well. (See the Resources section in the back of the book for font and clip-art manufacturers.)

THINK OF THE ENTIRE PAGE

If your presentation includes headings, footnotes and page numbers, be sure to take them into consideration as you create a design. Also think about the final form of the presentation. As discussed in Chapter 6, a bound book requires different design specifications than a single sheet being used as a handout. And remember, white space is a design element, too.

DON'T BOX YOURSELF IN

Misuse and overuse of borders and boxes is one of the biggest design pitfalls of spreadsheets. So, notes of caution about using borders and boxes are scattered throughout this book. When in doubt, leave the box out!

EXPERIMENT AND BORROW IDEAS

It can be a difficult and intimidating experience to turn a blank spreadsheet into a well-designed presentation. So look to others for ideas. Collect examples of effective spreadsheet output and refer to them for inspiration. You may be able to modify these examples. But don't be afraid to follow your instincts. Experiment. And if you're lucky, even your mistakes will produce some interesting and effective results.

MOVING ON

You're now ready to enter the world of spreadsheet publishing with a fundamental understanding of Quattro Pro's features. With this versatile software, your monitor and your printer, you can begin to construct effective reports that take full advantage of your system. The remaining chapters in this section of this book explain in detail all of Quattro Pro's powerful spreadsheet publishing features. You can apply this information as you read Sections II and III, "Putting It All Together" and "Design in Action," respectively.

Here are some things to check before moving on:

- Determine whether you're using Version 2.0 or 3.0 of Quattro Pro. (Features specific to Version 3.0 are so noted throughout this book.)

- Be sure your monitor is correctly identified by Quattro Pro.

- Designate your main printer and any alternate printer as 1st and 2nd printers in the Options-Hardware-Printers command. (Remember, you can use two modes of the same printer if desired.)

- Select the most appropriate palette for your system using the Options-Colors-Palettes command.

Now that you've covered the basics, you'll examine ways you can improve your spreadsheets with Quattro Pro in the next chapter.

Formatting Spreadsheets

2

A readable, attractive spreadsheet begins with a well-thought-out format for presenting the information. Until recently, a spreadsheet format was predictable: monotonous rows and columns of numbers that were difficult to sift through. However, Quattro Pro offers users a lot of versatility when it comes to formatting spreadsheet data. By carefully applying Quattro Pro's spreadsheet formatting options to your data, you can transform your reports into interesting and informative presentations.

This chapter explores some of the elements of spreadsheet publishing, such as column widths, data alignment, shading and other formatting options. While you're learning Quattro Pro's formatting capabilities and limitations, you'll also discover some useful design ideas for your spreadsheets.

Every time you discover a new option, go ahead and try it out. Then ask yourself whether that formatting adds to or detracts from the overall effect. Show your spreadsheet or graph to a friend and ask for his or her opinion. However, restraint and simplicity are often the basis of good design. An effective spreadsheet report isn't overloaded with information. It displays data clearly and calls attention to the information rather than the presentation.

CATEGORIZE YOUR DATA

Spreadsheet information falls into three general categories: *numbers, text* and *dates*. This is important for your spreadsheet calculations, since each data type requires different handling in formulas. But it's also an important distinction for formatting, because different types of information require different alignment, cell widths and formats.

To some extent, Quattro Pro assumes certain formatting norms for each type of information. For example, numbers and dates are always aligned with the right side of a cell, while text is aligned with the left. Generally, numbers appear in a default format (the General format) while dates need to be formatted as you enter them. Before you learn the basics of spreadsheet formatting (including column width, alignment and built-in formats), let's review Quattro Pro's definitions of numbers, dates and text.

Numbers are values that can be calculated with other values on the spreadsheet. A number is anything that begins with a numeric character, including any numeral, the decimal point (Period key) and the symbols +, − and (. When it's first entered, a numeric entry will always align with the right side of the cell. However, you can change this alignment, as you'll see in "Aligning Text, Numbers and Dates" later in this chapter.

Dates are values entered by first pressing Ctrl-D. These will appear as date entries in one of several different formats (depending on how you enter it). Technically, dates are just numbers representing the number of days elapsed since Dec 31, 1899, a value called the *date serial number*.

You can actually enter a date serial number as a standard numeric value and then reformat it to appear in one of the date formats. For example, the number 2 can be shown as the date Jan 2, 1900—two days after the date Dec 31, 1899. By using Ctrl-D before entering a date, Quattro Pro can automatically calculate the date serial number when you enter the date in a normal way. This lets Quattro Pro do the work for you.

Because they're actually numeric values, dates align themselves with the right side of a cell if entered properly. (In

---

ENTERING NUMBERS AND TEXT

1. Move the cell pointer to the desired cell using the Arrow keys.
2. Type the entry and press Enter.
3. Text will align with the left side, numbers with the right.

ENTERING DATES

1. Move to the desired cell using the Arrow keys.
2. Press Ctrl-D.
3. Type the date in the format MM/DD/YY and press Enter.
4. Dates will align with the right side of the cell.

"Aligning Text, Numbers and Dates," you'll learn how you can change this alignment.)

Text is everything that is not a date or number. Typically, text begins with a text character, which includes all letters of the alphabet and most special characters. At times, you may have to use a number as a text entry. To do so, type an apostrophe (') before making the entry. The resulting number will align itself with the left side of the cell as all text entries do. A number entered this way cannot be used in numeric calculations.

Now, let's examine ways these information categories and spreadsheets can be formatted.

ADJUSTING COLUMN WIDTH

You will usually want to adjust the column width in your spreadsheets. Data doesn't always fit in Quattro Pro's default column width of nine characters. If a numeric or date entry is too long for the column, Quattro Pro displays asterisks (*) in the cell to call attention to this fact. If a text entry is too long for the column, Quattro Pro will let it "spill over" to the next column (as shown in Figure 2-1), provided the next column contains no information.

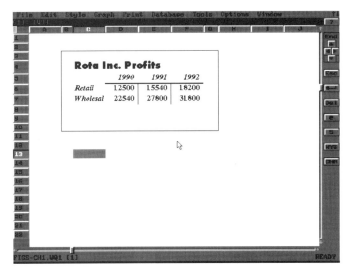

Figure 2-1: If a text entry is too large for its column, it will spill into the next column.

CHANGING A COLUMN'S WIDTH

1. Move the cell pointer to the desired column.
2. Press Ctrl-W.
3. Press the Right Arrow key to widen the column or the Left Arrow key to narrow it.
4. Press Enter when finished.

CHANGING THE WIDTH OF A BLOCK

1. Move the cell pointer to the first column.
2. Select the command Style Block Widths-Set Width by using the mouse or pressing /SBS.
3. Press the Period key.
4. Press the Right Arrow key until all desired columns are highlighted. Press Enter when finished.
5. Enter the desired column width and press Enter.

1. Select Style-Block Size-Auto Width.
2. Press Esc, then move the pointer to the first column whose width you want to change.
3. Press the Period key.
4. Press the Right Arrow key to highlight additional columns.
5. Press Enter.

Although your text can "spill" over from one column to the next, you might prefer to expand the column's width so the information appears within a single column. Also, information that is too small for a column may look better if you narrow the column, as shown in column B in Figure 2-2.

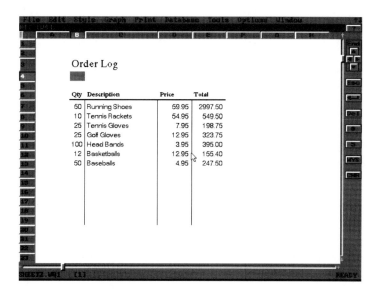

Figure 2-2: Adjust columns to fit the data.

One reason for allowing text to exceed the width of its column is to include headings above tables of data. A table may have specific column-width requirements, which you can't change for the headings. Therefore, headings that are too wide for the columns spill into the adjacent columns, as shown in Figure 2-3. You'll also occasionally want to exceed column widths when creating forms.

Quattro Pro can automatically change the widths of columns to match the widest entry in the column. This way, you don't have to figure out how wide a column should be. Just use the Style-Block Size-Auto Width command to do this. If a new entry exceeds the new column width, repeat the command.

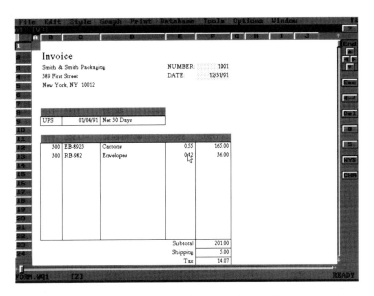

Figure 2-3: Headings for forms and tables often spill into adjacent columns.

The Auto Width command takes your fonts into consideration. If you use a large font in the column, it may require a larger cell width.

Column widths also affect the placement of lines on the spreadsheet. Lines can be drawn on the edges of cells. Widening or narrowing the right edge of a cell will change the appearance of the line. (This is discussed in more detail under "Using Lines, Borders and Shades" later in this chapter.)

Finally, column widths can increase or reduce the contrast between the various alignment options. A wider column will increase the difference.

CHANGING AND USING THE DEFAULT WIDTH

1. Select the Options-Formats-Global Width command.

2. Enter the desired width and press Enter.

3. Quit to return to the spreadsheet. All columns using the default will change to reflect the new default width.

4. Use the Style-Reset Width command to change columns from a custom width to the default width.

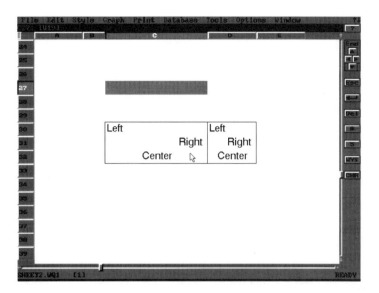

Figure 2-4: The wider a column, the more you will see differences in alignment.

You can return a cell to its default width by moving to the column and using the command Style-Reset Width. Quattro Pro also lets you change the default width by using the Options-Formats-Global Width command. This changes all columns in the spreadsheet that are currently set to the default width. This includes all columns that haven't previously been changed.

ADJUSTING ROW HEIGHT

Just as column width can be adjusted, you can also change the heights of the rows in your spreadsheet. Ordinarily, Quattro Pro adjusts the row heights according to the text size in the row. If you change the point size of the text, Quattro Pro adjusts the row's height, which will be slightly larger than the point size of the largest font used in the row. This gives you a little extra space above the text. It can also create awkward and uneven spacing when a single row contains different font sizes. (For information on changing fonts, see Chapter 4, "Fonts and Printers.")

NOTE:	When you want to communicate your message in a consistent way, avoid mixing different point sizes on the same row.

Figure 2-5: *Quattro Pro's automatic row heights adjust to the largest text in the row. In some cases, that can be unattractive.*

You can manually change the heights of the rows in Quattro Pro. Simply use the Style-Block Size-Height command. The row height you choose can be significantly larger or smaller than the size of the text in the row.

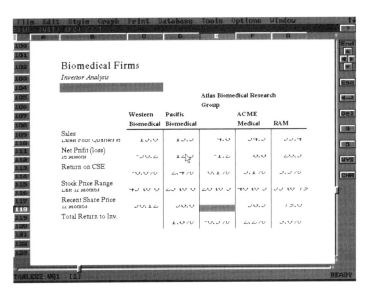

Figure 2-6: *Row heights can be made smaller or larger than the information in the row.*

When you make a row smaller than the text in it, Quattro Pro will truncate the text on the screen, as shown in Figure 2-6. But when you print the block the text will overlap with the row above it. In other words, it will spill over the top of the row, as shown in Figure 2-7.

Normal Row Height
Adjusted Row

Figure 2-7: Text that is taller than its row height will overlap with the text in the row above it.

Row heights can be used to manipulate the text on your spreadsheets and printouts. For example, you can use row heights to change the leading (the space between baselines) of your spreadsheet text.

A simple leading feature can be added to your spreadsheets by increasing the point size used in certain cells.

A simple leading feature

can be added to your

spreadsheets by increasing

the point size used for

certain rows.

Figure 2-8: Adjusting row heights acts like leading, since it changes space between lines of text.

Other text effects, such as mixing sizes, can also be achieved with row height adjustments, as shown in Figure 2-9.

48pt

Mix large text
and small text
side by side
by reducing the
height of the
larger row

Figure 2-9: Use row heights to display different point sizes together.
This example shows 48-point text in a 26-point row height.

In this case, the height of the row containing the large type is adjusted to the size of the small type, causing the large characters to spill over the top of the row. Changing the size of text is covered in Chapter 4, "Fonts and Printers."

Later in this chapter, you'll discover how to use row height adjustments as a way to change the thickness of a line. In Chapter 6, "Designing Effective Pages," you'll see an example of using row heights to achieve a superscript for footnotes.

ALIGNING TEXT, NUMBERS AND DATES

Quattro Pro lets you align information with the left, right or center of the column. As mentioned earlier, by default text aligns with the left; numbers and dates with the right. But you can change this at any time.

Usually, right alignment is best for numbers because it keeps them aligned when they've been formatted with a constant number of decimal places.

CHANGING ALIGNMENT

1. Move the cell pointer to the desired cell or, if you're aligning a block, move to one of the corner cells.
2. Select the command Style-Alignment.
3. Choose Left, Right, Center or General, depending on the type of alignment you want. General aligns numbers with the right and text with the left.
4. If you are aligning one cell, then press Enter. If you are aligning a block, press the Period key and use the Arrow keys to highlight the entire block. Then press Enter.

```
23.45
125.78
3.99
39.98
1124.56
342.99
```

Figure 2-10: Numbers are right-aligned to make the decimal places line up.

Most fonts use *monospacing*, or consistent spacing, for numbers. In other words, the number 1 is given as much space as the number 5, even though it's physically narrower. Monospaced numbers allow for easy decimal alignment when all values have the same decimal place.

Although numbers are often monospaced, most fonts use *proportional spacing* for all other characters. These fonts allot each individual character a varying amount of space determined by its width. For example, the letter *i* takes less space than the letter *m*.

Fonts such as Courier and Monospace are entirely monospaced fonts, using consistent spacing for all characters and numbers. These generally look less professional than proportional fonts.

Some font publishers offer monospaced versions of attractive proportional fonts. Bitstream, for example, offers both a monospaced and proportional Swiss font.

Still, numeric information is not aligned by the decimal place but by the right edge. Therefore, values that have a different number of decimal places will not be aligned—even with monospaced numbers.

You will undoubtedly find occasion to align numbers with the left side of a column. One example might be when numbers are entered with text in a column.

Loan Data

Name:	Arnold Meyers
Date:	04/15/92
Principal:	$5,000.00
Interest Rate:	13.5%
Term (months):	60
Payment:	$97.20

Figure 2-11: Sometimes, you'll have to align a number with the left side of a cell.

Another example might be numbers that don't contain decimal places, such as when they represent a counted value.

Sometimes you'll find that right-aligned columns run into adjacent left-aligned columns, causing a confusing display—especially when the right-aligned columns contain negative numbers formatted with the Currency format. These numbers will include a parenthesis in the rightmost position of the column, a position normally left blank.

Amount	Name
($355.00)	Lori Smith
$85.55	Randy Westin
$306.56	Frank Colavo
$125.45	Brian McNab
($54.99)	Sara Franklin
($23.50)	Joni Trescoluso
$455.12	Robert Jones

Figure 2-12: Some numeric formats compound the problem of adjacent columns. This is especially true when right-aligned data is next to left-aligned data.

INSERTING A COLUMN

1. Move the cell pointer to the desired position for the new column. The column on which you locate the pointer will move to the right when the new column appears.
2. Select the command Edit-Insert-Column and press Enter.

There are a few basic ways to cure this problem. First, you can avoid using the Currency format and live with a single space between the columns. (See "Formatting Numbers" later in this chapter for information about changing formats.) If you want more room, try inserting a blank column between the conflicting columns. Use the Ctrl-W command to narrow this extra column to an appropriate width.

Amount	Name
($355.00)	Lori Smith
$85.55	Randy Westin
$306.56	Frank Colavo
$125.45	Brian McNab
($54.99)	Sara Franklin
($23.50)	Joni Trescoluso
$455.12	Robert Jones

Figure 2-13: You can insert a blank column between two columns to separate them and provide a more attractive display.

One disadvantage of this technique is that the extra column may not be appropriate in your spreadsheet. It may force you to skip past this column each time you enter data into the spreadsheet. If inserting a column is inappropriate for your application, try using a vertical line to separate the two columns. (This is described in "Using Lines, Borders and Shades" later in this chapter.)

Note that you can change the default method of alignment for labels. In other words, Quattro Pro can be set to automatically center or right-align label entries. This is done with the Options-Formats-Align Labels command.

PLACING COLUMN HEADS

Centering a heading over several columns can be tricky since aligning it within its cell may not center it over the block. You can "pad" the heading with extra spaces to position it in the center of the block by simply pressing the space bar several times before typing the heading.

Mailing List

Name	Street	City	ST	Zip
Larry Smith	34 First St	San Diego	CA	92101
Greg Rand	7782 Orange Ave	Los Angeles	CA	90034
Lisa Burke	101 Broadway	San Mateo	CA	94402
Linda Perle	61 Idaho Bl	San Mateo	CA	94402
Samual Yin	902 Elm Ave	New York	NY	10012

Figure 2-14: Center headings by adding blank spaces to the beginning of the text. You may have to adjust this a few times for best results.

This works fine when you are using the WYSIWYG display mode and a non-PostScript printer, because you'll see exactly how the extra spaces will look on the final printout. So the screen will match the printed results. If you are using a PostScript printer, however, the screen will not match the printer exactly and you may have to print the spreadsheet to see the precise effects of your spacing. Then adjust the spreadsheet accordingly and print again.

If you are not using the WYSIWYG display mode, but one of the character (text) modes, the difference between the screen and printer will be even greater—especially if you use large fonts in the spreadsheet. In this situation, use the screen preview feature (print to screen) to see what the spreadsheet will look like before printing. Then return to the spreadsheet and adjust the heading accordingly.

FORMATTING NUMBERS

Numeric formats change the appearance of numeric information, including dates and times. This can be done for both aesthetic and informative reasons. Use the Style-Numeric Format command to select a format for numbers, dates and times. The next few sections explain each of the numeric formats in Quattro Pro.

FORMATS

Numeric formats control the decimal places and special characters added to numeric information. The following are Quattro Pro's numeric formats:

Fixed displays numbers with a fixed number of decimal places. If a value has no decimal value, then the format will pad with zeros (for example, 45 will become 45.00). If a value has more than the specified number of places, then the format rounds the value to the specified number of places. Negative numbers include a minus sign and values between 1 and −1 include a leading zero, as in 0.34.

Scientific displays numbers in scientific notation with one integer digit, for example, 8.23E+3.

Currency displays numbers with dollar signs, commas and a fixed number of decimal places (usually two), as in $4,306.50. Negative numbers are shown in parentheses and values between 1 and −1 include a leading zero.

, (comma) displays numbers with commas and a fixed number of decimal places, for example, 5,234,102.45, when two places are specified. Negative values are shown in parentheses.

General displays only as many decimal values as are needed for the number entered. No special symbols are used. For example, if you enter 5.50, Quattro Pro displays 5.5. If you enter 5.6782, Quattro Pro enters 5.6782.

+/− displays numbers as a series of symbols for use in text graphs. Positive values show as + symbols, negative values as − symbols, and zero as . (period) symbols.

Percent displays numbers as percentages. This multiplies values by 100. For example, if you enter 1, Quattro Pro displays 100%. Therefore, convert values to their decimal equivalents by multiplying them by .01. To get 1%, type .01 into the cell. You can also enter 1% (include the percent symbol) and Quattro Pro will convert the value for you. This format includes a fixed number of decimal places.

All number formats, except General, let you specify a number of decimal places to display. Remember that this will add zeros when a value does not fulfill the required number of decimal places. For example, if you specify 2 decimal places and enter the value 4.5, Quattro Pro will display 4.50 to fill out the two decimal places. This fixed number of decimal places is useful for making a spreadsheet consistent. Remember that this requires wider cells in some cases.

If your spreadsheet contains mostly financial information, consider changing the default numeric format to the Fixed or , (comma) format. Then you can use the Style-Numeric Format command to change the exceptions.

The most common mistake made in number formats is to repeat the Currency format throughout a spreadsheet when the values all represent dollar amounts. This makes the spreadsheet look amateurish and can distract the audience. It can also require wider cells to accommodate the dollar signs and commas.

CHOOSING NUMERIC FORMATS

1. Select Style-Numeric Format.
2. Choose the desired format from the list.
3. Specify the desired block to format using the mouse or keyboard.
4. Press Enter.

CHANGING THE DEFAULT NUMERIC FORMAT

1. Select the command Options-Formats-Numeric Format.
2. Select the new default format.
3. Select Quit, then Update to save the changes.
4. Quit or Esc back to the spreadsheet.

Assets		Liabilities	
Checking Account	$50,000.00	Notes Payable - Bank	$35,000.00
Savings Account	$22,000.00	Notes Payable - Credit Union	$15,000.00
Other Checking	$50.00	Secured Notes	$1,500.00
		Other Investments	$12,000.00
Marketable Securities	$15,500.00	Mortgage	$350,000.00
Non-Marketable Sec	$545,000.00		
Life Insurance	$2,500.00	Credit Card	$2,000.00
		Margin Accounts	$4,000.00
Real Estate - Other	$33,594.00	Income Taxes Payable	$20,100.00
Real Estate - Res	$650,000.00	Life Insurance Loans	$4,000.00
Real Estate - Investment	$445,000.00	Other	$0.00
IRA, KEOGH, Pension	$24,000.00	Other Insurance	$24,000.00
Deferred Income	$25,000.00	Notes Payable - Personal	$25,000.00
Personal Property	$145,000.00	Other Property Tax	$1,525.00
		Association Fees	$3,000.00
Art, Collectables	$54,000.00	Real Estate	$150,000.00
Other	$15,000.00	Other	$0.00

Figure 2-15: Avoid overuse of the Currency format. It makes your reports look amateurish.

Try using either the , (comma) or Fixed format instead. You don't need to clutter the spreadsheet with $ symbols. The audience will know that your values represent money because of the context of your presentation. Reserve the Currency format for column totals or other main values of the spreadsheet.

As another design consideration, determine whether your values can be displayed without decimal places. Perhaps they all contain zeros. Or maybe the decimal values are insignificant to the message. In that case, you can include a footnote on the page, such as "Values rounded to nearest dollar."

ROUNDING NUMBERS

Remember that when Quattro Pro rounds numbers to adhere to the specified number of decimal places, it's not actually changing the value in the cell. Instead, Quattro Pro is merely displaying the number "as if" it were rounded. Calculations made using the value will be made with the full, unrounded number. In short, number formats only *appear* to round numbers.

Assets		Liabilities	
Checking Account	50000	Notes Payable - Bank	35000
Savings Account	22000	Notes Payable - Credit Union	15000
Other Checking	50	Secured Notes	1500
		Other Investments	12000
Marketable Securities	15500	Mortgage	350000
Non-Marketable Sec	545000		
Life Insurance	2500	Credit Card	2000
		Margin Accounts	4000
Real Estate - Other	33594	Income Taxes Payable	20100
Real Estate - Res	650000	Life Insurance Loans	4000
Real Estate - Investment	445000	Other	0
IRA, KEOGH, Pension	24000	Other Insurance	24000
Deferred Income	25000	Notes Payable - Personal	25000
Personal Property	145000	Other Property Tax	1525
		Association Fees	3000
Art, Collectables	54000	Real Estate	150000
Other	15000	Other	0

Figure 2-16: Consider whether you can remove decimal values entirely. Some financial reports work well this way.

By using the @ROUND function, you can round values in a spreadsheet and actually change the original value to the rounded value. This will affect calculations that refer to the rounded value.

@ROUND(Value, Places)

Enter the value to be rounded and the number of places to round off, as indicated. You can use this function to round values to the nearest 10 dollars by entering –1 for the number of decimal places. For example, @ROUND(3389.45,–1) will display 3390 in the cell. Enter –2 to round to the nearest 100 dollars. To remove the trailing zeros, try this formula:

@ROUND(3389.45,–2)/100

This rounds the value to the nearest 100 dollars, and then removes the two trailing zeros. The cell displays 34. This can be useful for annual reports or other financial spreadsheets that show values in thousands or millions of dollars.

When using the Percent format, consider whether you need any decimal places. Often, one decimal place is perfect for percentage values.

FORMATTING DATES

Handling dates can be one of the trickiest things to do in a spreadsheet—especially when you have to make date calculations. This section provides some useful information and techniques for formatting dates. Let's start with Quattro Pro's built-in date formats:

Format	Example
DD-MMM-YY	02-Dec-91
DD-MMM	02-Dec
MMM-YY	Dec-91
Long International	12/02/91 or 12.02.91 or 91-12-02
Short International	12/91 or 12.91 or 91.12

The International formats, intended for documents that must adhere to international standards, can assume one of three different styles. Normally, the international mode is set to the United States standard of 12/02/91. To change this, use the Options-International-Date command to select the desired format. (This applies to the International formats only.)

Sometimes your dates may not require that the day value be displayed. This may be true for monthly financial comparisons that assume the last day of the month. In these cases, you should use either the MMM-YY or Short International formats to make the spreadsheet look cleaner.

Quarterly Sales		Quarterly Sales	
Date	**Amount**	**Date**	**Amount**
01/01/89	4,500	Jan-89	4,500
04/01/89	4,800	Apr-89	4,800
07/01/89	3,446	Jul-89	3,446
10/01/89	6,600	Oct-89	6,600
01/01/90	6,790	Jan-90	6,790
04/01/90	8,000	Apr-90	8,000
07/01/90	9,870	Jul-90	9,870
10/01/90	9,890	Oct-90	9,890

Figure 2-17: Use the date format most appropriate for your application. Often simple date formats look cleaner than longer formats.

Another advantage to the shorter formats is that they fit into narrower cells than the others. (Note that dates in the year 2000 and beyond will require wider columns. That's because the year portion is displayed with the full year value to distinguish it from years prior to 2000.)

You may need formats other than those offered by Quattro Pro. For example, you might want to display only the month, in abbreviated or long fashion, in a cell. Or you might want to display a full version of the date, such as December 2, 1991. The easiest way to accomplish this is simply to type the date as a label (or text entry) in the cell. The only drawback is that you cannot use the date for date math calculations. If date calculations are not required, consider entering dates as text values, even when you don't need a custom format.

When you require a custom format and must use date calculations, you can use a formula to create a custom format. You can display any portion of a date (day, month or year) by using the functions @DAY, @MONTH or @YEAR. If cell C5 contains the date 12/02/91, then these functions will produce the following values:

@DAY (C5)   02

@MONTH (C5)   12

@YEAR (C5)   91

To convert the month number into its appropriate month name requires a simple formula using the @MONTH function along with the @CHOOSE function:

@CHOOSE(@MONTH(C5),"","Jan","Feb","Mar","Apr","May", "Jun","Jul","Aug","Sep","Oct","Nov","Dec")

If you want the format December 2, then try this formula:

@CHOOSE(@MONTH(C5),"","January","February","March", "April","May ","June","July","August","September","October", " November"," December ")&&@STRING(@DAY(C5),0)

Notice that each month name includes a blank space at the end. When displaying just the year portion, you might want to include the entire year—not just the two-digit abbreviation. Here's a formula:

@IF(@YEAR(C5)<2000,@VALUE("19"&&@STRING(@YEAR (C5))),@YEAR(C5))

These formulas work best when you need to convert a date that's already entered into a different cell of the spreadsheet. That's because you need to refer to a cell containing a date (cell C5, in this example). Date calculations should be made using the original date entry.

FORMATTING TIME

There are only so many ways to format time. Quattro Pro covers the bases pretty well with the following built-in time formats:

HH:MM:SS AM/PM	06:30:10 PM
HH:MM AM/PM	06:30 PM
Long International	18:30:10 or 18.30.10 or 18,30,10
Short International	18:30 or 18.30 or 18,30 or 18h30m

Use the Options-International command to determine which of the International date formats is used.

USING LINES, BORDERS AND SHADES

Quattro Pro's line drawing features give you the tools you need to create forms and professional-looking reports directly from the spreadsheet. At first glance, the line drawing may seem rudimentary; but with some creative ideas and design basics, these tools can provide a wealth of possibilities. There are several types of lines and shades you can apply to your spreadsheets.

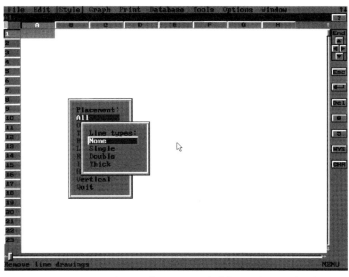

Figure 2-18: You can choose from several different line styles for your spreadsheets.

Lines can be applied to all sides of a block of cells: the top, bottom, left and right. Just specify the desired block of cells, and then choose the line placement options. Your block can consist of one cell or many. If your block contains several cells, you can also apply lines both vertically and horizontally.

APPLYING LINES TO A BLOCK

1. Select Style-Line Drawing.
2. Highlight the desired block and press Enter.
3. Choose a line position.
4. Choose a line type.
5. Press Esc twice to return to step 2 or use Q to quit.

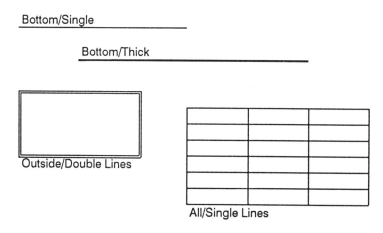

Figure 2-19: You can apply lines to various sides of your block of cells. If the block contains more than one cell, consider adding lines vertically or horizontally.

Shading applies to a block of cells also. The block you specify will be shaded entirely; each cell will be completely filled, even if it contains data. If your shaded cells contain text, then that text will be "reversed" (printed in white) when you use the black shade and will be normal (printed in black) when you use the gray shade. Using bold fonts can improve the readability of shaded text. (See Chapter 4 for details about using bold fonts.)

APPLYING A SHADE TO A BLOCK

1. Select Style-Shading.
2. Select the shade style.
3. Highlight the desired block and press Enter.

Figure 2-20: *Using bold fonts can improve the readability of shaded text—both black and gray shades.*

1 point	
2 points	
3 points	
4 points	
5 points	
6 points	
7 points	
8 points	
12 points	
15 points	

Figure 2-21: *By shading a row of cells and then adjusting the height of that row, you can get several line thicknesses for underlining and spreadsheet highlights.*

As you can see, lines and shades are affected by the width of your columns and the height of your rows. You can deliberately adjust the height of a row to alter the thickness of the shaded block. This can give you a variety of line weights for your spreadsheets.

You don't get the same variety in vertical lines because column widths cannot be controlled to the same extent that row heights can.

MOVING ON

This chapter has introduced you to Quattro Pro's spreadsheet formatting features and provided some ideas for using these features in creative ways on your spreadsheets. As you create your spreadsheets, apply some simple rules as you go and your reports will be more presentable. The rules of good design apply at every stage of your work with spreadsheets. The information in this chapter applies to basic data entry and number formatting.

In order to make your basic spreadsheet design pleasing and efficient, you should ask yourself these questions:

- Have I allowed enough space in the columns and enough space between the columns?

- Have I used appropriate number formats and avoided overusing the Currency format?

- Have I avoided all uppercase headings and made appropriate use of larger point sizes?

- Have I overused shading or lines?

Remember to use appropriate number formats and avoid excessive use of lines and shades. These ideas alone will make a big difference in your work.

Creating Effective Graphs

3

Graphics are an effective tool for business communication, and Quattro Pro gives you some of the best graphing features available in a spreadsheet program. With Quattro Pro you can select from numerous graph types, such as bar graphs, XY graphs and a host of 3D graphs. Each of these has its own design considerations and communicates its values in a unique way. Line graphs, for example, are excellent for expressing a trend, whereas area graphs compare component parts of a whole over time.

Besides basic graphing features and graph selections, Quattro Pro offers numerous ways to customize graphs. Customization lets you communicate your message more effectively. For example, you can choose values for the vertical axis (Y-axis) of a graph to reveal high and low points for the values. Other customization features are designed to give you better-looking graphs. For example, you can add borders around various parts of a graph and use numerous fonts for the titles and other graph text.

This chapter will show you Quattro Pro's graphing procedure and explain its numerous customization options. At the same time, you'll learn how to apply these options to create attractive, well-designed graphs that communicate effectively. In addition to explaining commands and design ideas, this chapter gives you the steps for each important graphing process; these appear along the sides of the pages and will serve as a reference later. (For additional graphing examples and ideas, refer to the makeovers in Chapter 11.)

The first step in mastering Quattro Pro's graphing capabilities is learning the basic elements of a graph—as well as some graphing terminology.

LEARNING THE LANGUAGE

To really understand the structure of a graph, it's important to become familiar with basic graphing elements. The following are some important graphing terms and definitions that you should know. Refer to Figure 3-1 when learning about each element.

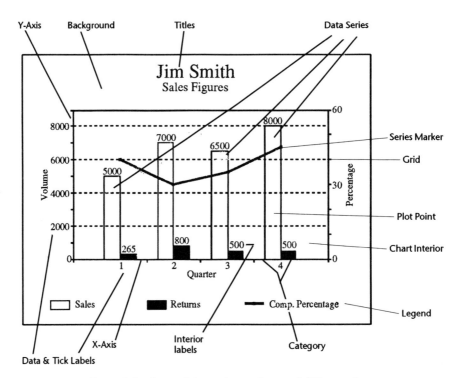

Figure 3-1: A graph is made up of several different elements.

Data series—A series of values that apply to the same item. A data series usually consists of several plot points but can sometimes have only one. All plot points within a series have the same pattern. Figure 3-1 shows three data series: two represented as bars, and one as a line.

Series marker—A symbol, usually used in line and XY graphs, that represents the plotted values (or plot points) on the graph.

Plot point—Every value you include in the graph. A plot point is represented by a bar, series marker or other element.

Category—A grouping of different plot points along the X-axis. Often, several groups (or categories) appear along the X-axis, depending on the number of plot points in the data series. For example, if a data series has four plot points (i.e., four bars) then you'll get four categories. Usually, all the data series are given the same number of categories. (Figure 3-1 shows a graph with four categories.)

X-axis—The horizontal axis that contains the graph's category divisions. Note that XY graphs show values, rather than labels, along the X-axis. The X-axis is the vertical axis on a rotated bar graph.

Y-axis—The vertical axis that contains the graph values. On a rotated bar graph, the Y-axis is the horizontal axis.

Legend—The name of the graph's data series. This provides a "key" to the graph, showing each data series name, color and pattern. This usually appears along the side of the graph or at the bottom.

Background—The area on which the graph is drawn. You can change the color of the background if desired.

Chart interior—The area on which the data series and grid lines (see below) appear. This area appears just inside the two axis lines and often appears in a different color than the background.

Grid—The vertical and/or horizontal lines that appear in the chart interior. These lines extend the axis tick marks to reveal exact placement of values in the graph. You can add or remove these grid lines if desired.

Data & tick labels—The values that appear along the X-axis and Y-axis. You can change the font, color and style of these labels if desired. Note that data labels are also known as interior labels.

Titles—The various headings on the graph. Titles include the first line heading, second line heading, X-axis title and Y-axis title. You can change the font, size, style and color of each title individually.

Interior labels—The labels that appear inside the graph and correspond to each plot point. You can add these labels to your graphs if desired.

STARTING THE PROCESS

There are two basic ways to create a graph in Quattro Pro. You can use the Fast Graph feature, which creates graphs in one easy step, but forces you to arrange data in a certain way. If your data doesn't fit these requirements, you can identify the graph data manually using the Graph-Series command. The following sections describe both of these methods.

FAST-GRAPH IN ONE STEP

The easiest way to create a graph is by selecting the Graph-Fast Graph command and highlighting the entire block of graph data on the spreadsheet. Quattro Pro immediately creates a stacked bar graph from the data you highlighted. You can then customize the graph as desired.

The Fast Graph command uses the block of cells you specify as graph values. It assumes that each row contains a different data series. So the more rows you have, the more data series appear in the graph. The first cell in each row (that is, the first column of the block) should contain the names of the data series. Each subsequent cell in the row designates a new category. Finally, place column headings above each of these columns of values; these will act as X-axis labels (category labels). Figure 3-2 shows an example of a Fast Graph block and the graph it creates.

NOTE: If the number of rows in your data block is equal to or greater than the number of columns, Quattro Pro will use the columns as data series and the rows as categories. If you do not want this orientation, use the method for identifying data series individually, as described in the next section.

FAST GRAPHING

1. Select the Graph-Fast Graph command.
2. Highlight the block of cells containing the values to be graphed. This block should adhere to the Fast Graph requirements.
3. Press Enter and Quattro Pro displays the graph for you. Press Enter to return to the Graph menu.
4. Name the graph with the Graph-Name-Create command.

	First	Second	Third	Fourth
Smith	5000	7000	6500	8000
Jones	5500	8600	7000	9000
Miller	6400	8000	8200	9200

Figure 3-2: The Fast Graph feature uses a special configuration of cells to create the data series for a graph. This shows a block of cells and the graph it creates.

When finished, you may want to make some changes to the graph, such as changing the graph type or adding headings. These procedures are covered under "Doing Your Own Thing" later in this chapter.

It's not usually difficult to enter your data into the Fast Graph structure on the spreadsheet. You may already be using this structure—it's a natural way of organizing data. However, if your data cannot be entered into such a block, you can specify each data series individually.

EXERCISE YOUR OPTIONS

You are not forced to enter your data series into rows as required by the Fast Graph command; you can enter data series in columns, if desired. And all the data series do not have to be adjacent; they can be spread throughout the spreadsheet. To graph such data, however, will require that you identify the data series individually.

1. Select the Graph-Series command.
2. Select the 1st Series option.
3. Highlight the row or column that contains the values for the first series, then press Enter.
4. Repeat steps 2 and 3 for the remaining series in the graph.
5. Select the X-Axis Series option.
6. Highlight the cells containing the X-axis labels (category labels) and press Enter.
7. Quit to return to the spreadsheet.
8. View the graph with the Graph-View command.

1. Select Graph-Graph Type.
2. Click to select the desired graph type from those offered, or use the arrow keys to highlight the desired type.
3. Select View to display the new graph.

Identify the data series using the Graph-Series command and choosing up to six series from the list. Generally, each block of cells you identify should have the same number of cells as every other block. This will keep the number of categories consistent for each data series (each cell creates a new category for the series you are identifying).

After identifying the data series, use the Graph-Series-X Axis command to identify the X-axis labels. In the Fast Graph format, these appear above each column; but with this graphing method, they can appear in any block of cells on the spreadsheet. You should include as many cells in this block as appear in each data series. For example, if you have five cells in each data series, you should have five X-axis labels.

When finished, you can quit the series options and view the graph with the Graph-View command. At this point, you may want to customize the graph to make it appear more to your liking. Graph customization is described next.

DOING YOUR OWN THING

Once you have created a graph using either method described above, you are ready to customize it. Customization includes

- Changing the graph type.
- Adding titles and other text to the graph.
- Changing the patterns and colors of data series.
- Changing the Y-axis labels.
- Changing the X-axis labels.
- Creating a legend.
- Adding a second Y-axis.

The next few sections address these customization procedures. Afterward, you'll learn some important tips for choosing the right graph type.

TAKE YOUR PICK

After you specify the data series and X-axis labels for the graph, the next step is to select the desired graph type. Quattro Pro offers several from which to choose, including some 3D graphs.

Take some care in selecting the graph type—different graph types reveal different things about data. A detailed discussion of each type appears later in this chapter under the heading "The Right Graph Type." This will show you the advantages and disadvantages of each type and tips for making them look their best.

ADD TEXT

The Graph-Text command controls the standard text labels that you can add to the graph. These are shown in Figure 3-3.

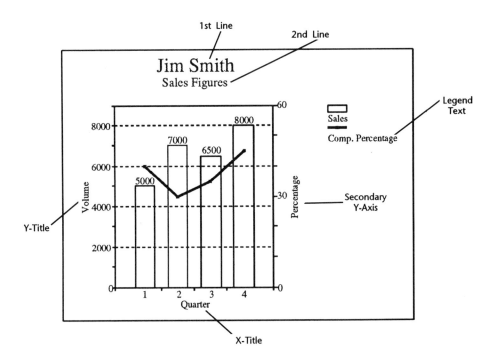

Figure 3-3: Each graph can have several different labels. You can insert these labels individually if desired.

1. Select the Graph-Text-Fonts option.
2. Choose the item whose font you want to change.
3. Select the desired font options (Typeface, Color, Point Size, Style.) See Chapter 4 for details about fonts.
4. Quit to return to the spreadsheet.

ADDING TEXT TO
THE GRAPH

1. Select the Graph-Text command.
2. Select from the list of titles and labels (the Legends option is discussed under "Use a Legend" later in this chapter).
3. Enter the desired text and press Enter.
4. Complete any other items in the list.
5. Quit to return to the spreadsheet.

1st Line—The main title that appears at the top of the graph. This title starts out in 24-point Swiss and is centered above the graph.

2nd Line—The subtitle that appears just below the main title. This title starts out in 18-point Swiss.

X-Title—The title that appears below the X-axis to explain what the axis labels represent. (Often, this is obvious and an X-title is not needed.) This title starts out in the 18-point Swiss font.

Y-Title—The title that appears along the Y-axis to explain its values. This title starts out in the 18-point Swiss font.

Secondary Y-Axis—The title that appears along the right (or secondary) Y-axis. You must add a secondary Y-axis before this title appears. Details about adding this axis appear in the "Adding and Formatting a Second Y-Axis" sidebar on page 96.

Legends—The labels that appear in the legend. Adding these labels makes the legend items appear on the graph. Details about adding legends appear in the "Creating a Legend" sidebar on page 62.

Completing one of these options causes the text to appear on the graph and the graph adjusts to make room for the text. To remove the text from the graph, return to the appropriate Graph-Text option and remove the entry.

Instead of entering text for each of these titles, you can tell Quattro Pro to use the text in a particular cell of the spreadsheet. Do this by typing a backslash (\) and then the cell address as the text. For example, to use the text in cell A5 as the main graph title, you would type \A5 after entering the command Graph-Text-1st Line.

Quattro Pro uses standard fonts, point sizes, styles and colors for the text labels, but you can change them if you like. To change these fonts, use the Graph-Text-Font command. Each title can be changed individually and you can select the Data & Tick Labels option to change the font used for the Y-axis values and X-axis labels. See Chapter 4, "Fonts and Printers," for details about using fonts.

CHANGE COLORS

You can change the colors that Quattro Pro applies to the data series in your graph. Just use the Graph-Customize Series-Colors command. Your monitor and the palette you've selected in Quattro Pro affect the appearance of color on the screen (see Chapter 1, "Spreadsheet Publishing Power"). Your printer affects the appearance of color or gray shades on the printout (see Chapter 7, "Printing Reports").

If you are not printing in color or with shades of gray, you should ignore this command and use fill patterns to distinguish data series from one another. Fill patterns are described next. (For information about appropriate use of color in your graphs, see Chapter 8.)

CHANGING SERIES COLORS

1. Select Graph-Customize Series-Colors.
2. Select the series whose color you want to change.
3. Select the color from the list or gallery provided.
4. Quit to return to the spreadsheet.

CHANGE PATTERNS, MARKERS AND LINES

Another type of customization includes changing the fill patterns of the graph's data series. This helps you distinguish one data series from another when printing or viewing them in black and white. Quattro Pro offers the following fill patterns for your data series.

CHANGING SERIES PATTERNS

1. Select Graph-Customize Series-Fill Patterns.
2. Select the series whose pattern you want to change.
3. Select the pattern from the list or gallery provided.
4. Quit to return to the spreadsheet.

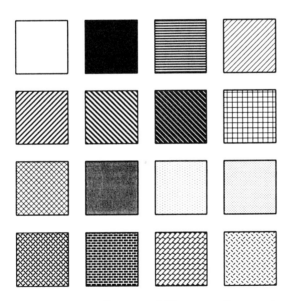

Figure 3-4: *Quattro Pro offers several fill patterns for your data series.*

For ideas on using fill patterns effectively, see the discussion of bar graphs under the heading "The Right Graph Type" later in this chapter.

Changing fill patterns does not apply to line or XY graphs because they have no space to fill. For these graphs, you can change the styles of the series lines and markers. Quattro Pro offers the following line styles and marker styles.

CHANGING SERIES LINES

1. Select Graph-Customize Series-Markers & Lines-Line Styles.
2. Select the series whose line you want to change.
3. Select the line style from the list or gallery provided.
4. Quit to return to the spreadsheet.

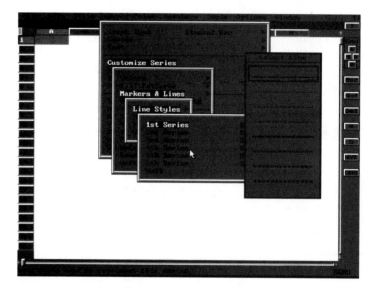

Figure 3-5: Quattro Pro offers several line styles for your line and XY graphs.

For more information on selecting markers and lines, see the discussion of line graphs under the heading "The Right Graph Type" later in this chapter.

ADD INTERIOR LABELS

Interior labels are special text entries that explain the plot points in a graph. Usually, these appear above the bars of a bar graph and display the values of each bar.

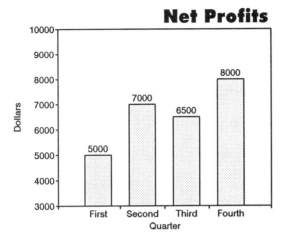

Figure 3-6: You can add interior labels to a graph to explain the value of each plot point.

You can use any block of cells on the spreadsheet as the interior labels for a data series. But the block should contain the same number of cells as the data series. In other words, match one interior label with each plot point in the data series. You can type these labels into a block of cells on the spreadsheet or you can take values from the existing graph data. Often, interior labels use the same cells as the data series.

After you specify the block of cells, Quattro Pro asks you to position the labels relative to the plot points. This helps you avoid overlapping the interior labels with other chart elements (or with each other) and it applies to line, XY, hilo and 3D line charts only. Interior label positions are fixed for the other graph types, and the position you select will have no effect. You should avoid using interior labels with stacked graphs, such as stacked bar and area graphs.

Note that the font, size, style and color of interior labels is set by the Graph-Text-Font-Data & Tick Labels command.

CHANGE GRID LINES

Normally, Quattro Pro includes grid lines in your graphs. Usually, these appear horizontally to display the Y-axis values, but they may also appear vertically.

CHANGING SERIES MARKERS

1. Select Graph-Customize Series-Markers & Lines-Markers.
2. Select the series whose markers you want to change.
3. Select the line style from the list or gallery provided.
4. Quit to return to the spreadsheet.

ADDING INTERIOR LABELS

1. Select Graph-Customize Series-Interior Labels.
2. Choose the desired series from the list.
3. Highlight the range of cells containing the labels. Each cell will correspond to one plot in the series, so the block should have as many cells as there are plot points in the series. Press Enter when finished.
4. Choose a label position.
5. Repeat the procedure for other series if desired.
6. Quit to return to the spreadsheet.

Using the Graph-Overall-Grid options, you can control the appearance of grid lines on your graph. They can appear horizontally, vertically, both or neither. And if you display grid lines, you can also control their color and style. Figure 3-7 shows some examples.

CHANGING GRID LINES

1. Select the Graph-Overall command.
2. Select Grid.
3. Add grid lines using the Horizontal, Vertical or Both option. Remove grid lines using the Clear option.
4. Use the Grid Color option to change the color of the grid lines.
5. Use the Line Style option to change the thickness and style of the grid lines.
6. Use the Fill Color option to change the color of the chart interior where the grid lines are drawn.
7. Quit to return to the spreadsheet.

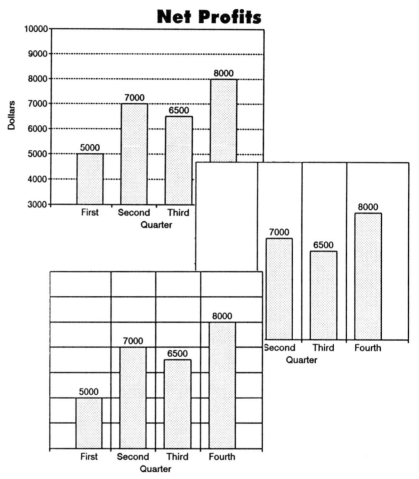

Figure 3-7: You can control the grid lines used in a graph and their colors and styles.

ADD BORDERS

Quattro Pro lets you add a border to three main elements of a graph: the titles, the legend and the graph itself. Figure 3-8 illustrates these borders.

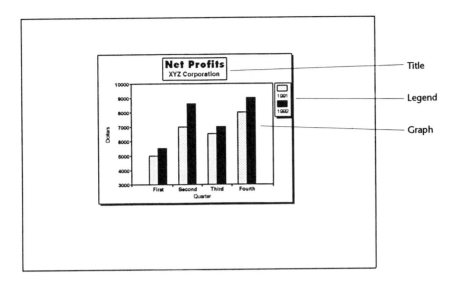

Figure 3-8: Three types of graph borders can be added to a graph.

You can select from seven different border styles as shown in Figure 3-9.

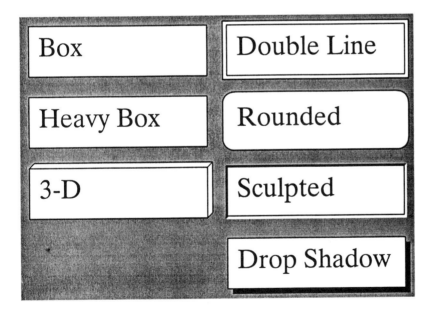

ADDING BORDERS AND BOXES

1. Select Graph-Overall-Outlines.
2. Select the element around which you want an outline.
3. Select one of the outlines from the list. The None option removes the outline from the selected element.
4. Quit to return to the spreadsheet.

Figure 3-9: Quattro Pro offers seven different border styles for your graph borders.

Remember that too many boxes and outlines in your graph can be distracting. It's often better to avoid using borders than risk overusing them.

CUSTOMIZING Y-AXIS VALUES

1. **Select Graph-Y Axis-Scale-Manual.**
2. **Choose High, and enter the high value for the axis.**
3. **Choose Low, and enter the low value for the axis.**
4. **Choose Increment, and enter the increment for the scale.**
5. **Press Q to return to the spreadsheet.**

CUSTOMIZE THE Y-AXIS

The vertical axis determines the graph's numeric range. Usually, Quattro Pro's automatic selections for the Y-axis minimum and maximum values are acceptable, but changing these values can make a dramatic change on the graph. One reason for changing these values is to show how the graph's values differ from a particular high or low value. For example, Quattro Pro may set the high value to 50 because no data point is larger than 50. But you want to show how the data points relate to the maximum available value of 100. This change can make a vast difference in the message implied by the graph and used improperly can sometimes mislead. Consider the two graphs in Figure 3-10 that show a change in values over time .

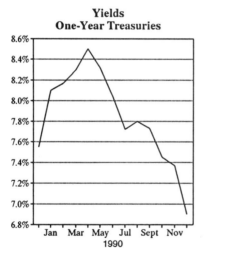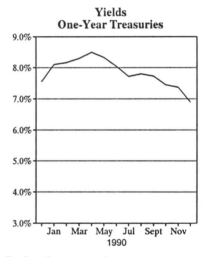

Figure 3-10: Two graphs that display the same values can appear to show different values. This is done by adjusting the Y-axis values.

The first graph appears to have a greater variance in the values. Actually, it just uses a smaller range of minimum and maximum Y-axis values.

This change also has the effect of minimizing the peaks and valleys of the line and the overall downward trend. Sometimes, this is desirable; sometimes it's not. The decision should be based on the graph's purpose. However, it can be distracting when a graph has dramatic differences in data points; changing the axis values is an excellent way of "turning down the volume." Check that your minor tick marks are divisible evenly into the major marks.

If the axis values appear in the graph itself via the Graph-Customize Series-Interior Labels command, you can sometimes eliminate the Y-axis completely.

ADDING X-AXIS LABELS

1. Select Graph-Series-X Axis Series.
2. Highlight the block containing the X-axis labels and press Enter.
3. Quit to return to the spreadsheet.

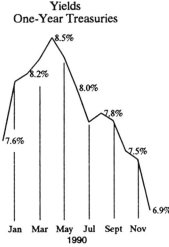

Figure 3-11: *The Y-axis values are not required if your graph is well annotated. In this example, the Y-axis is covered up.*

In this example, the Y-axis values were covered up by a rectangular object of the same color as the background. This was done in the Annotator (see Chapter 5, "Using the Annotator"). Also, drop lines were added to the plot points to emphasize their position on the X-axis. This was done using the line tool in the Annotator.

CUSTOMIZE THE X-AXIS

Most graphs use the X-axis to display the category labels for the graph. These come from the block of cells you specified with the Graph-Series-X Axis Series command.

The most common problem with the X-axis is that it doesn't adequately display the X-axis labels. Often, the labels are too long or there are too many of them to fit comfortably along

ALTERNATING X-AXIS LABELS

1. Choose Graph-X Axis-Alternating Ticks-Yes.

CREATING A LEGEND

1. Select Graph-Text-Legends.
2. Select the desired series.
3. Type the legend entry for that series or refer to a cell.
4. Repeat these steps for other series.

the axis. There are several ways around this problem. First, you can split the labels onto two lines using the Graph-X Axis-Alternating Ticks command. In some cases, you can enter shorter versions of the label in a different area of the spreadsheet and refer to this area for the X-axis labels. This is useful when the X-axis labels are dates.

You can also skip labels along the axis so that every other one—or every third one—appears. To skip labels, move to the X-Axis Series range and delete or hide the labels you don't want to appear. If this is not appropriate for the spreadsheet, consider using a different block of cells for the X-Axis Series data. Other ideas include using a more compressed typeface or a smaller point size for the axis labels. This is done with the Graph-Text-Font-Data & Tick Labels command.

Be sure that your font choice works well with other type on the graph and that you don't use all uppercase letters.

USE A LEGEND

Sometimes a graph's annotation is sufficient to describe each data series shown. Other times, you need to include a legend. Legends should be as simple to understand as possible. They should be in a visible area of the graph, but should not be too large or overbearing.

Quattro Pro automatically inserts a legend on your graph when you fill out the legend text entries using the Graph-Text-Legends options. Entering text into any of the legend options causes the legend to appear. Therefore, to remove a legend, you must remove the text entries from each of the Graph-Text-Legends options.

MOVING THE LEGEND

1. Select Graph-Text-Legends-Position.
2. Choose from the list of positions.
3. Quit to return to the spreadsheet.

You can type the legend entry for each data series, or refer to a cell containing the data. Refer to a cell by typing the cell address preceded by a backslash (\), as in "\B5."

You can change the font, size, style and color of the legend entries by using the Graph-Text-Font-Legends command. Font options are discussed in Chapter 4, "Fonts and Printers."

Quattro Pro offers several standard locations for a graph's legend. It originally appears at the bottom of the graph, but you can move it to another standard location using the Graph-Text-Legends-Position command.

If you don't like the standard locations, you can move the legend anywhere on a graph by using the Annotator. Another idea is to use annotation tools to create a custom legend.

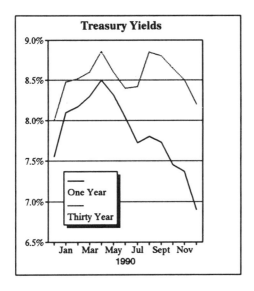

MOVING THE LEGEND
MANUALLY

1. Enter the Annotator.
2. Press the Tab key until the legend is highlighted.
3. Press Shift with the Arrow keys.
4. Press Enter when finished.

Figure 3-12: You can use the Annotator to move the legend to any location on the graph.

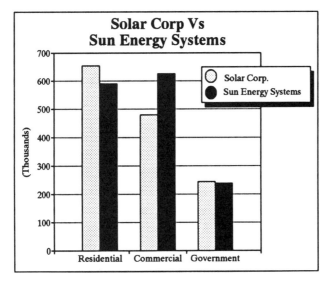

Figure 3-13: The Annotator can be used to create a custom legend for the graph.

These custom legend ideas can be interesting and attractive without taking away from the graph. (For more details about using the Annotator, see Chapter 5.)

WHAT'S IN A NAME?

You can create and save numerous graphs on each Quattro Pro spreadsheet if you like. Simply give each one a unique name (with the Graph-Name-Create command) after you create it. This places it into a list of graphs for the spreadsheet, and you can view any of the listed graphs by using the Graph-Name-Display command.

When you save the spreadsheet with the File-Save command, the named graphs are also saved and will appear the next time you use the spreadsheet.

When you first create a graph—and before you name it— Quattro Pro keeps the graph in a temporary location called the "current graph." It's important to name the current graph before creating a new graph because the new graph will replace the previous current graph. In short, the current graph is the graph on which you are currently working. All the graphing commands and options apply to the current graph. When you're done working on it, name it.

You can make changes to a previously named graph by copying it into the current graph storage place and then changing it. Do this simply by displaying the graph with the Graph-Name-Display command. Remember that this removes whatever graph was previously in the current graph location. After changing the graph, you can then re-store the graph under its previous name, or type a new graph name to store the modified version as a separate graph. In this way, you can use any named graph as the starting point for other graphs.

NAMING AND SAVING A GRAPH

1. Create the graph and view it with the Graph-View command, then press Esc to return to the Graph menu.
2. Choose the Graph-Name-Create command.
3. Enter a name for the graph and press Enter.
4. Save the spreadsheet with the File-Save command.
5. Repeat the procedure for any other graph you create on the same spreadsheet. (You may want to reset the graph after naming it.)

REMOVING A GRAPH

1. Select Graph-Name-Erase.
2. Select the desired graph from the list provided.
3. Save the spreadsheet with the File-Save command.

VIEWING A PREVIOUSLY NAMED GRAPH

1. Select the Graph-Name-Display command.
2. Select the desired graph from the list provided.

Using a previously named graph as the starting point for new graphs is a handy feature. But what if you want to start a graph from scratch? It appears that there is always one graph or another in the current graph location. Hence, all graphing commands will be modifying that graph.

To start a fresh graph from scratch, reset the current graph using the Graph-Customize Series-Reset-Graph command. You can then start your graphing commands on a blank current graph.

THE RIGHT GRAPH TYPE

Earlier in this chapter, you read about changing the graph type using the Graph-Graph Type command. This is an essential part of the graphing procedure. Here you'll discover some important considerations for choosing each of the graph types in Quattro Pro.

LINE GRAPH

Line graphs are very effective for presenting fluctuations in data over time. Usually, the X-axis represents a progression of time in even increments, such as months or years.

(Because they can handle so many plot points, line graphs are excellent alternatives to bar graphs that have too many categories—see "Bar Graph" later in this chapter.)

RESETTING A GRAPH

1. Select the Graph-Customize Series-Reset-Graph command.

REMOVING SERIES MARKERS

1. Select Graph-Customize Series-Markers & Lines-Formats.
2. Choose the series from which you want to remove markers.
3. Select Lines.
4. Press Esc until you return to the spreadsheet.

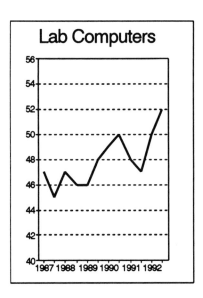

Figure 3-14: Line graphs are best for showing fluctuation of data over time.

Technically, only the plot points of a line graph are accurate. The line connecting these points is placed there for visual effect. Any point on the line between the plot points doesn't necessarily reflect an accurate value. That's why line charts often use special symbols to indicate plot points. For line charts that include more than one line, the symbols may be different for each line; however, this is usually not necessary. You can use various colors and styles to differentiate between the lines. Line colors and styles are discussed under "Change Patterns, Markers and Lines" earlier in this chapter.

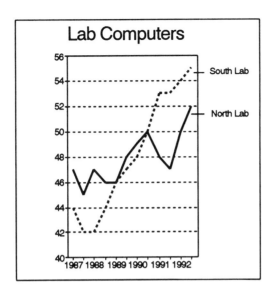

Figure 3-15: Use various line styles (or colors) to differentiate between lines in a line graph. This is an alternative to using markers.

Sometimes, each line of a chart is marked with a caption instead of symbols. This can be done in the Annotator and eliminates the need for a legend.

Line graphs are also good for showing future trends. Consider including extra (blank) categories in each data series to provide room on the graph for supposition.

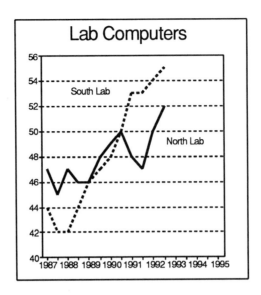

*Figure 3-16: Adding some blank cells to each data series in a line
graph adds extra room on the graph for supposition.*

While line graphs work well with a lot of categories, avoid
using too many lines (data series) on the same graph. This
can cause confusion.

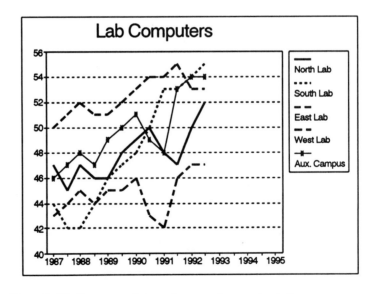

Figure 3-17: Too many data series on a line create clutter.

The example in Figure 3-17 is very cluttered with elements, such as boxes, series markers and grid lines (we'll talk more about these elements later in the chapter). In such cases, ask yourself whether the graph can be split into two or more graphs. Perhaps each line could have its own graph in a presentation, as shown in Figure 3-18.

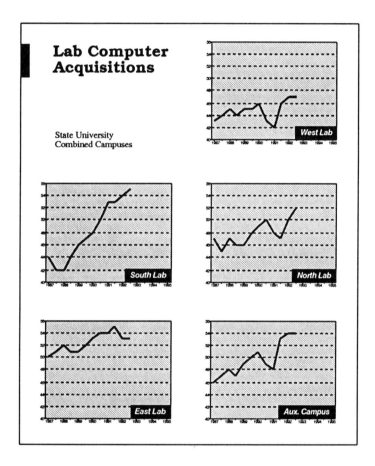

Figure 3-18: If a line graph has too many lines, try splitting the data series into individual graphs and combining them on a page.

The audience can make comparisons among these graphs without needing to see all the lines piled on top of each other. In this example, each graph was created from one of the data series in the original graph—resulting in five separate graphs. Printing them together on a page is done by inserting the graphs onto the spreadsheet. This procedure is discussed in Chapter 6, "Designing Effective Pages."

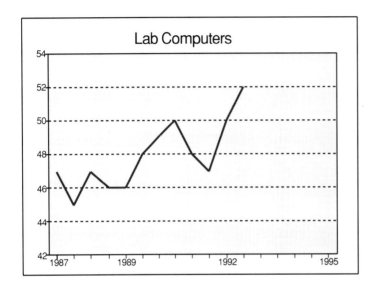

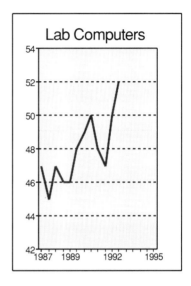

Figure 3-19: You can make a graph taller than normal to emphasize the fluctuation in lines. This can be done in the Annotator or by inserting the graph into a tall block on the spreadsheet.

CHANGING GRAPH PROPORTIONS

1. **View the graph using Graph-View or Graph-Name-Display.**
2. **Press the Slash (/) key to enter the Annotator.**
3. **Press Tab until the graph is "highlighted."**
4. **Press the Period (.) key.**
5. **Press the Left and Up Arrow keys to change the proportions.**
6. **Press Enter when finished.**

Because line charts emphasize fluctuations in data, consider how you might emphasize this fluctuation. One way is to make the chart tall and thin—giving the optical illusion of a larger fluctuation.

Horizontal grid lines are often needed to make a graph clearer and the plot points easier to evaluate. But keep the grid lines understated and subordinate to the lines themselves. Vertical grid lines are seldom needed.

Using heavy plot lines helps attract attention to the graph's message and away from subordinate elements, such as grids and annotation.

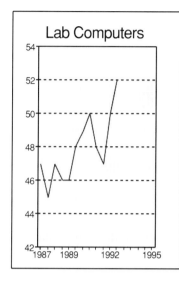
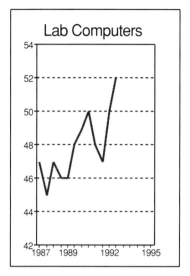

Figure 3-20: Thick lines lend contrast to the graph and make the lines easier to follow.

BAR GRAPH

Bar graphs are probably the most common type of graph used for business. Their purpose is to show how plot points compare to one another over time and/or for different categories. A single data series can be compared over several categories; multiple data series can be compared to each other and over several categories.

Although the X-axis can represent time, the chart does not emphasize the time element as well as a line chart could. Instead, the bar chart focuses on the bar heights in comparison to one another. If you keep the data series to a minimum,

CHANGING LINE THICKNESS

1. Choose Graph-Customize Series-Markers & Lines-Line Styles.
2. Choose the series you want to change.
3. Choose the desired line style.
4. Repeat the procedure for other lines.

you can easily compare one bar to the next within a single category, and you can easily follow the change in each series across several categories. Too many data series can make the graph too complex to be easily understood, as shown in Figure 3-21.

CHANGING SERIES WIDTH

1. Choose Graph-Customize Series-Bar Width.
2. Enter the desired width (a larger number will make the bars wider).

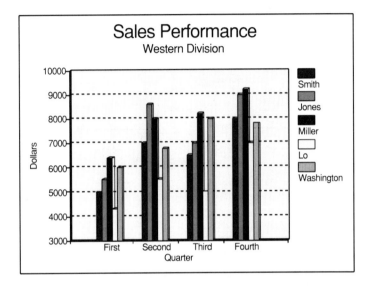

Figure 3-21: Too many data series in a bar graph create visual clutter.

To simplify this graph, try turning off the 3D effect on the bars. This is described in more detail under "3D Effects" later in this chapter. (Using the 3D bar graph may also make the graphs easier to read.)

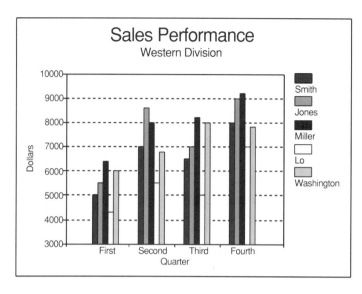

Figure 3-22: You can turn off the 3D effect on the data series to simplify the graph.

You may also try widening the bars and changing the grid lines to make the graph easier to read.

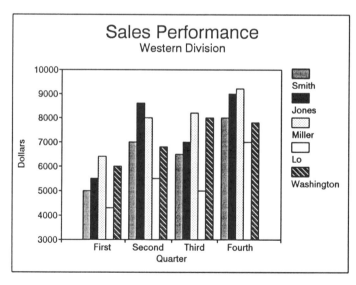

Figure 3-23: Another way to increase readability is to change the widths of the bars.

If your graph requires many series, put the information into several graphs, instead of one, to simplify the comparisons. For example, Figure 3-23 can be split into five column charts that compare dollar sales per quarter for each individual salesperson. Then you can compare salespeople to each other in a bar or stacked bar graph showing sales totals.

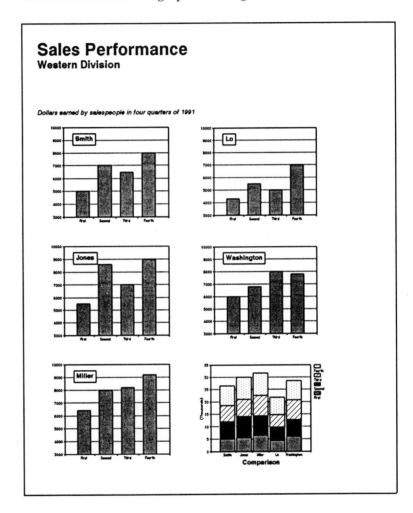

Figure 3-24: Try splitting each data series into a separate bar graph and combining them on a page. This is useful when your graphs have too many data series.

Details about inserting graphs onto the spreadsheet and printing graphs are covered in Chapter 6, "Designing Effective Pages."

Avoid using wild patterns or colors for the bars, which can distract the audience from the chart's message. Simple pattern contrast is sufficient to be effective for black-and-white business charts.

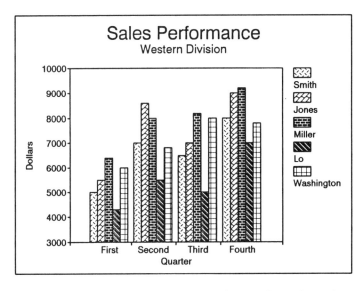

Figure 3-25: Wild patterns and colors can distract the audience from the point of the graph.

As with line charts, you can emphasize the difference in data points on a bar chart by changing the graph's proportions (increasing its height) and by using a minimum number of values on the Y-axis.

XY GRAPH

XY graphs are also called scatter graphs because they can show plot points in a sort of scattered pattern along X- and Y-axes. But they can also be used as line charts that have values along both the X-axis and the Y-axis. The primary purpose of an XY graph is to show the relationship of the plot points to one another. The patterns of plotted points often reveal trends.

CUSTOMIZING SERIES PATTERNS

1. Select Graph-Customize Series-Fill Patterns.
2. Choose the desired data series.
3. Choose the desired pattern.

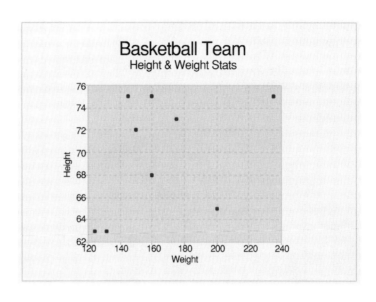

Figure 3-26: XY graphs are useful for showing statistical data plotted along two value axes.

To create an XY graph, you need exactly two data series—one defined as the 1st Series and the second defined as the X-Axis Series. Quattro Pro will automatically scale both the X and Y axes, but you can customize the axes as described earlier in this chapter. Finally, use the Graph-Customize Series-Markers & Lines-Formats-Graph-Symbols command to remove the series' lines, leaving only the plot-point markers. This is also explained earlier in this chapter, under the heading "Change Patterns, Markers and Lines."

XY graphs are somewhat technical and require some expertise to use and interpret. They are typically used to graph sample statistics and population analyses, and often include a regression line plotted among the points.

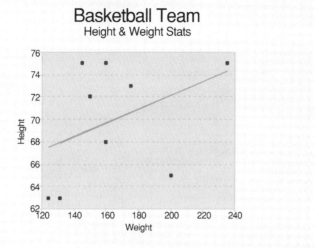

Figure 3-27: *You can add a regression line to an XY graph to show trends.*

To add a regression line, you must calculate a series of values that will be plotted and displayed as a line on the graph. The calculations are made with Quattro Pro's regression analysis features.

Start with your two basic data series for the graph. These should be plotted as 1st Series and X-Axis Series. (Use series markers and not lines to plot these values on the graph.) Quattro Pro's regression analysis takes your X-Axis Series values and calculates the "intercept" values required to form a regression line along the Y-axis. In other words, given a set of values for the X-axis, the regression calculation specifies values along the Y-axis that will form a regression line. The intersection of the X-axis values and the calculated Y-axis values forms the line. The X-axis values are called the Independent Variables, because they're not dependent on other values. The Y-axis values are Dependent Variables because they depend on the X-axis values.

Using the Tools-Advanced Math-Regression options, specify the Independent and Dependent values as the current X-Axis Series and 1st Series ranges, respectively.

ADDING A REGRESSION LINE

1. Select the Tools-Advanced Math-Regression command.
2. Specify the X-Axis Series values as the Independent range.
3. Specify the 1st Series values as the Dependent range.
4. Specify an output range for the regression calculations.
5. Select Go.
6. Calculate a new series of values by multiplying each X-axis value by the X-Coefficient and adding the Constant.
7. Plot the new calculated values as the 2nd Series for the graph.
8. Use the Graph-Customize Series-Markers & Lines-Formats-2nd Series-Lines command to display the *2nd series* as a Line.

Next, highlight a cell to indicate the output range. This is where Quattro Pro will display the regression calculations. Make sure you have at least four columns and ten rows for the output. Use the Tools-Advanced Math-Regression-Go option to create the regression calculations.

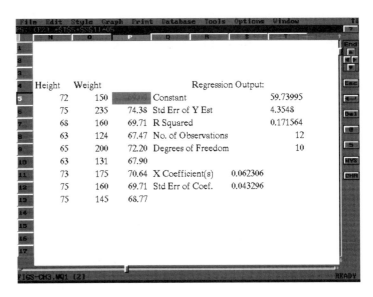

Figure 3-28: The Advanced Math tools provide commands for regression analysis.

This simply gives you the values on which you can calculate the desired data series values for the graph. To do this, multiply each value in the current X-Axis Series by the X Coefficient value in the regression output range. Then add the Constant value to this. Using the previous figure, an example would be

P5: T5+S11*O5

Repeat (or copy) this for each value in the X-axis range, and you have the values needed for the 2nd Series. Add these to the graph using the Graph-Series command.

The final step is to display the new data series as a line, by selecting the Graph-Customize Series-Markers & Lines-Formats-2nd Series-Lines command.

If the regression line is the main point of the graph, make it stand out using techniques described for line graphs earlier in this chapter.

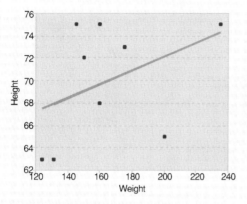

Basketball Team
Height & Weight Stats

Figure 3-29: Make the regression line stand out by using a thick line style.

Note that XY graphs show precise relationships between plot points and require a square graph perspective. Changing the orientation of the graph could distort the information—since one axis would be longer than the other.

STACKED BAR GRAPH

The stacked bar graph is a bar graph that stacks data series on top of each other. Each data series comprises a portion of the total bar. The number of bars equals the number of categories in your data series. For example, if you have several data series but only one category in each, then you'll have only one bar. The height of the stacked bars represents the combined data series for that category—so you can quickly compare totals by looking at the bar heights (assuming you have more than one data series). You can also examine in detail the bar's component parts and how much each data series contributes to the bar.

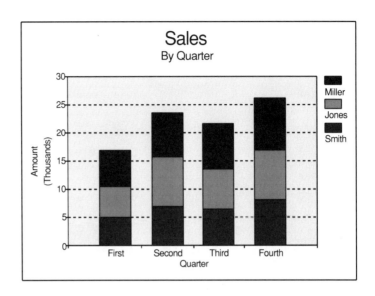

Figure 3-30: A stacked bar graph is useful for showing how individual values make up the totals of several bars.

Like most graphs, stacked bar graphs work best with a minimum of data series; however, if you keep the graph simple and uncluttered, you can compare several categories effectively, as shown in Figure 3-31.

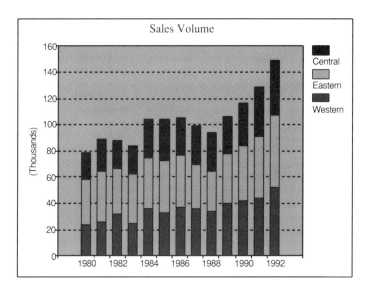

Figure 3-31: Stacked bar graphs can work well with numerous categories (bars).

If you begin to accumulate too many categories or categories are time-oriented, consider using an area graph (described in detail later in this chapter) instead of a stacked bar.

Avoid using interior labels to display values in the stacked bars. Stacked graphs simply cover up the labels and make them useless. Instead of interior labels, you can use annotation to indicate the graph's values. Alternatively, consider using pie graphs or column graphs instead. A separate pie or column would be necessary to show the information in each bar, but this would provide plenty of space for labels. A simple bar graph can chart and compare the totals of these pies or columns.

CREATING A PIE GRAPH

1. Select the Graph-Series-1st Series command.
2. Highlight the block of data representing the pie slices.
3. Press Q to quit the Series menu.
4. Select the Customize Series command.
5. Select Reset.
6. Select 2nd Series.
7. Quit to return to the spreadsheet.

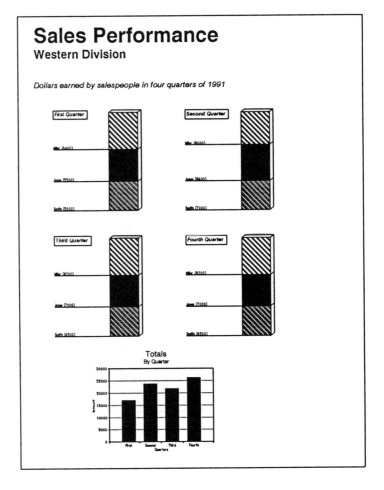

Figure 3-32: Try using column graphs when you need to label individual elements of each bar.

You can use a different color for each pie or column, and various patterns to differentiate the series inside. Then, use the same color sequence for the bars in the simple bar chart.

PIE GRAPH

The pie graph is a classic example of how parts make up a whole. The "slice" metaphor seems to be universally understood. But pie graphs have certain limitations. For example, a pie graph created with Quattro Pro shows only one data series. Therefore, when you define the data series for a pie graph, select only the 1st series option in the Graph-Series command. In fact, you should make sure the second series is empty by using the Graph-Customize Series-Reset-2nd Series command.

Each cell in the first data series will create a slice of the pie, and Quattro Pro will give it a unique pattern and color. However, Quattro Pro has only nine color/pattern combinations to assign to the slices, so if you include more than nine cells in the data series, Quattro Pro will repeat the first nine colors and patterns beginning with slice 10. (In other words, slice 10 will be the same as slice 1.) In some cases, this will limit you to nine slices. But in most cases, repeating the patterns and colors will not change the message.

If you don't like the colors and patterns used by Quattro Pro, you can create a different set. This is done with the Colors and Patterns options in the Graph-Customize Series-Pies command. To use only colors with no patterns, choose the empty pattern from the list of patterns. You can also avoid using colors by choosing Bright White for each of the slices.

Keeping the slices to nine is a good idea if the pie would be confusing with duplicated colors and patterns. Another reason for limiting the slices is to avoid crowding the labels, as you can see in Figure 3-33.

CHANGING THE COLORS OF PIE SLICES

1. Select Graph-Customize Series-Pies-Colors.
2. Choose the slice whose color you want to change. You can choose from the first nine slices.
3. Select from the list (or palette) of colors.

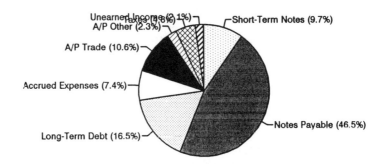

Liabilities

Figure 3-33: Pie graphs can have overcrowded labels. This is especially common when pies have numerous slices.

CHANGING THE PATTERNS OF PIE SLICES

1. Select Graph-Customize Series-Pies-Patterns.
2. Choose the slice whose pattern you want to change. You can choose from the first nine slices.
3. Select from the list (or palette) of patterns.

REMOVING PIE LABELS

1. Select Graph-Customize Series-Pies-Label Format-None.
2. Select Graph-Customize Series-Reset-X Axis Series.

Another idea is to eliminate the automatic labels and add them as a legend.

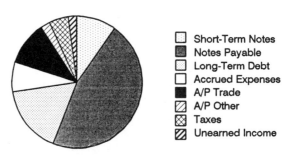

Liabilities

Figure 3-34: Remove the pie graph labels by resetting the X-axis series. You can then use the Annotator to create a legend.

You can eliminate all the labels using the Graph-Customize Series-Reset-X Axis Series command. You can also remove the percentage values and leave only the labels using the Graph-Customize Series-Pies-Label Format-None command. The legend shown in Figure 3-34 was created in the Annotator (see Chapter 5).

Pie graphs are often used to show companywide data, since the company is represented by the whole pie as one data series. But, as with stacked bar charts, you can use several pies to compare categories. You can also manually adjust the pie size as shown in Figure 3-35. However, a stacked bar chart is better for this type of comparison.

1991

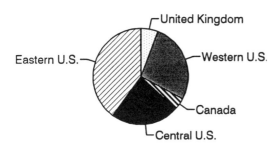

1992

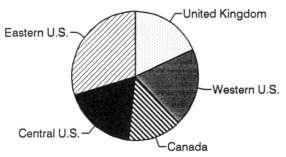

EXPLODING A PIE SLICE

1. Select Graph-Customize Series-Pies-Explode.
2. Choose the desired slice.
3. Choose Explode.

Figure 3-35: You can manually adjust the sizes of pie charts and print them together. This represents the overall comparison in the pies' volumes.

This sizing is accomplished by placing the graphs on the spreadsheet using different-size areas, then printing them with 4:3 aspect turned off. (More on adding graphs to your spreadsheets in Chapter 6, "Designing Effective Pages.")

The most common way to emphasize information on a pie graph is to explode a slice—or two. But if you explode more than two, you may weaken the effect.

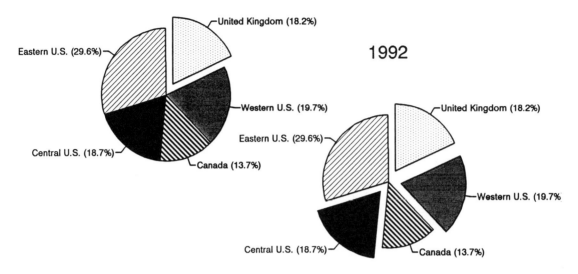

Figure 3-36: Explode only a slice or two for emphasis.

If you need to explode a slice beyond the ninth slice, you'll have to use a special technique. First, type sequential numbers (beginning with 1) for each slice of the pie. For example, if the pie has 14 slices, enter the numbers 1 through 14 into a block of cells on the spreadsheet.

Now go back and add 100 to any of the numbers whose corresponding slice is to be exploded. For example, to explode slice 12, change the number 12 to 112. Next, use the Graph-Series-2nd Series command to highlight this block of cells as the data for the second series. Then display the pie again.

When exploding one slice, place the slice between 0 and 60 degrees (between 12:00 and 3:00). Never position the slice between 60 and 180 degrees (3:00 and 6:00) because the eye is led downward and off the page. Also, facing the slice downward tends to create a negative feeling (this effect is not as strong with a 3D pie graph).

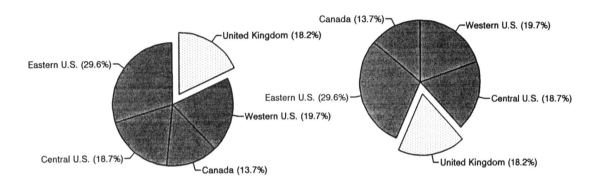

Figure 3-37: *When exploding slices, try positioning the slice in the upper right quarter of the pie.*

When exploding two slices, place them on opposite sides of the pie for the best effect.

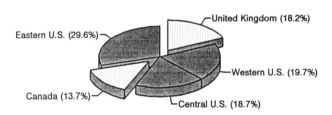

Figure 3-38: *When exploding two slices, place them on opposite sides of the pie.*

For emphasis, use a different pattern for exploded slices, as in Figure 3-38. You can do the same with color. Choose patterns that don't clash and avoid heavy parallel lines on large slices because they cause eye strain. And don't overlook black and white as "colors."

AREA GRAPH

An area graph is to a line graph what a stacked bar graph is to a bar graph. In other words, you could consider an area graph a "stacked line graph." But the purpose of the area graph is to show how parts make up a whole when viewed over time. For this reason, area graphs and pie graphs serve a similar purpose.

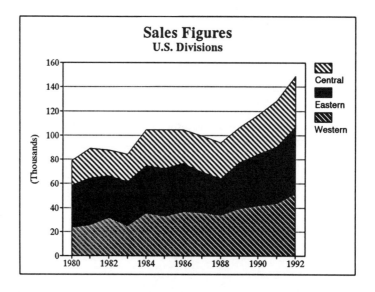

Figure 3-39: Area graphs are useful for showing how parts make up a total over time. They are similar to pie and stacked bar graphs.

The line at the top of each layer does not represent the performance of that data series. The line's valleys and peaks can be misleading because, except for the first line, the plot points don't originate from zero but from the top of the series below. The graph shows the area between the lines as a portion of the total. By examining the thickness of each area, you can see how layers change over time in terms of their contribution to the total.

Changing the graph's proportions can change the overall effect, making the line fluctuations more obvious.

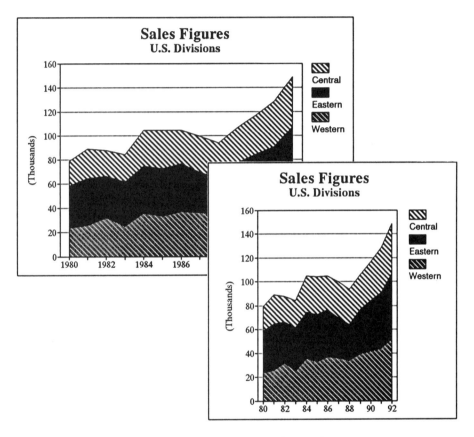

Figure 3-40: Change a graph's proportions to emphasize the fluctuation of values. This is done in the Annotator.

ROTATED BAR GRAPH

A rotated bar graph is a bar graph turned sideways. This orientation is especially useful for showing performance or merit among several series.

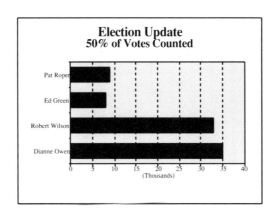

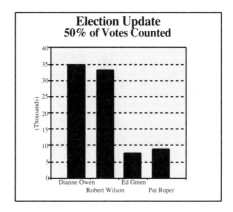

Figure 3-41: A rotated bar graph is useful for showing performance among several items.

Comparing the bar to the rotated bar, you'll probably find the rotated bar graph gives an impression of more competition between the elements because the bars seem to run from left to right. A standard bar chart, on the other hand, plots values on an axis, which emphasizes quantity. You can do anything with a rotated bar graph that you can do with a standard bar; and many of the graphic rules discussed for bar charts apply here also.

Rotated bar graphs are usually best when they show only one category or only a few series within a number of categories.

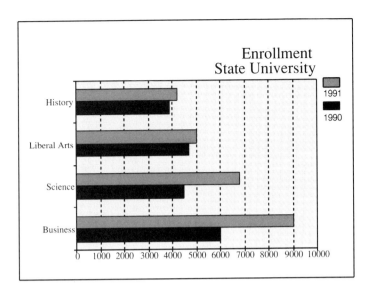

Figure 3-42: Rotated bar graphs are best when they show only one category of data, or only one series.

As shown in Figure 3-42, rotated bar graphs have plenty of room for axis labels. Note that the X-axis and Y-axis have changed positions; the X-axis is now vertical and the Y-axis is horizontal. However, if you use the Graph-X Axis command, it will affect the Y-axis on this graph (the horizontal axis) and the Graph-Y Axis command will affect the X-axis (the vertical axis).

Rotated bar graphs don't effectively emphasize changes in time; standard bar charts or line charts are best for this. When time is used in rotated bar graphs, it's often a benchmark for comparing the performance of the rotated bars, as in Figure 3-42.

Rotated bar graphs are often arranged in descending order. That is, the best performing bar is placed on top and others are in order beneath it. This keeps your eye on the page rather than making it scan downward and off the page.

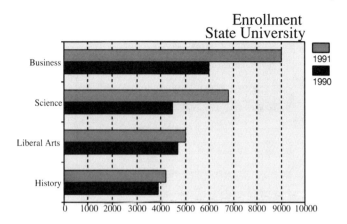

Figure 3-43: *Arrange bars in descending order on a rotated bar graph. This keeps the eye on the page.*

Often, you can eliminate the horizontal axis labels and use annotation to demonstrate the bar values. See Chapter 5 for details.

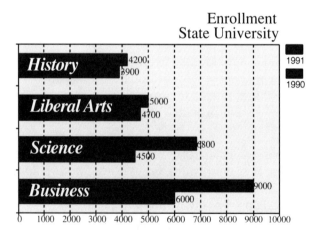

Figure 3-44: *You can annotate the graph to show detail for each bar. This is done in the Annotator.*

Other types of annotation and graphics work well with rotated bar graphs.

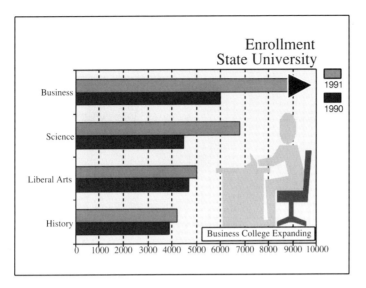

Figure 3-45: Rotated bar graphs have plenty of space for annotation.

COLUMN GRAPH

You might think a column graph is like a stacked bar graph with only one bar. That's true in some ways, but a column graph is more like a rectangular pie graph: by dividing a column into segments, it shows how parts make up the whole. It's useful in the same ways a pie graph is useful.

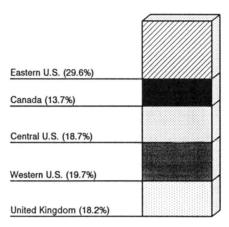

Eastern U.S. (29.6%)

Canada (13.7%)

Central U.S. (18.7%)

Western U.S. (19.7%)

United Kingdom (18.2%)

Figure 3-46: Column graphs are useful for showing how parts make up a total. They are similar to pie graphs.

Quattro Pro automatically adds labels to the column, as it does with pie slices. (And you can remove them in the same way.) Graph customization options for column graphs are identical to those for pie graphs (except you can't explode parts of a column graph). A column graph, like the pie graph, uses one data series, and each category (cell) in that series becomes a segment of the whole. A *stacked* bar graph, however, charts several data series—each comprising a segment of the bar. A column chart allows nine segments (or more, if you don't mind repeating patterns) whereas a stacked bar allows only six.

TEXT GRAPH

A text graph is simply a blank screen on which you can draw or type text using the Annotator. It's useful for creating organizational charts, flow charts and illustrations (these design elements are discussed in Chapter 6, "Designing Effective Pages). See Chapter 5 for details about using the Annotator's tools to draw or type onto text graphs.

COMBINATION GRAPH

A combination graph combines two or more contrasting graph types within one graph screen. Combination graphs are effective for charting two data series that present two different types of information.

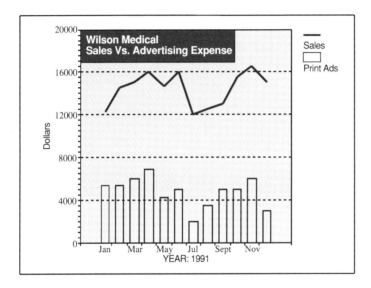

Figure 3-47: *Combination graphs are useful for showing two data series that use two different types of graphs. This contrasts one element with the other.*

CREATING COMBINATION GRAPHS

1. Start with a normal graph.
2. Select Graph-Customize Series-Override Type.
3. Select the series that you want displayed in a different graph type.
4. Choose Bar or Line for the type. Default returns the series to the same type as the other series.

To create a combination graph, you simply specify which data series you want displayed in a different type. When choosing graph types for combinations, use the same criteria discussed throughout this chapter. Different graph types reveal different things about the data, and this should be the main factor in your combination choices.

Some combinations won't work: a stacked graph cannot be combined with any other type of graph, including stacked bar, pie and area graphs. If you were to combine a stacked bar graph with, say, a line graph, the stacked totals would be inaccurate because the data series used to create the line would be included in the totals for the stacked bars. The stacked bars would then represent one too many values. Also, Quattro Pro doesn't allow you to stack a 3D graph with any other graph.

One useful technique is to use a combination graph to show the same data series in two different ways. This can emphasize the change in bars, for example.

ADDING AND FORMATTING A SECOND Y-AXIS

1. Choose Graph-Y Axis-2nd Y Axis.
2. Choose options for the second axis.
3. Choose Graph-Customize Series-Y Axis.
4. Select the series that applies to the 2nd Y-axis.
5. Choose Secondary Y-axis.

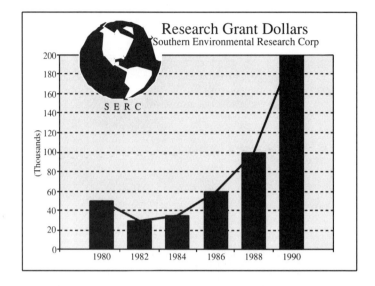

Figure 3-48: *You can use a combination graph to plot the same values twice—once using a bar graph and once using a line graph.*

This is done by repeating the same block of cells in both the 1st series and 2nd series, then showing one series as a bar graph and the other as a line graph.

If your combinations require two different Y-axis scales, be sure that each data series can be matched with its respective axis. Color coding and annotating are two ways to do this.

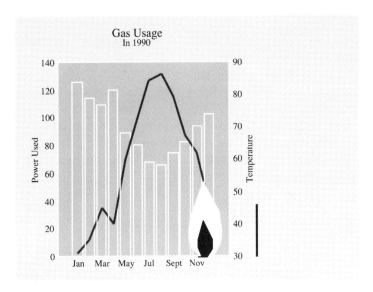

Figure 3-49: *If you use two different Y-axes for the combination graph, be sure to make it clear which series goes with which axis.*

Also, consider manipulating the axis scale of the Y-axes to make the data series fit well with each other.

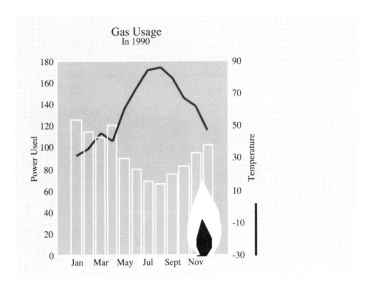

Figure 3-50: *Adjust the scale of both axes to make the data series fit together. In this case, the secondary Y-axis was changed to place the line farther up on the chart.*

3D GRAPH

Generally, 3D graphs serve the same purpose as the 2D graphs they resemble. They can effectively show one or many data series. But because 3D graphs separate data series onto different levels of a "depth" axis, there are some fundamental differences between 3D and other graph formats. For one thing, 3D graphs (except ribbon graphs) require your data series to be progressively smaller, so you should select the series with the largest values as the 1st series, then proceed in order from largest to smallest.

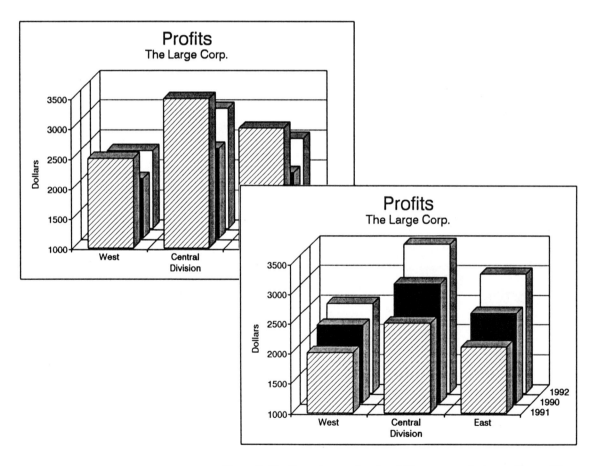

Figure 3-51: Your data series should be progressively smaller on 3D graphs. This is because bars in front cover bars in back.

This may require you to rearrange your specified data series order, which can distort your message. In Figure 3-51, re-arranging the data has destroyed its chronological order. In addition, the 3D effect creates a subtle optical illusion that makes it difficult to accurately compare the series. Two bars with the same value can appear to be different heights.

Horizontal grid lines can reinforce optical illusions in 3D graphs; removing them can help to eliminate this problem, since only the rear series is "close" enough to the grid to show accurate measurement.

Many people consider 3D graphs more attractive than their 2D counterparts and use them almost exclusively. But attractiveness should not take precedence over using the best type of graph for the message you want to get across. In many instances, your viewers can grasp the meaning of a 2D graph quicker than they can sort out angles and depths in a 3D construction.

Use 3D graphs only when data series have progressively larger values and when differences between series are dramatic. The exception to this is the 3D line, or ribbon, graph.

While 2D graphs show how series compare to one another within a single category, 3D graphs compare series to one another across all categories. Therefore, a 3D graph can be more effective for charting multiple data series.

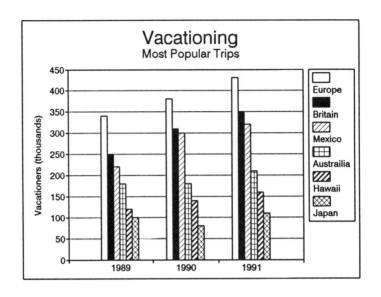

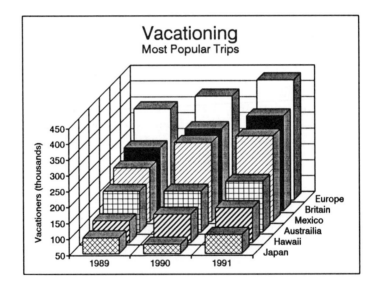

Figure 3-52: 3D graphs are effective for showing several data series. You can easily compare one series to another.

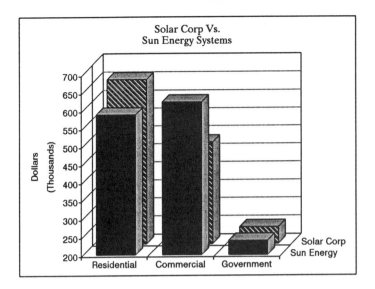

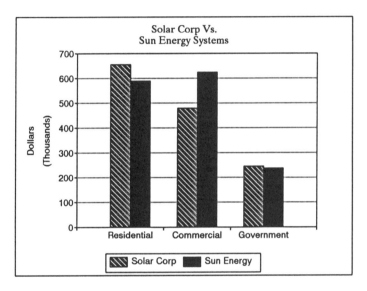

Figure 3-53: Normal 2D graphs can be more effective than 3D graphs. In particular, they show a more accurate comparison of values.

The 2D graph in Figure 3-53 gives a clearer picture of how one company compares to the other. The comparisons are shown precisely in the bar heights. The 3D version is overkill.

In graphs with frequently intersecting lines, *3D ribbon graphs* cán be more effective than 2D line graphs. The third dimension makes it easy to follow each line. In ribbon graphs, it's less important to use different patterns for each line—since there's little chance of confusing one line with another.

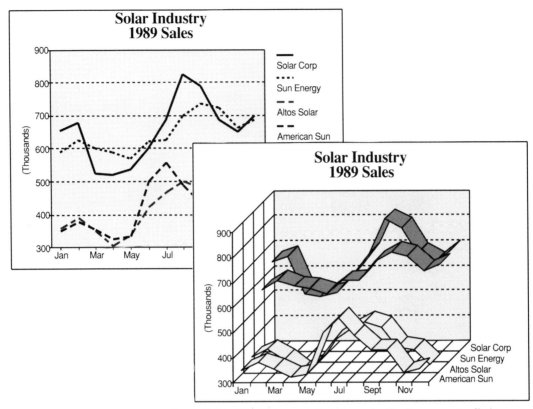

Figure 3-54: 3D ribbon graphs help make the lines easy to distinguish from one another.

3D area graphs are very different from 2D area graphs, which stack the data series on top of each other and emphasize the layers. A 3D area graph places each area behind the other with the values originating from zero. Therefore, the 3D chart is more like a line chart that "fills in" beneath the lines. It offers very little that a line chart does not offer. However, it can be useful for combination charts (described earlier in this chapter).

3D Effects

Quattro Pro offers two types of 3D effects for your graphs. The 3D graph types, including bar, ribbon, step and area, are true 3D graphs. They use three axes—vertical, horizontal and depth—instead of two. The viewing angle is slightly above and to the right of the graph, to emphasize the depth. Data series are split onto different "rows" of the depth axis. But you cannot control the depth axis independently, rotate the graph on an axis (change the viewing angle), or alter its perspective (that is, the distance of vanishing points).

The other type of 3D effect includes the depth added to the data series themselves. These can appear in 2D and 3D graphs alike.

USING 2D AND 3D SERIES

1. Select Graph-Overall-Three D.
2. Choose Yes or No.

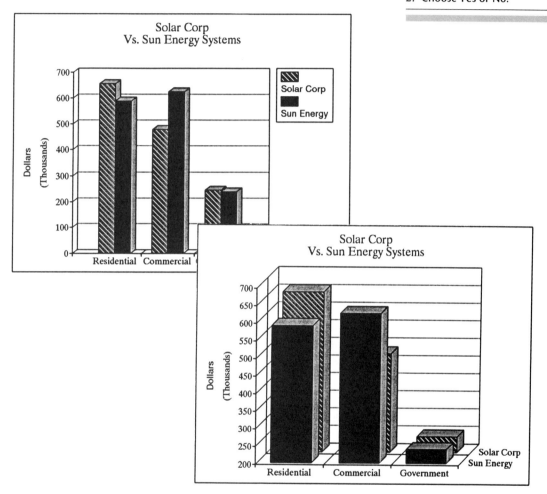

Figure 3-55 : The 3D effect appears in both 2D and 3D graphs.
It adds depth to the bars in a bar graph.

You can also turn this effect off for both 2D and 3D graphs. This is done with the Graph-Overall-Three D-No command.

Showing two-dimensional data series on a 3D graph type can give the graph some additional eye appeal.

MOVING ON

Just being proficient with Quattro Pro does not guarantee that your graphs will be effective and attractive. But knowing Quattro Pro's graphing capabilities will help. When creating graphs, be sure to follow three primary rules:

- Select the best graph for the information you're conveying. Sometimes, one type of graph suggests a different message than another.

- Emphasize your message. Although graphs are an effective way to show numeric information, a poorly designed graph can confuse the message; Quattro Pro's graph annotation tools help you make your point.

- Finally, keep graphs simple and interesting. Graphs lose impact when they become too cluttered or try to convey too much information.

The following checklist offers a more detailed look at how to implement these rules.

- Keep the graph's data series to a minimum. Too many series will dull the graph's impact.

- Fully annotate the graph to emphasize your message, but avoid over-annotating (see Chapter 5).

- Use fonts that work well together and don't distract from the graph itself (see Chapter 4).

- Make sure axis labels fit comfortably along the axis lines and aren't awkwardly formatted.

- Consider whether the background, grids, legends and other elements add to the graph or make it cluttered.

- Add interest to the graph by using color, graphics or special effects—provided they don't detract from the message.

You should now be ready to build attractive graphs for your spreadsheet reports or slide shows. But you may find some other chapters helpful in this process. Chapter 5 provides details about annotating your graphs with graphics and text. Chapter 7 shows you how to print graphs effectively and compose attractive pages. Chapter 8 shows you how to use graphs in your slide shows.

Fonts and Printers 4

Fonts probably affect black-and-white graphic presentation more than any other design element. A font often sets the tone for a page, overhead or slide. Some typefaces convey formality, while others create a casual, more relaxed feeling.

Quattro Pro takes full advantage of today's font technology. You can easily change fonts, install new fonts and even access your printer's built-in fonts throughout your spreadsheets.

In this chapter, we'll look at Quattro Pro's extensive font capabilities, starting with a description of computerized fonts and font fundamentals. In addition to learning how to use Quattro Pro's fonts, you'll see how font selections influence the readability and effectiveness of your spreadsheets and graphs.

ABOUT TYPEFACES

Like other areas of graphic design, typography has its own vocabulary and specifications. For spreadsheet publishing purposes, there are three key areas of type which you should become familiar with: typeface, type size and type style.

When you hear the term "font" in spreadsheet or desktop publishing, it refers to a particular typeface in a specific size and style (bold, regular, italic, etc.) Let's begin our exploration of typography by looking at the typeface.

A typeface is a particular graphical design of letters and numbers. Commonly used typefaces include Dutch (similar to Times), Swiss (the same as Helvetica) and Goudy. You can usually distinguish one typeface from another quite easily, although some typeface designs may differ only slightly from each other.

Make way for Dutch
Make way for Baskerville
Make way for Goudy Old Style

Figure 4-1: A typeface is the graphical design of letters and numbers. The differences can be subtle.

Typeface design by tradition is an art form, and many designers consider these subtle differences very important. But it's the major differences that really count in a presentation visual.

First, all fonts are either serif or sans-serif typefaces. Serif typeface characters have "feet" or finishing lines and strokes, while sans-serif designs are unadorned by these strokes.

Serif   **This is Dutch**
This is Slate
This is Goudy Old Style

Sans-Serif   **This is Swiss**
This is Hammersmith
This is Futura Condensed

Figure 4-2: Serif fonts have finishing lines; sans-serif fonts do not.

Some studies have concluded that serif typefaces are easier to read than sans-serif faces; other studies have proved just the opposite. However, most people agree that serif faces are more businesslike, or "professional," and that sans-serif faces are more casual and friendly. But this isn't always the case.

Futura Extra Bold is a sans-serif face

University Roman is a serif face

Figure 4-3: Serif fonts are not always "serious"; sans-serif are not always "casual."

That's why typeface selection is more art than science—it involves subjective criteria.

Another way to group typefaces is to categorize them as headline faces, decorative faces and body faces.

Body
This is Swiss
This is Dutch
This is Humanist
This is Goudy Old Style
This is Futura Light
This is Baskerville
This is Hammersmith

Headline

This is Charter

This is Futura Bold

This is Cooper Black

This is Goudy Extra Bold

Decorative

This is Script

𝔗𝔥𝔦𝔰 𝔦𝔰 𝔆𝔩𝔬𝔦𝔰𝔱𝔢𝔯 𝔅𝔩𝔞𝔠𝔨

This is University

Figure 4-4: You can classify fonts into headline faces, decorative faces and body faces.

Most faces fit clearly into one category; but some lie on the border. You can easily guess that reading a large document of decorative type, designed more for appearance than readability, would become tiresome.

Decorative faces often combine sharply contrasting thick and thin lines in each character. This design device is called *stress*. In small amounts, heavily stressed type can be interesting and eye-catching. But if you use too much of it, you may burden your reader. That's why you should use decorative fonts rarely and only for short pieces of text.

Faces with heavy stress can be difficult to read When used in blocks of text. Stick with body fonts for most of your work. Reserve decorative fonts for fancy headlines. This is Broadway.

Figure 4-5: Decorative faces should be avoided in long bodies of text.

Some typeface designs are inherently strong (or bold). This strength is referred to as a typeface's "weight." Because of their weight, these heavier typeface designs may not be available in bold styles. Similarly, script faces do not usually include an italic style.

TYPE STYLES CONSIDERED

Styles are effects, such as boldface and italic, added to a typeface. Quattro Pro gives you bold and italic as styles in the spreadsheet. In the Annotator, Quattro Pro also provides the shadow and underline styles.

Normally normal
Brashly bold
Intensely italic
Better with bold & italic
<u>Undoubtedly underlined</u>
Drastically drop shadowed

Figure 4-6: Quattro Pro offers several type styles for your fonts.

Color is also available for fonts used in the spreadsheet and Annotator. Color is considered a style, too.

SIZING UP TYPE

The size of a typeface is defined in points, the traditional measurement units of printers and typesetters. A point is about 1/72 of an inch. Hence, a 72-point type produces characters approximately one inch tall.

Figure 4-7: A point size of 72 gives you letters about one inch tall.

LETTERSPACING AND LEADING

Letterspacing and leading are special font characteristics. Letterspacing refers to the space between letters. Quattro Pro doesn't let you control the letterspacing of a font. However, you can add space between letters by using the space bar; the effect simulates true letterspacing.

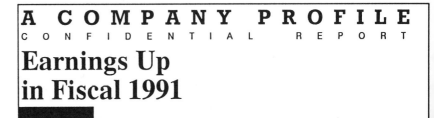

Figure 4-8: By adding space between letters you can simulate letter-spacing effects.

In the Annotator, you can also remove space between letters. See Chapter 5 for details.

Leading is the space between lines of type. You can control leading in your spreadsheets by adjusting the row heights. In the Annotator, you can control leading by placing each line in a separate text box and stacking the boxes on top of one another. If you enter two or more lines in the same text box, you cannot control the leading. (See Chapter 2 for more information on changing row heights and Chapter 5 for details about using type in the Annotator.)

FONT TECHNOLOGIES

The two most prevalent font technologies in the computer industry are bitmapped fonts and scalable fonts. A bit-mapped font is made up of tiny dots that are combined in a particular pattern or matrix. Dot-matrix printers always use bitmapped fonts.

Figure 4-9: Bitmapped fonts are made up of tiny dots.

Programs that use bitmapped fonts store the font patterns in individual font files. And printers that accept bitmapped fonts require that the maps be sent in a particular way. Hence, bitmapped fonts can be cumbersome to use and time-consuming to print. Quattro Pro uses bitmapped fonts exclusively, but minimizes inconvenience through intelligent programming and font handling.

A scalable font is not created with dots. Instead, the program uses advanced math (called vector graphics) to calculate the size and shape of each font, based on a set of instructions. So a scalable font is just a series of instructions that "describe" its shape.

The instructions for describing a font are created with a "Page Description Language." The most common of these is Post-Script. A PostScript printer can interpret these instructions and use them to construct the fonts and other elements of a page using the printer's particular technology (for example, 300-dpi laser technology).

The advantage of scalable fonts is that they require less storage space. Rather than save individual font files, the program saves a single "description" of the font. Any size and style can be calculated from that one description. Scalable fonts generally print much faster than bitmapped fonts.

Although Quattro Pro doesn't use scalable font technology, it lets you use your printer's scalable fonts, if your printer has them built in.

USING FONTS IN QUATTRO PRO

Quattro Pro allows you to use eight fonts in each spreadsheet. Within a spreadsheet, you can format some data with Dutch 12 point, other data with Dutch 18-point bold, and so on until you have used eight individual fonts. You can view a spreadsheet's eight fonts by using the Style-Fonts command.

APPLYING A FONT TO SPREADSHEET DATA

1. Choose the command Style-Font.
2. Choose the desired font from the list and press Enter.
3. Specify the cell or range to which this font should apply.
4. Repeat these steps to apply other fonts throughout the spreadsheet.

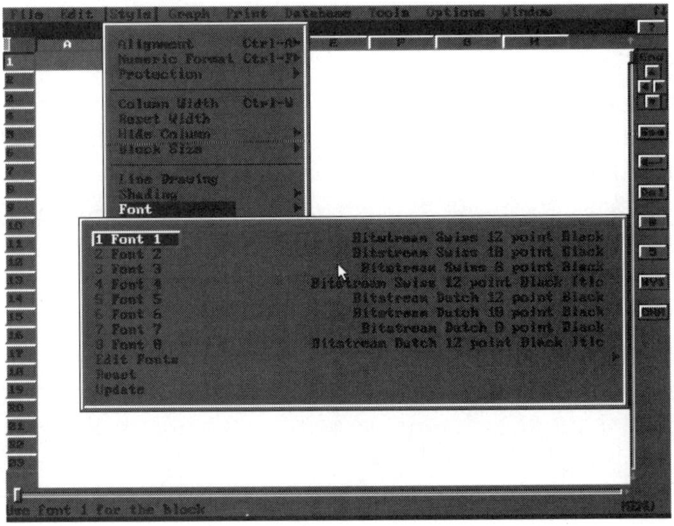

Figure 4-10: Quattro Pro allows you to choose eight fonts in each spreadsheet.

You can apply a font to one cell of data or a block of cells; then apply another font to a different block. If you don't specify a font, Quattro Pro will automatically apply Font 1 to it. Because Font 1 is the default font for all spreadsheet data, Quattro Pro makes it a small font (12-point Swiss), appropriate for most spreadsheet data.

CHANGING FONTS

You're not stuck with the eight fonts that Quattro Pro provides for your spreadsheet. You can swap one of the eight for a new font. That way, you can use larger point sizes or more style variety for a particular typeface.

Quattro Pro gives you a number of fonts to choose from. Choose the eight you think will be most useful in each spreadsheet. The entire set of fonts that comes with Quattro Pro is shown in Figure 4-11.

Say it in Swiss
Say it in Dutch
Say it in Courier
Say it in Roman

Say it in Sans-Serif

Say it in Script

Say it in Old English

Say it in Eurostyle

Say it in Monospace

Figure 4-11: Quattro Pro offers many fonts to choose from.

These come in different styles, such as bold, underline, shadow and italic, and in point sizes ranging from 6 to 72.

Remember that you can select fonts for each spreadsheet independently. When you save a spreadsheet, the font selections are saved along with it. When you return to the spreadsheet later, your chosen fonts are still active.

If you change a font that's currently being used in the spreadsheet, all data using that font will change to the new font. Thus, eight fonts are still active on the spreadsheet.

FONTS IN TEXT-BASED SYSTEMS

If you're not using EGA (or better) graphics with Quattro Pro, you'll notice a considerable difference between your screen and the illustrations in this book (and with your own print-outs). Most important, when you select fonts for spreadsheet data, the screen does not display the change—the screen

---

CHANGING THE EIGHT FONTS

1. Select Style-Font.
2. Choose Edit Font.
3. Choose the font that you want to change.
4. Choose Typeface.
5. Select from the list of typefaces.
6. Choose Point Size.
7. Select from the list of point sizes.
8. Repeat these steps to select another font or return to the spreadsheet by pressing Esc or selecting Quit.

shows only Quattro Pro's normal Text mode. Nevertheless, all the data you see on the screen is being formatted with one font or another, as your printed copy and the screen preview will show.

The default font (Font 1) is slightly larger than the text size on your screen display, so your printouts won't match the screen, even when you leave the spreadsheet data in Font 1. Often, column widths that work fine on the screen are too narrow when the text is printed out in a 12-point font, especially if you've used uppercase letters.

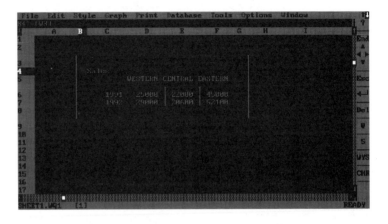

Sales			
	WESTER	CENTRA	EASTERN
1991	25000	22000	45000
1992	29000	20600	52100

Figure 4-12: In Text mode, your screen font may not match the print-out—even if you don't change fonts.

One way to solve this problem is to change Font 1 to a smaller point size that comes closer to the screen type size. Try using 10-point Swiss, or any typeface in a small point size.

Another way around this problem is to use the Screen Preview mode before printing. This preview shows you what the spreadsheet will look like when it's printed with all its fonts. If columns are too narrow in this display, you can return to the spreadsheet and expand them. Preview the spreadsheet again to see if your changes were effective. You'll probably find yourself using this preview feature regularly, even before you're ready to print. Quattro Pro treats the screen as another destination for printing. To Quattro Pro, there is little difference between printing a spreadsheet to the screen (preview) and printing it to the printer.

Finally, you can use the Style-Block Size-Auto Width command to have Quattro Pro change the widths of the columns to accommodate the data within them.

SCREEN PREVIEW

1. Choose the Print-Block command.
2. Specify the desired block to print and press Enter.
3. Set any other print options, such as margins and formats.
4. Choose Destination.
5. Choose Screen Preview.
6. Choose Spreadsheet Print.

QUATTRO PRO'S HERSHEY FONTS

Eight of Quattro Pro's built-in fonts are Hershey fonts. These are useful for any non-PostScript printer and especially for plotters. They're designed with an outline and, sometimes, lines inside the outline, which are visible when you use larger point sizes or enlarge the spreadsheet.

Figure 4-13: Hershey fonts are created from an outline and fill lines. They are made especially for plotters.

A plotter can trace this font outline and produce an attractive report. But these fonts are also useful for dot-matrix and laser printers. Figure 4-14 shows some Hershey fonts printed on a plotter, a low-cost dot-matrix printer and a laser printer.

Figure 4-14: **The Hershey fonts look considerably different on different types of output devices.**

Although the Hershey fonts look quite good, if you compare them with the Bitstream fonts shown later, you'll notice some distinct differences, especially at the larger point sizes. Hershey fonts include Roman, Roman Light, Sans Serif, Sans Serif Light, Script, Monospace, Old English and Eurostyle.

QUATTRO PRO'S BITSTREAM FONTS

Bitstream fonts are widely used in the PC world. Borland gives you three complete sets of these fonts with Quattro Pro: Dutch, Swiss and Courier. They can be used in point sizes from 6 to 72 and boldface and italic styles. With all of these font versions to choose from you can do some wonderful things.

NOTE: If you have purchased Version 3.0 of Quattro Pro, you may have gotten the ProView PowerPack with your purchase. This package includes two additional Bitstream fonts, called Slate Bold and Script. When you install the ProView PowerPack disks, these fonts will be added to the list in Quattro Pro. (If you took advantage of the low-cost upgrade from Version 2.0, you may not have gotten the ProView PowerPack. You can purchase it separately.)

Quattro Pro calls Bitstream fonts "final quality" because they're professionally designed to take full advantage of a printer's resolution up to 300 dpi. (See "Printers and Output Devices" later in this chapter.) Figure 4-15 shows examples of these fonts, printed on a Panasonic KX-P1180 dot-matrix printer and on a Hewlett-Packard LaserJet II.

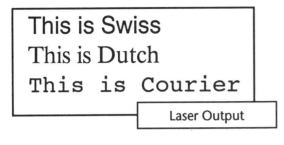

This is Swiss
This is Dutch
This is Courier

Laser Output

This is Swiss
This is Dutch
This is Courier

Dot Matrix Output

Figure 4-15: Bitstream fonts can take advantage of your printer's 300-dpi resolution.

As you can see, these fonts look good when printed on dot-matrix printers and still better on laser printers. And because these fonts are created from 300-dpi bit maps, they can be used on any non-PostScript printer supported by Quattro Pro (more on PostScript printers later). This makes them versatile and uncomplicated to use.

As mentioned earlier in this chapter, bitmapped fonts can be rather bulky and slow, and require large amounts of disk storage space. This is because they're built from special compressed files. When you use a final-quality font, Quattro Pro must decompress the font file, a process known as *building* the font. This process, which can take several minutes, must be performed before printing or displaying fonts in WYSIWYG mode on the screen, in the print preview or in the Annotator. If you change printers, Quattro Pro must re-create the fonts when you print, since each font file specifies a particular printer.

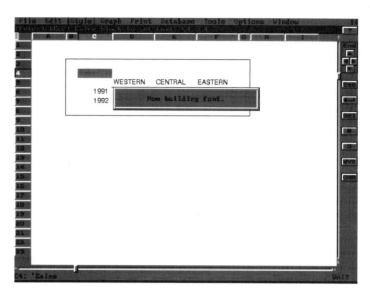

Figure 4-16: Quattro Pro may pause to "build" fonts for the screen or printout.

The decompressed files are 300-dpi bit maps stored on disk. If you use several fonts (including multiple sizes and styles), you'll find several of these files on your disk, taking several megabytes of disk space. Thankfully, they look good enough to make it all worthwhile—and Quattro Pro stores them in an out-of-the-way location on your hard disk (in the C:\QPRO\FONTS directory path). If your hard disk has plenty of space, a megabyte or two for great-looking fonts will probably be worth it. And a fast computer will reduce the time required to build the fonts.

The good news is that the fonts have to be created and saved only once. Once saved on disk, they're available for all your spreadsheets. Hence, no extra time or disk space is required to use them. Once you've used several of these final-quality fonts, you may forget they're there.

Quattro Pro offers several ways to further minimize the font inconvenience: first, a Draft mode, for creating and proofing your work. The Draft mode temporarily turns font generation off while you work. You can return to Final mode before printing your spreadsheets or before previewing them for final proofing. (Draft and Final modes are explained in detail later in this chapter.)

PRE-BUILDING FONTS AFTER INSTALLATION

1. Select the File-Open command.
2. Choose INSTALL.WQ1 which is located in the QPRO directory.
3. Press Enter after reading the short message that appears.
4. Choose the font set you want to build (the Limited set contains a small number of Swiss fonts).

Second, you can build fonts "on the fly," so that only the fonts you use are built and stored on disk. If you use a few fonts over and over, Quattro Pro will require a minimum amount of disk space. Since the program builds fonts as you use them, this requires a delay each time you request a new font.

Third, with a process called "pre-building," Quattro Pro lets you build fonts when you install the program. This way, all the waiting and saving delays are lumped into one session, eliminating periodic delays while you're using the program. You can build a full set of high-quality fonts, including most sizes and styles of Dutch, Swiss and Courier. Or you can build only the Swiss and Dutch fonts, or just the Swiss font.

If you have already installed Quattro Pro without pre-building the fonts, you can still have Quattro Pro pre-build the fonts for you (see "Pre-building Fonts After Installation" sidebar). Be sure the correct printer is active by using the Options-Hardware-Printers command. (You may also want to pre-build fonts if you change printers.)

Another space-saving option is to remove unwanted font files from your disk. You can remove some or all of the files that contain the .FON extension in the C:\QPRO\FONTS directory. This is especially useful if you permanently switch printers, or if you no longer use certain fonts that you once used frequently. If Quattro Pro ever needs the font file again, it will simply rebuild it at that time. (Steps for removing all font files appear in the sidebar.)

REMOVING ALL FONT FILES

1. From the DOS prompt, type
   ERASE
   C:\QPRO\FONTS*.FON
2. Press Enter.

You can also remove a few font files from the disk. To do this, switch to the C:\QPRO\FONTS directory and examine the .FON files. Remove any .FON file you don't want, except the INDEX.FON file. (You can also use a DOS file manager to erase the .FON files.)

TIP: You can save a lot of disk space by copying Quattro Pro's library of clip art and sample spreadsheets to floppy disks. If you need them in the future, you can access them from the floppy disk. After copying the files to floppy disks, remove them from the QPRO directory. All files in the QPRO directory that end in the extensions .WQ1, .CLP and .CGM can be moved and then erased—except the INSTALL.WQ1 file.

ADDING NEW BITSTREAM FONTS

You can add any Bitstream or Bitstream-compatible font to your Quattro Pro directory and to the existing list. Bitstream fonts can be found at your local computer dealer or ordered directly from Bitstream. (See the Resources section of this book for ordering information.) Figure 4-17 shows a sampling of Bitstream's font library:

**ADDING NEW
BITSTREAM FONTS**

1. Exit Quattro Pro and return to the DOS prompt.
2. Type CD C:\QPRO and press Enter.
3. Insert your Bitstream font disk in Drive A (or your floppy drive). Do not use the scalable fonts for this purpose. If there are two disks, you'll probably only need the first one.
4. Type BSINST and press Enter.
5. Follow the instructions on the screen.

Futura Light

Light		ABCDEFGabcdefg 12345?$&¢[:!?
Light Italic		*ABCDEFGabcdefg 12345?$&¢[:!ß*
Medium Cond.		ABCDEFGabcdefg12345?$&¢[:!ßœÊáéñÿ£¥ƒ§
Extra Black		**ABCDEFGabcdefg12345?$&**

ITC Souvenir®

Light		ABCDEFGabcdefg12345?$&¢[:!
Light Italic		*ABCDEFGabcdefg12345?$&¢[:!*
Demi		**ABCDEFGabcdefg12345?$&**
Demi Italic		***ABCDEFGabcdefg12345?$&***

Bodoni

Book		ABCDEFGabcdefg12345?$&¢[:!ßœ
Book Italic		*ABCDEFGabcdefg12345?$&¢[:!ßœÊ*
Bold		**ABCDEFGabcdefg12345?$&¢[:**
Bold Italic		***ABCDEFGabcdefg12345?$&¢[***

Figure 4-17: Bitstream offers numerous fonts that you can add to Quattro Pro.

You may feel that you have an overwhelming number of font choices to make for your spreadsheets. But remember that each point size and each style (such as bold and italic) of each typeface is a separate font. Actually, putting together a useful family with a bold and an italic version will probably use all eight font selections. (Advice on choosing fonts for your spreadsheets appears later in this chapter.)

Using Final and Draft Modes

If you use Bitstream fonts in your spreadsheets, you'll notice Quattro Pro's "Now Building Font" message. This can occur during your work when you're trying to format your spreadsheets with new fonts. The interruption occurs when you

* Change fonts in the WYSIWYG mode.
* Reduce or enlarge the WYSIWYG view.
* Use fonts in the Annotator.
* Display graphs.
* Preview pages on the screen.
* Print.

Quattro Pro's Draft mode lets you turn the font-building off to avoid delays. To turn font-building off, switch to Draft mode with the Options-Graphics Quality-Draft command. This is particularly useful for formatting an entire spreadsheet at one time. You can make all your font changes, then return to Final mode when you're through, with only one pause instead of several. Draft mode is also useful for printing rough drafts of your spreadsheets. With Draft mode active, Quattro Pro will not pause to build fonts before printing.

Don't let the word Draft mislead you. Draft mode doesn't necessarily lower the quality of the fonts on the screen and printout. Draft mode simply stops font-building. Any fonts already built will still be used in Draft mode—on the screen and in the printout.

But what about fonts not already built? In Draft mode, Quattro Pro substitutes the Hershey fonts or any Bitstream font that's already built for unbuilt fonts. Therefore, your screen, Draft, and Final printouts may all be different from each other. Draft mode is especially useful when you're doing a lot of chart manipulation or when you need to reduce or enlarge the WYSIWYG view.

CHOOSING DRAFT-QUALITY PRINTING

1. Select Options-Graphics Quality-Draft.

CHOOSING FINAL-QUALITY PRINTING

1. Select Options-Graphics Quality-Final.

CHOOSING FONTS

When selecting the eight fonts for a spreadsheet, remember that each spreadsheet can have a different set of eight fonts. So choose fonts appropriate for the specific spreadsheet. But if you find that you use the same eight fonts for most spreadsheets, using the Style-Font-Update command after you select the desired fonts makes your list of fonts the default for all new spreadsheets.

You might find that you use two or three different sets of fonts, depending on the application. Rather than switch between these sets, save three blank spreadsheets, each with a different set of fonts. Use these spreadsheets to begin new applications instead of using the File-New command. (Be sure to save your data under a new name so you don't replace the blank copy.)

Another thing to remember when selecting your fonts is that Font 1 is always used as the default font. So you should always make it a small font appropriate for the body of the spreadsheet. Of course, you can apply some other font to the data, but it's easiest to leave most data in Font 1. Unless you change it, Quattro Pro sets Font 1 as 12-point Swiss.

Consider the fonts used for your headings carefully. You may need a large point size for main headings and smaller size for subheadings. You may need bold or italic fonts for these headings.

Once you determine these needs, you'll probably find that two typefaces are about all Quattro Pro can handle with only eight fonts to a spreadsheet. The good news is that you shouldn't be using more than two different faces in the same spreadsheet anyway. You're much better off with several sizes of the same face. Often, a larger point size can be used instead of boldface.

The next few illustrations in Figure 4-18 show suggested font combinations for your spreadsheets and example spreadsheets that use them. Some of these combinations require Bitstream fonts that must be purchased separately.

PRICE LIST

American Nuts & Bolts Corp.
PRICES AS OF JANUARY 1, 1990

Arlington Industries
Spun Aluminum Bolts

Order Number	Price
RX-2388	$ 12.50
RX-2389	12.50
RX-2390	14.99
KS-51180	23.50
KS-51210	23.50
PR-10012	25.99
PR-10013	29.99

Maddington Premium
Cast Steel Bolts

Order Number	Price
MD-112	$ 35.99
MD-113	35.99
MD-4510	42.99
MD-4550	42.99
MD-9000	59.99

Arlington Industries
Spun Aluminum Nuts

Order Number	Price
AR-3410	$ 11.24
AR-3420	11.24
AR-3430	11.24
AR-10	14.99
AR-12	14.99
AR-14	16.99
AR-123	19.99
AR-124	19.99

Figure 4-18a: Font combinations of Swiss (roman and bold) and Goudy (roman, bold and italic).

National Business Group

Consolidated Balance Sheets

	Fiscal Year End: December 31		1990
Assets	Current Assets:		
	Cash and Equivalents	$	22.9
	Accounts and Notes Receivable		684.8
	Inventories		767.0
	Other		212.3
	Total Current Assets		1687.0
	Property, Plant & Equipment		3855.1
	Accumulated Depreciation		-877.2
	Property, Plant & Equip. - Net		2977.9
	Land		103.9
	Goodwill		1089.8
	Other		395.1
	Total Assets	$	6253.7
Liabilities	Current Liabilities:		
	Notes Payable	$	66.4
	Current Portion LTD		286.0
	Accounts Payable		355.9
	Income Taxes Due		71.1
	Accrued Liabilities		293.2
	Total Current Liabilities		1072.6
	Long-Term Debt		2598.0
	Subordinated Debt		671.1
	Other Long-Term Liabilities		78.6
	Deferred Taxes		185.8
	Total Non-Current Liabilities		3533.5
	Stockholders' Equity:		
	Common Stock		556.8
	Retained Earnings		1090.8
	Total Stockholders' Equity		1647.6
	Total Liabilities and Equity	$	6253.7

Figure 4-18b: Font combinations of Charter (roman) and Dutch (roman, bold and italic).

Mailing List
From Advertisement

Name	Street	City	ST	Zip
Larry Smith	34 First St	San Diego	CA	92101
Greg Rand	7782 Orange Ave	Los Angeles	CA	90034
Lisa Burke	101 Broadway	San Mateo	CA	94402
Linda Perle	61 Idaho Bl	San Mateo	CA	94402
Samual Yin	902 Elm Ave	New York	NY	10012

Figure 4-18c: Font combinations of Futura (extra-bold) and Swiss (roman, bold and italic).

Notice that serif and sans-serif fonts can be mixed successfully when one is used only as a heading font. Otherwise, be careful when mixing these types of fonts. As mentioned earlier, many people consider sans-serif fonts casual and contemporary and serif fonts businesslike and formal. This is generally but not always true.

Remember that your spreadsheet data should be easily readable, so avoid fancy scripted faces and extra-bold, extra-narrow or otherwise dramatic faces. Italic should also be used with restraint.

When you add graphs to your spreadsheets, you may be changing your font needs. Your graphs may benefit from fonts that are not needed for the spreadsheet—especially larger sizes for headlines. Luckily, you can use additional fonts in your graphs, over and above the eight spreadsheet fonts. However, avoid using completely different typefaces for a graph, especially when it will be printed with spreadsheet data. Too many faces on the same page can be distracting. Instead, use this capability to add extra point sizes and styles to the graph's fonts.

Note that graphs are often reduced when printed, especially when you insert them into the spreadsheet; therefore, the point sizes you choose for the graph will be reduced accordingly. Quattro Pro will take care of this for you. See Chapter 3 for details about graphs.

PRINTERS AND OUTPUT DEVICES

Your printer largely determines the quality of your output. The resolution at which it prints, measured in dots per inch (or dpi), determines how smooth, sharp and clean the type and graphics will be. In general, the higher the resolution, the better the printout.

Each type of output device—daisy-wheel, dot-matrix, thermal-transfer, inkjet, bubble-jet or laser printer or phototypesetter—has its own capabilities and limitations. If you haven't already chosen a printer, make a full comparison of these technologies (or those within your price range) and their output quality.

You'll probably find that the high-end printers always have their own built-in fonts. Many have scalable or PostScript font capabilities. The next sections focus on how to access a printer's built-in fonts and how to get the most from your PostScript, LaserJet or dot-matrix printer.

USING YOUR PRINTER'S BUILT-IN FONTS

If you have a PostScript or an HP laser printer, Quattro Pro will access your printer's built-in or cartridge fonts and make them available for your printouts. As soon as you select your printer (as described in the "Selecting Your Printer" sidebar), Quattro Pro adds the printer's fonts to the master font list. You can then swap one or more of the eight spreadsheet fonts with these printer fonts and use them in your spreadsheets.

SELECTING YOUR PRINTER

1. Choose Options-Hardware-Printers.
2. Choose either 1st Printer or 2nd Printer.
3. Choose Type of Printer.
4. Select the printer's manufacturer in the list provided.
5. Select the printer model in the list provided.
6. Select the desired print mode from the list provided.
7. Press Q twice, then U to update the program with your selections.
8. Press Esc or Quit to return to the spreadsheet.

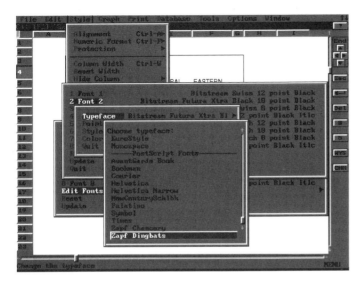

Figure 4-19: When you select a printer that has built-in fonts, its fonts appear in the fonts list.

These fonts take full advantage of the printer's resolution, since they're made for the printer. But because Quattro Pro doesn't have a copy of these fonts, it must substitute a reasonable alternative on the screen. Normally, Quattro Pro substitutes the closest match from any of the Bitstream or Hershey fonts in its list. Often, the Swiss, Dutch and Courier fonts will match well with equivalent printer fonts.

Dutch   Times
Swiss   Helvetica

Figure 4-20: Bitstream's Dutch and Swiss match perfectly with PostScript's Times and Helvetica.

But Quattro Pro may have to substitute fonts that don't look at all like Swiss or Dutch. Furthermore, if Draft mode is active, Quattro Pro substitutes the closest match using only the Hershey and Bitstream fonts that are already built. This could make the screen/printer discrepancy even greater since Quattro Pro can't build new fonts to match those you've chosen from your printer.

For the closest possible match between the screen and your printer's built-in fonts, use Quattro Pro's Final mode. Even better, expand Quattro Pro's Bitstream font list by purchasing new Bitstream fonts to match those built into your printer. Chances are, you can find Bitstream fonts identical to your printer fonts. Quattro Pro will substitute the matching Bitstream font for the screen display. Details about PostScript and HP LaserJet printers follow.

POSTSCRIPT AND COMPATIBLE PRINTERS

A PostScript printer can use only PostScript fonts. And, since Quattro Pro doesn't come with PostScript fonts, your printing will involve font substitution. Font substitution takes place when your screen fonts don't match the printer's fonts. Most PostScript and PostScript-compatible printers come with several built-in fonts, including those in Figure 4-21.

Times

Helvetica

`Courier`

AvantGarde Book

Bookman

Helvetica Narrow

NewCentury Schoolbook

Palatino

Σψμβολ (Symbol)

Zapf Chancery

✿✛⁘✤✥✦✧★☆✪✯✵ (Zapf Dingbats)

Figure 4-21: Many PostScript printers come with these eleven fonts built in.

As you can see, Times, Helvetica and Courier are dead ringers for Quattro Pro's Dutch, Swiss and Courier. Figure 4-22 shows all the matching Bitstream fonts for the built-in PostScript fonts.

Times	Dutch
Helvetica	**Swiss**
Courier	Courier
AvantGarde Book	ITC Avant Garde Gothic
Bookman	ITC Bookman
Helvetica Narrow	Swiss Condensed
NewCentury Schoolbook	Century Schoolbook
Palatino	Zapf Calligraphic
Σψμβολ (Symbol)	───── (No Symbol Equivalent)
Zapf Chancery	*ITC Zapf Chancery*
✿✛✜❖✤◆✦✧★☆✪★✹ (Zapf Dingbats)	✿✛✜❖✤◆✦✧★☆✪★✹ (Symbols)

Figure 4-22: You can find Bitstream fonts to match the PostScript fonts in your printer, but you'll have to purchase many of these separately.

If you have all these Bitstream fonts, Quattro Pro will substitute them for the PostScript versions whenever necessary. If you don't have them, Quattro Pro will substitute the ones that come the closest.

One type of substitution can occur when you use Bitstream fonts in your spreadsheet and print the spreadsheet to a PostScript printer. This might happen if you buy a new PostScript printer and use it to print a spreadsheet created for your old non-PostScript printer.

Or you may have used the Bitstream fonts instead of the printer's built-in fonts for your spreadsheet. Of course, if the font you've used in the spreadsheet matches one of the printer's built-in fonts, the substitution will not result in a noticeable difference between the screen and printout. However, if you've used special Bitstream fonts that don't match your printer's fonts, there may be a very noticeable difference. In this case, you can correct the problem by changing the fonts in your font list. Swap the printer's built-in fonts for the Bitstream fonts. You'll have to do this for every individual spreadsheet.

If you've purchased a special Bitstream typeface, it may not match any of the printer's built-in fonts. In this case, you can download the PostScript version of the font into the printer, thus adding to the printer's existing fonts. Bitstream fonts come with PostScript (scalable) versions as well as the versions required by Quattro Pro. You'll need a font-downloading utility to accomplish this (see the Resources section in the back of this book). But your printer must be able to store downloaded fonts. If all goes well, Quattro Pro will match the spreadsheet font with the one you've downloaded into the printer.

Another type of substitution occurs when you select one of the printer's built-in fonts for the spreadsheet. Since Quattro Pro doesn't actually use PostScript fonts, it substitutes Bitstream fonts *on the screen* when you select your printer's fonts from the font list. As before, the difference will be negligible if you have Bitstream fonts that match your printer's fonts. You already have matching fonts for Times, Helvetica and Courier. If you need more, consider purchasing them.

UNSUPPORTED POSTSCRIPT PRINTERS

You can print your spreadsheet on a PostScript device that doesn't appear in Quattro Pro's printer list. Just select the "PostScript" printer from the printer list.

If you're printing a graph without the spreadsheet, you can save the graph as an EPS (Encapsulated PostScript) file on disk. The EPS file can be printed from a program that supports the printer. It can also be sent directly to the printer via programming codes. All PostScript devices can print EPS files in one manner or another. See Chapter 9 for details about using EPS files for graphs and slides.

Another solution to the quandary is to use one of your printer's emulation modes (if it has any). Often, PostScript printers emulate HP LaserJet printers. When the LaserJet emulation mode is set, you can use the printer as a LaserJet. (See the following section for details.)

HEWLETT-PACKARD LASERJET AND COMPATIBLE PRINTERS

If you have a Hewlett-Packard LaserJet printer, Quattro Pro will produce some outstanding results. Any Bitstream font can be printed to your LaserJet in resolutions as high as 300 dpi. You can set the resolution when you choose your printer from the Options-Hardware-Printers-1st Printer command. You might find it handy to switch between two different print resolutions. You can set different 1st and 2nd printer resolutions to apply to and different modes of the same printer. (See Chapter 1 for details.)

You'll find the Bitstream fonts quite professional looking on your HP printer, but you might also want to use the printer's built-in fonts. Any fonts that come with your HP printer will be available in Quattro Pro when you select your printer from the printer list. If you select the LaserJet II printer, for example, the fonts in Figure 4-23 appear in the fonts list.

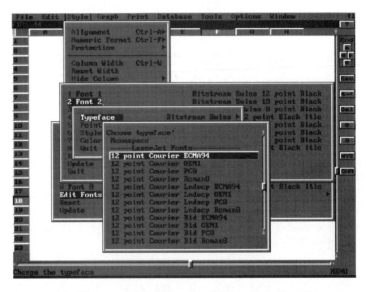

Figure 4-23: The LaserJet II adds several fonts to the font list.

Using the Style-Fonts-Edit Fonts command, you can select these fonts for your spreadsheets. Notice that the LaserJet fonts have predetermined point sizes. When you choose a built-in font from the LaserJet, you also choose its point size; therefore, Quattro Pro's point-size setting is deactivated. To display these fonts on the screen, Quattro Pro substitutes one of its existing fonts. If Quattro Pro is in Final mode, this will be any chosen Bitstream font that's available. If Quattro Pro is in Draft mode, this will be any already built Bitstream font.

If you use the Bitstream fonts in your spreadsheet, Quattro Pro won't substitute a LaserJet font when you print; it will simply print the spreadsheet using the Bitstream font, so there's no reason to purchase Bitstream fonts just to make your screen match the printer's built-in fonts. Having a Bitstream font makes the built-in font unnecessary. The rule: If you have a built-in font that does not match any of the Bitstream fonts in Quattro Pro, use it only if you like it enough to put up with differences between the screen and printer. However, go ahead and use the built-in fonts that match Quattro Pro's Swiss, Dutch and Courier. You may find that using the built-in fonts speeds the printing process slightly.

Quattro Pro will also access the cartridge fonts in your LaserJet printer. These will be added to the built-in fonts in the font list. Like the built-in fonts, these fonts appear on the printer but require substitutes for the screen.

ACCESSING LASERJET CARTRIDGE FONTS

1. Choose Options-Hardware-Printers-Fonts-LaserJet Fonts.
2. Choose Left Cartridge or Right Cartridge.
3. Choose the desired cartridge from the list.
4. Use Esc or Quit to return to the spreadsheet.

DOT-MATRIX PRINTERS

A dot-matrix printer is anything but PostScript- or LaserJet-compatible. It may use impact, laser, inkjet or bubble-jet technology. Quattro Pro will take full advantage of your printer's various capabilities, such as resolution or print density. You can select the resolution when you choose the printer (Quattro Pro calls this a printer mode).

Your printer can print Bitstream and Hershey fonts when you choose Graphics Printer with the Print-Destination command before printing. The Text Printer option uses your printer's built-in draft font. This will print quickly but without formatting. Some dot-matrix printers have several draft fonts available. Usually, these are set with DIP switches or mode buttons on the printer. However, these draft fonts are available only through Quattro Pro's Text Printer destination.

PLOTTERS

When using a plotter with Quattro Pro, you should select only the Hershey fonts in your spreadsheets, since Hershey fonts are made specifically for plotters and will give you the best results. Also, select Graphics Printer with the Print-Destination command.

SCALING YOUR SPREADSHEET

Quattro Pro can enlarge or reduce your spreadsheets when it prints. This is called scaling and it can be done for any printer (except daisy-wheel printers) regardless of the fonts you choose. When you scale the printout, Quattro Pro adjusts the point sizes of the spreadsheet's fonts to match the percent scaling you've set.

Quattro Pro will enlarge fonts to a maximum of 72 points—even if the scaling requires a larger font. Therefore, if you begin with a 72-point font and then use 200% scaling to make the printout larger, Quattro Pro will not increase the size of this font by 200% because it's already at the maximum size.

NOTE: Although Quattro Pro will not scale a font beyond 72 points for printing, it will do this when you "zoom" into the screen in WYSIWYG mode. For example, if you have a 72-point font on your spreadsheet and increase the WYSIWYG zoom to 200%, you will get a 144-point font on the screen. However, this has no effect on the printout—it's merely a screen view. You can increase the WYSIWYG view using the Options-WYSIWYG Zoom% command.

SCALING THE PRINTOUT

1. Select the Print-Layout-Percent Scaling command.
2. Enter the desired scaling percent from 1 to 1000 percent (100 percent is normal size).
3. Print the desired block.

Figure 4-24: Quattro Pro can enlarge your printed fonts to a maximum of 72 points, but on-the-screen fonts can be twice that size.

The Print reduction feature is used automatically in the new Print-Print to Fit command. This command reduces the current block so it fits onto as few pages as possible using reasonable font sizes. You could use the Percent Scaling command in the same way, but it might require several tries to get the printout onto one page.

The Percent Scaling option adjusts *all* fonts in the print block, so you can't use it to adjust individual cells. However, you can create a spreadsheet with an enlarged size in mind. Just set the WYSIWYG mode to the same enlargement as your Percent Scaling value. This shows you on-screen what the sizes will look like on the printer. Smaller point sizes will be more readable, and you can create more dramatic differences in headings.

MOVING ON

You can't design effectively without taking fonts into consideration. Attractive fonts alone can make a presentation look more professional and command the audience's attention. When using fonts in your Quattro Pro spreadsheets, remember the following points:

- A font is a combination of typeface, type size and type style.

- Each spreadsheet can use eight different fonts and these are saved with the spreadsheet.

- You can change the eight spreadsheet fonts at any time.

- It's better to select a variety of point sizes and styles than to have several different typefaces on a spreadsheet.

- Use a maximum of three different faces on your spreadsheets.

- If you use Swiss, Dutch and Courier, you will probably not notice any difference if your printer substitutes equivalent fonts for the final printout.

- If you select your printer's built-in fonts that match Swiss, Dutch and Courier, you will probably not notice any difference when Quattro Pro substitutes fonts on the screen.

Chapter 5 is about the Annotator, which you can use to enhance graphs or to produce slides for presentations. You'll find the font information in this chapter useful when you use the Annotator.

Using the Annotator 5

The Annotator is an area inside Quattro Pro for drawing and constructing graphics. It's called the Annotator because it's often used to annotate graphs; that is, to embellish them with graphics, text, colors and patterns. Figure 5-1 shows a graph before and after annotation.

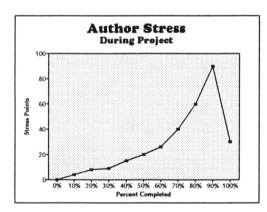 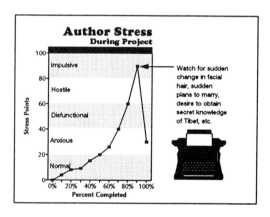

Figure 5-1: The Annotator can be used to embellish graphs with text and graphics.

**ENTERING THE
ANNOTATOR WITH
A GRAPH**

1. Display the desired graph
   by choosing the Graph-
   Name-Display command.
2. Select the desired graph
   from the list.
3. With the graph on the
   screen, press the Slash key
   (/) to enter the Annotator.

Besides adding new elements to a graph, you can use the Annotator to change a graph's existing elements, such as colors and fonts used in its titles. These are changes that can also be made outside the Annotator by using the Graph menu options described in Chapter 3, "Creating Effective Graphs." But you'll probably find the Annotator the easiest way to make changes to a graph.

The Annotator does more than just annotate graphs. You can use it to simply draw illustrations or type text. This is primarily used to enhance your spreadsheets with logos and other graphics or to create slides for use with slide shows or screen shows. Figure 5-2 shows such a slide created in the Annotator.

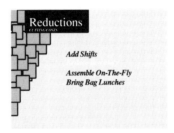

*Figure 5-2: The Annotator can be used to create slides and other
illustrations that do not contain graphs.*

This chapter explains all the Annotator's capabilities and some tricks for using the Annotator's tools. It also explains some useful design tips for annotating graphs.

ANNOTATOR REVEALED

All Quattro Pro's drawing features are found in the Graph Annotator. Its primary purpose is to provide an area where you can enhance your graphs. However, you can also use the Annotator's tools to create drawings that can be added to the spreadsheet or used as presentation slides.

To enhance a graph using the Annotator's tools, first create and display the graph. Then use the Graph-Annotate command to enter the Annotator with the graph simultaneously in view. Much of your annotation work will involve this kind of graph enhancement. You can also bring a graph into the Annotator by pressing the Slash key when you are viewing the graph.

To use the Annotator to create illustrations and slides, you should enter the Annotator with a Text graph type. This provides a totally blank screen for you to use to draw your own creations. You can enter the Annotator from the spreadsheet by typing /GGTA.

When you complete the illustration, you should exit the Annotator and save the graph or slide using the Graph-Name-Create command—the same way you'd save any graph. (See Chapter 3, "Creating Effective Graphs," for details.)

Once you are inside the Annotator, you'll see the tools shown in Figure 5-3.

ENTERING THE ANNOTATOR WITHOUT A GRAPH

1. Select the Graph-Graph Type command.
2. Choose the Text type.
3. Select the Graph-Annotate command.

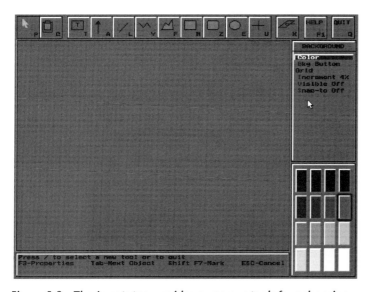

Figure 5-3:   The Annotator provides numerous tools for enhancing graphs and creating slides.

Let's take a quick look at the purpose of each of these tools. Then, the rest of this chapter will show you how to use them.

Pointer—Activates the pointer arrow. Use this tool when you want to select or manipulate objects.

Clipboard—Copies illustrations to and from disk and changes the "layer" on which an object appears.

Text—Creates a box containing text. You can use the Properties list to change the font, size, style and color of this text.

Arrow—Creates arrows using various points and line types.

Line—Creates straight lines at any angle.

Polyline—Creates lines with multiple segments, including curved lines. An example is a zig-zag line.

Polygon—Creates multi-sided objects.

Rectangle—Creates rectangles.

Rounded Rectangle—Creates rectangles with rounded corners.

Ellipse—Creates ovals.

Restricted Line—Creates straight lines vertically and horizontally.

Link—Links objects to parts of a graph.

Help—Brings up Quattro Pro's help screens.

Quit—Exits the Annotator.

Properties List—Displays options for changing the properties of objects. This includes an object's color, line style, fill pattern and more.

Palette—Lists the colors, patterns or line styles available to a particular Properties option.

Many of the Annotator's tools create objects; the remaining tools manipulate those objects. As you'll see, everything in the Annotator is an object—lines, boxes, rectangles, even the graph itself is an object. The rest of this chapter shows you how to manipulate these various objects.

SAVING YOUR ANNOTATED GRAPHS AND SLIDES

1. Click the Quit button or press /Q to quit the Annotator.
2. Select the Graph-Name-Create command.
3. Enter a name for the graph and press Enter.
4. Choose File-Save to save the spreadsheet.

MANIPULATING OBJECTS

If you entered the Annotator with a graph, you already have at least one object on the screen—the graph itself. If the graph contains a legend, you have two objects. A main title makes three separate objects.

But you can also draw your own objects on the screen by using the Annotator's drawing tools. Let's take a look at some of the objects you can draw, then we'll examine how to manipulate objects in the Annotator.

USING BASIC OBJECTS

Quattro Pro's graphic objects may seem limited at first glance, but actually you can create a number of useful graphics with them. While you can't compose freehand drawings or complex illustrations, you can create logos, graphic icons and fancy text displays to use in your spreadsheets and charts. You can also import CGM (Computer Graphics Metafile) files into the Annotator.

The objects you can draw include arrows, lines, polylines (including curved lines), polygons (including rounded shapes), ovals, rectangles, rounded rectangles and restricted lines.

DRAWING BASIC OBJECTS

1. Click on the desired object tool with the mouse. Using the keyboard, press the Slash (/) key and the letter of the desired object.
2. Click and drag on the annotation screen, then release the mouse. The object will appear on the screen. Using the keyboard, simply press the Period key and then use the Arrow keys to draw the object. Press Enter when finished.

USING THE GRID FOR PERFECT CIRCLES AND SQUARES

1. Click on the background or a blank area of the annotation screen. The Background properties should appear on the right side of the screen. Using the keyboard, press /P to view the Background properties.

2. Choose the Visible option to toggle the grid marks on and off.

3. Choose the Snap To option to toggle the snap-to feature on and off.

4. Choose the Increment option and type the desired increment for the grid.

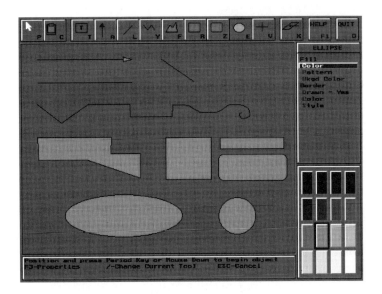

Figure 5-4: Objects you can draw in the Annotator include lines, arrows, polylines, polygons, ovals and rectangles.

Except for the polygon and polyline objects, drawing an object's shape requires a simple click-and-drag motion of the mouse. Just click on the desired tool, then click and drag on the screen to draw the object. If you're using the keyboard, press / and the letter of the desired tool. Then position the pointer (crosshairs shape) and press the Period key to begin drawing; then move the pointer again and press Enter.

You can create perfect squares and circles by applying the Snap To Grid feature. With the Snap To feature on, all your movements with the mouse or keyboard will adhere to the grid's increments. The Increment setting determines the distance between the grid points.

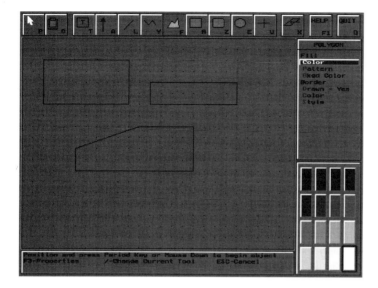

Figure 5-5: The Annotator's grid feature makes everything line up with the grid's increments.

You can also use the grid with the Snap To option off, to provide a visual guide without restricting the mouse or pointer movement. The grid is also useful for aligning objects vertically or horizontally.

Drawing polylines and polygons requires a slightly different approach: with the mouse, click and drag for the first segment of the line or shape, then click on the screen to create each new side. When there are enough sides, click twice. You can return to the starting point or finish the line or shape at some other point. Quattro Pro will connect the beginning and ending points if you're drawing a polygon.

You can draw curved lines and shapes using either the polyline or the polygon tool along with the Shift key. You must have a mouse to access this feature, and it's recommended that you turn off the Snap To Grid feature when drawing curves. However, you may want to leave the visible grid on to help you draw geometric shapes that contain curves.

Drawing curved lines can be useful for freehand drawings, but it requires some practice and a steady hand.

DRAWING POLYLINES AND POLYGONS WITH A MOUSE

1. Click on the polyline or polygon tool.
2. Click and drag on the screen to draw the first segment of the line or shape.
3. Click anywhere to position the second segment.
4. Repeat step 3 for any additional segments.
5. Click twice to complete the line or shape.

DRAWING POLYLINES AND POLYGONS USING THE KEYBOARD

1. Press /Y or /F to select the Polyline or Polygon tool.
2. Tap the Arrow keys to position the pointer on the screen, then press the Period key.
3. Tap the Arrow keys to move the pointer and press Enter to complete the first segment.
4. Repeat step 3 for additional segments.
5. Press Enter twice to finish the line or shape.

1. Click the polyline or poly-gon tool.
2. Hold the Shift key down or press the Scroll Lock key.
3. Draw the curved line using the mouse. Draw slowly.
4. Release the Shift key or press the Scroll Lock key to draw straight segments.
5. Release the Shift key, then click two times to complete the curved line or shape.

TIP: When drawing curved objects, try drawing them as large as possible on the screen, then reduce them to the desired size as described in the following section, "Selecting, Moving and Sizing Objects." This practice may help "clean up" imperfectly drawn images.

SELECTING, MOVING AND SIZING OBJECTS

Once you draw an object onto the screen, you may want to move it or change its overall size and shape. These procedures are simple if you have a mouse, but you can also accomplish them without a mouse.

To move an object with the mouse, you must first select the object. Do this by clicking on the Pointer tool and then on the object. When the object is selected, it will have small squares, called size boxes, around its edges.

MOVING OBJECTS WITH THE MOUSE

1. Click on the Pointer tool.
2. Click on the object you want to move and release the mouse. The object should be selected and should have small squares (size boxes) around its edges.
3. Click on the object again and drag to another location on the screen, then release the mouse.

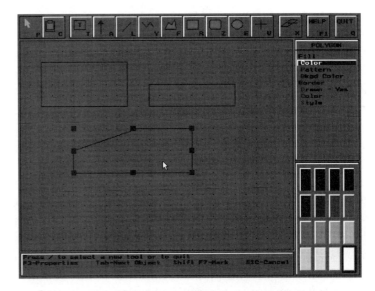

Figure 5-6: Selected objects have size boxes around their edges.

If you have trouble selecting an object (sometimes, very small objects can be stubborn), try clicking directly on one of its edges, or lines. Click on the Pointer tool again and try once more. If you're still having trouble, you can select an object by clicking on the background outside the object and dragging to "surround" the object as shown in Figure 5-7.

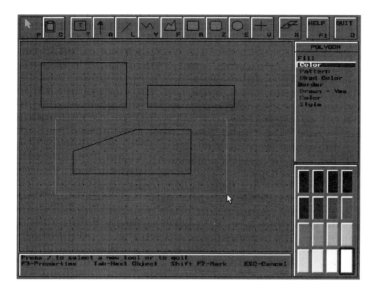

Figure 5-7: You can select an object by surrounding it with the Pointer tool's highlight box.

MOVING OBJECTS WITH THE KEYBOARD

1. Press Tab until the desired object is selected.
2. Press the Arrow keys to move the object slowly.
3. Press Shift with the Arrow keys to move the object more quickly.
4. Press Enter when finished.

When you release the mouse, the object will be selected. Another way to select objects is to press the Tab key. Each time you press Tab, a different object on the screen is selected; keep pressing Tab until the desired object is selected. Pressing Shift-Tab cycles through the objects in reverse order. Use the Tab key to select objects when you don't have a mouse.

After the object is selected, click on it with the mouse and drag to a new location. If you don't have a mouse, use the four Arrow keys to move it. Pressing Shift with the Arrow keys moves the objects more quickly.

You can move an object past the edge of the screen, but anything not showing on the screen will not print either. Nevertheless, it can be useful to push an object slightly off the edge to create various effects.

Figure 5-8: You can move an object past the edge of the screen, although anything not showing will not print.

To change an object's size and shape, first select the object as described above. Then, click on any of the size boxes that surround the object (small squares) and drag on them. Make sure you click directly on one of the size boxes; if you miss, you may have to reselect the object and try again. Depending on where you release the mouse, the object's size and shape will change.

You can also use the keyboard to size objects. Just press Tab to select the object, then press the Period key. After this, the four Arrow keys will change the object's size and shape. Try this with graphs to change their proportions.

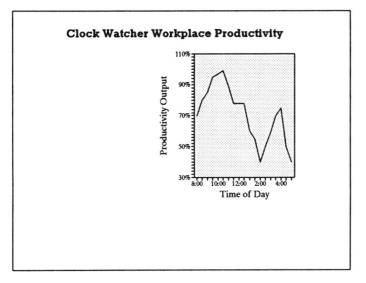

Figure 5-9: You can resize any object in the Annotator, including graphs.

You can "flip" an object horizontally or vertically by dragging one edge inward past the other edge. For example, if you drag the left edge past the right edge, you'll flip the object horizontally. Dragging the top edge past the bottom edge flips the object vertically.

SIZING OBJECTS WITH THE MOUSE

1. Click on the Pointer tool.
2. Click on the object you want to resize and release the mouse. The object should be selected.
3. Click and drag on any of the four corners of the object (directly on one of the size boxes), then release the mouse.

SIZING OBJECTS WITH THE KEYBOARD

1. Press Tab until the desired object is selected.
2. Press the Period key.
3. Press the four Arrow keys to resize the object slowly.
4. Press Shift with the four Arrow keys to resize the object more quickly.
5. Press Enter when finished.

Figure 5-10: Drag one edge past the other to flip an object vertically or horizontally.

CHANGING OBJECT COLORS AND PATTERNS

Before an object can have a color, it must have a pattern. If you remove an object's pattern (which you can do with the Patterns option in the Properties list), then you effectively remove its color also, and the object becomes transparent.

CHANGING AN OBJECT'S COLOR

1. Select the desired object as described earlier in this chapter.
2. Using a mouse, click on the Color option in the Properties list. With the keyboard, press F3 and use the Down Arrow key to highlight the Color option, then press Enter.
3. Select the desired color from the palette. The object changes when you select the color. If the object has a pattern, the pattern changes to the selected color.
4. If the object has a pattern, use the Bkgd Color option in the Properties list to change the background color of the object.

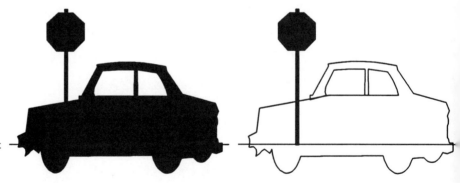

Figure 5-11: Removing an object's pattern also removes any colors, making the object transparent.

If you apply a pattern to an object, then you can add color to the object also. This makes the object opaque, so it will "cover up" any objects beneath it. (Details about overlapping objects appear later in this chapter.)

NOTE: Your graphs will probably appear to be opaque on the screen, covering up objects beneath them. However, they may print differently, depending on your printer. For a discussion of black-and-white printing, see Chapter 7, "Printing Reports."

All patterns have two colors: a foreground color and a background color. The foreground color determines the color of the pattern itself and the background color is the color on which the pattern is drawn. For example, Figure 5-12 shows a pattern using opposite foreground and background colors.

CHANGING AN OBJECT'S PATTERN

1. Select the desired object as described earlier in this chapter.
2. Using a mouse, click on the Pattern option in the Properties list. Using the keyboard, press F3 and use the Down Arrow key to highlight the Pattern option, then press Enter.
3. Select the desired pattern in the palette. The "No" pattern makes the object transparent.

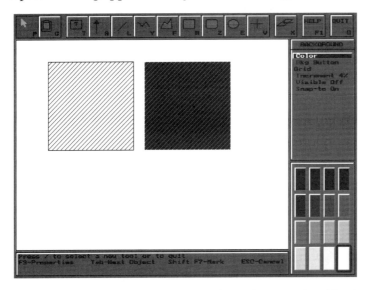

Figure 5-12: A single pattern can use different foreground and background colors for different effects.

The foreground color is set with the Color option in the Properties list. The background color is set with the Bkgd Color option.

NOTE: Colors and patterns do not always print the way they appear on the screen. See Chapter 7 for details about printing colors and patterns on black-and-white printers.

NOTE: The solid pattern makes the Bkgd Color setting unimportant because it uses a solid version of the foreground color.

CHANGING OBJECT BORDERS AND LINES

You can change three properties of an object's border: its color, its style, and whether or not it's displayed. These border options appear in the Properties list when you select an object.

If your object is an arrow, then an additional Property appears in the list. The Arrowhead-Color option changes the color of the arrow's tip.

TIP: You can easily duplicate the formatting used on previous objects without having to reselect the properties options. Just select the object containing the desired formatting and then click on the drawing tool to draw the new object. The new object will automatically appear with the formats of the selected object.

OVERLAPPING OBJECTS

Complex drawings can be created using object "overlapping" in strategic ways. When you draw an object, it automatically appears above (or on top of) objects previously drawn. Each object rests on its own "level" according to the order in which it was drawn. You can change the overlap order of objects by using the Clipboard's To Top and To Bottom commands.

Objects with patterns are opaque and will "cover up" objects beneath them. This can be used for special effects. For example, you can create arcs by covering parts of a circle. And partially covering a rectangle with another rectangle can create a "shadow" effect.

CHANGING AN OBJECT'S BORDERS AND LINES

1. Select the desired object as described earlier in this chapter.
2. Choose the Draw option in the Properties list to show or hide the border.
3. Choose the Border-Color option in the Properties list to change the border's color. Select from the palette of colors.
4. Choose the Style option to select a line type for the border.

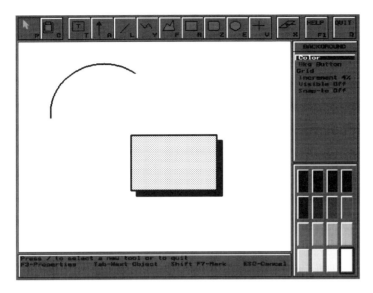

Figure 5-13: Overlap objects for various effects.

In this example, two boxes were used to cover up part of the circle. These boxes are the same color as the background and their borders have been removed. This makes them blend into the background, leaving only a portion of the circle showing. The shadow effect on the box is emphasized by making the bottom rectangle black.

Overlapping can be used to create custom border designs. In these examples, the bottom rectangles are formatted with various patterns and another rectangle is placed on top, revealing only the edges of the box below.

OVERLAPPING OBJECTS

1. Click on the Pointer tool on the desired object to select it. Using the keyboard, press the Tab key until the desired object is selected.

2. Click on the Clipboard tool. Using the keyboard, press /C.

3. Select the To Bottom or To Top option in the Properties list.

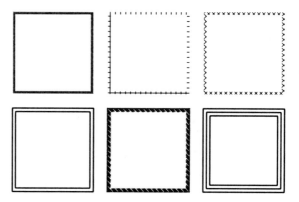

Figure 5-14: Use overlapping to create special borders.

You can take this concept even further by adding other shapes and patterns to the mix.

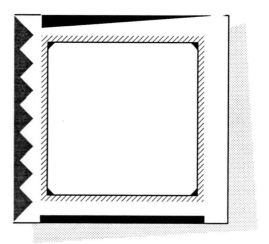

Figure 5-15: By combining and overlapping various objects, you can create some complex illustrations.

Note that graphs will appear opaque on your screen and will cover up any objects beneath them. However, on some printers, the graphs will appear transparent and objects beneath them will show through. This can be useful for certain types of graph annotation, such as highlighting a section of the graph or placing graphics behind the graph.

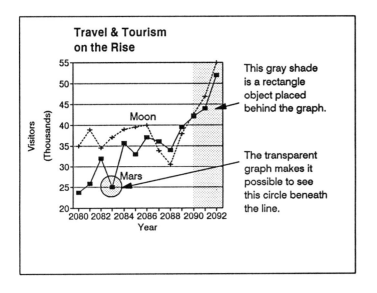

Figure 5-16: If your printer treats graphs as transparent objects, you can perform special types of annotation.

Remember, this is a function of how Quattro Pro handles your printer and it may not be available for your equipment. For a complete discussion of printing, see Chapter 7, "Printing Reports."

MANIPULATING OBJECTS IN GROUPS

You've seen that annotation options normally require you to first select an object. But you can also select several objects at a time and apply formatting properties to them all at once. You can move and resize objects as a group, and you can change a group's colors, patterns and borders in one shot.

To select a group, hold the Shift key down as you click on each object. All selected objects will have size boxes around their edges. If all the objects in the group appear together on the screen, you can select them all at once by clicking on the

SELECTING A GROUP OF OBJECTS

1. Click on the first object. Using the keyboard, press Tab to select the first object.

2. Hold down the Shift key and click on other objects. Using the keyboard, press Shift-F7, then press Tab to select the next object. Repeat this procedure for more objects.

3. You can manipulate the object group now or press F7 to "combine" them as a single object—then manipulate the group. This retains the spacing of each object relative to the others as the objects are moved.

Pointer tool and then clicking and dragging on the spreadsheet to surround the objects with the selection box. When you release the mouse, all the objects inside the selection box will be selected.

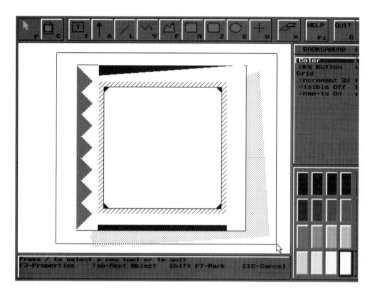

Figure 5-17: Use the mouse with the Pointer tool to surround all objects you want to handle as a group.

If you don't have a mouse, you can group objects by selecting each object with the Tab key and pressing Shift-F7 before tabbing to the next. When you press Shift-F7, the selected object will remain selected as you cycle through other objects. If you cycle all the way through the objects, the selected ones will return to normal.

Once you've selected a group, you can format and move it as a single object. First, press F7 to make all the individual objects in the group appear as a single object.

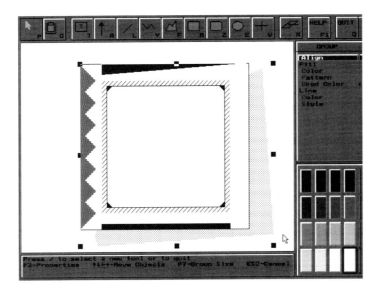

Figure 5-18: Pressing F7 after selecting the group turns all the objects into a single object.

Now you can handle the group as a single object. Anything you can do with a single object, you can do with a group. If the group becomes "unselected" you will have to repeat the procedure. This is because objects in a group return to their normal state when you finish manipulating them.

You can align a group of objects using the Align option in the Properties list (after you select the group). You can align the objects along the left side, right side, top or bottom. You can also center the selected objects vertically or horizontally.

DUPLICATING OBJECTS

You can copy objects or groups by using the Clipboard tool's Copy and Paste options. First, select the desired object or group, then copy it. You can then paste the object to make a copy on the same screen as the original. When you paste, the new copy will appear directly on top of the original and you should move it to view them both.

ALIGNING OBJECTS IN GROUPS

1. Select the desired objects as a group.
2. Select the Align option in the Properties list.
3. Choose from the alignment options.

COPYING AN OBJECT OR GROUP

1. Select the object or group.
2. Select the Clipboard tool or press /C.
3. Select the Copy command from the Properties list.
4. Select the Paste command from the Properties list.
5. Press F7 and then drag the copy to a new location.

1. Select all the objects as a group.
2. Click on the Clipboard tool or press /C.
3. Select the Copy To option in the Properties list.
4. Enter a name for the file (include an entire directory path if desired), then press Enter.

1. Click on the Text tool. Using the keyboard, press /T.
2. Click on the spreadsheet approximately where you would like to place the text. Using the keyboard, press the Arrow keys to position the Pointer, then press Enter.
3. Type the desired text. Press Ctrl-Enter to create a second line. Press Enter when finished.
4. To edit the text, select the text box and press F2.

If a group of objects forms a useful picture or graphic, consider saving it as a clip-art file on disk. This makes it available for all your Annotator graphics. Saving the image also serves as a backup, in case you need to start over again with a fresh copy of the illustration.

Use the Clipboard's Copy To option to save an image to disk for future use.

NOTE: You cannot copy graphs, graph titles or legends using these procedures.

MANIPULATING TEXT

In the Annotator, text appears in a box on the screen. You can add individual pieces of text to your Annotator graphics by adding text boxes and typing text into these boxes. Each box can contain one or more lines of text formatted with a particular font, size, style and color. Add as many text boxes as you like; you can manipulate the boxes much like you manipulate other objects.

To create text in the Annotator, simply click on the Text tool (or press /T) and then click on the spreadsheet and begin typing. The text will appear in a box which expands as you type. Pressing Ctrl-Enter starts a new line and pressing Enter completes the text box entry. You can then click on the spreadsheet to create another text box—or use one of the other Annotator tools.

You can move and size a text box as you would a rectangle object. Just click on the Pointer tool, then on the text box to select it. You can then drag it to another location or use its size boxes to change its overall size. However, the size of a text box is primarily controlled by the text it contains; you cannot shrink or expand the box very much.

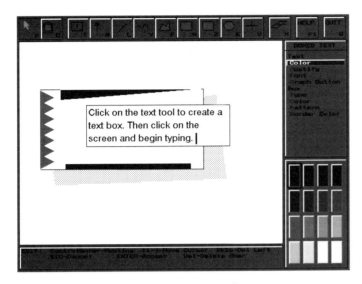

Figure 5-19: Create text boxes by clicking on the Text tool and then the spreadsheet before typing.

Like any other object in the Annotator, text boxes can be grouped and overlapped with other objects. And you can duplicate them as described earlier in this chapter for other objects.

To edit text inside a text box, click on the Pointer tool, then on the desired text box to select it. Next, press F2 to make the cursor appear inside the text box. Finally, use basic editing commands (such as the Backspace, Delete and Arrow keys) to change the text, and press Enter when finished.

TEXT BOX PATTERNS, BORDERS AND SHADOWS

Text boxes have border color and fill properties similar to rectangles. You can select a color for the interior of the text box by selecting the text box and using the Box-Color option in the Properties list. You can also change the fill pattern of the text box. Normally, this is set to a solid pattern—giving you a solid color inside the box. Your box color change will change this solid pattern to whatever color you select. However, if you have a different pattern active in the text box, changing the box color will change only the color of the pattern itself.

For example, if you start out with red dots in a blue box and then change the box color to green, you get green dots in a blue box. So how do you change the background color of the text box when you are using a nonsolid pattern? First, click on the Rectangle tool, then use the Bkgd Color option in the Properties list to select the desired background color. Also, choose the fill pattern and box color at this time. Now return to the Text tool and create a text box; it will have the background color, foreground color and pattern you selected.

By using the "No" pattern in a text box, you can create a transparent box that will show objects beneath it.

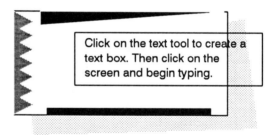

Figure 5-20: Changing a text box pattern to "No" gives you a transparent box.

Change the border style of the text box using the Box-Style option in the Properties list after selecting the text box. You can also make text "float" on the page with no border, by using the "None" box style.

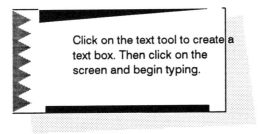

Figure 5-21: By changing a text box style to "None" you can make text float on the page.

NOTE: All properties can be applied to text boxes and other objects *before* you draw them. Just select the desired properties after selecting the desired tool but before drawing the object. Properties you've selected for one object are automatically applied to the next object you draw, unless you change them first.

Other text box border styles include a special sculpted box type and automatic drop shadows. (These aren't available for other objects.) Of course, you can create your own shadows for text boxes, as described earlier in "Overlapping Objects."

Note that when printing on a black-and-white printer, your text box patterns and colors may give unexpected results. On many black-and-white printers, Quattro Pro simply removes the text box patterns and colors and prints text black on white. (See Chapter 7, "Printing Reports," for a complete discussion of black-and-white printing.)

TEXT FONTS, COLORS AND STYLES

The most important change you can make to a text box is to change the font, color and style of its type. To change the font, select the Font option in the Properties list after selecting the text box. The font dialog box appears on the screen.

CHANGING TEXT BOX FONTS

1. Select the text box.
2. Select the Font option in the Properties menu.
3. Choose the Typeface, Style and Point Size for the font.
4. Select the Quit command.

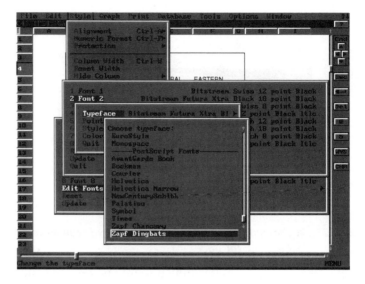

Figure 5-22: The Annotator offers a font dialog box for choosing typefaces, styles and sizes.

CHANGING TEXT COLOR

1. Select the desired text box.
2. Select the Color command in the Properties list (this may already be selected).
3. Choose the desired color from the palette.

CHANGING SHADOW COLOR

1. Return to the spreadsheet.
2. Select Graph-Overall-Drop Shadow Color command.
3. Select the color whose drop shadow color you want to change.
4. Select the drop shadow color from the palette (or list) provided.
5. Quit to return to the spreadsheet.

Select the Typeface option to select from any of Quattro Pro's fonts (including any you've added). You can mix any fonts you like in the Annotator—you're not limited to the fonts used in the spreadsheet. In fact, you can mix any typeface, size, style and color you like in the Annotator—provided the typeface you select comes in the style you select. And the Annotator includes three font styles not available in your spreadsheets.

Shadow text is ideal for color presentations, since the shadow is a different color from the text itself. In black and white, however, the shadow and text are both black.

You can change the colors of text and text shadows if you like. Quattro Pro contains a listing of each text color (16 different colors) and the shadow color that goes with it. You can combine text colors with shadow colors for use in all your Annotator text boxes. For example, green text may always have a brown shadow and blue text, a gray shadow. You simply combine text and shadow colors. Do this with the Graph-Overall-Drop Shadow Color command. The color combinations appear in a list.

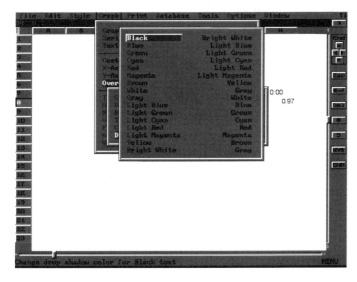

Figure 5-23: The Graph-Overall-Drop Shadow Color command
shows color combinations for drop shadows.

The left side of this list contains each of the 16 colors available in Quattro Pro. The right side contains the shadow color that corresponds to this color. To change the shadow color, select the desired color from the left side of the list and press Enter. Then choose a color for the drop shadow from the palette provided. Change as many combinations as you like.

When you're finished, return to the Annotator and use the drop shadow type style on some text. Then, change the color of that text and see what color you get for the shadow.

CUSTOMIZING TEXT

You can simulate special kinds of text formatting by using special techniques. For example, you can mix fonts within what appears to be the same box by placing several text boxes together, each with its own font. Remove the borders from the text boxes and place them beside each other (or on top, depending on your design). You can also shrink the text boxes to draw the individual text elements as close together as possible. (See sections on sizing objects earlier in this chapter.)

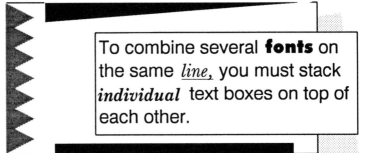

Figure 5-24: Combine several text boxes to get different fonts and styles on the same line or in the same box.

Notice that the text is not placed on top of existing text, but over spaces that were deliberately left blank. (On monochrome systems, this will be difficult to manage on the screen because the text boxes don't appear to be transparent and part of the box may overlap other text.) Note that on-screen text is sometimes slightly different from the printout, depending on your printer. So you may need to adjust the text after printing it.

Another way to customize text is to change the space between letters. You can insert space between letters by tapping the space bar several times between each character you type. You can then adjust the number of spaces that appear after you print the image to preview it.

To bring the letters closer together requires that you type each letter into a separate text box. For best results, remove the border of the first text box you type and set its various formatting options before creating the rest. Then, you can just click to create each letter. The same formats will apply to each letter you create. After you type each character, move them into position beside each other.

REPORTING ON:

Teen-Age
Run-Away Socks

AN AMERICAN TRAGEDY

Figure 5-25: Add spaces to your text to create special headings.

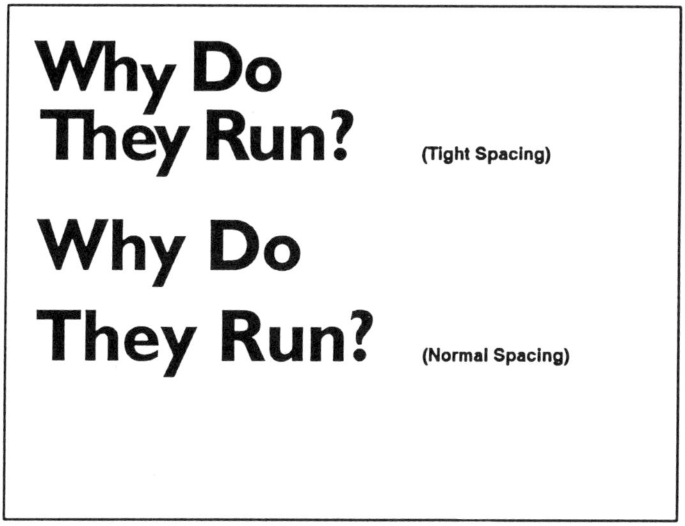

Why Do
They Run?   (Tight Spacing)

Why Do
They Run?   (Normal Spacing)

Figure 5-26: You can close up the space between letters by placing each letter in a separate text box and manually moving the boxes close together.

You can align all the bottoms by using the Annotator grid and Snap To feature (described earlier in this chapter) or by selecting all the letters as a group and using the Align option in the Properties list (also described earlier in this chapter).

Another way to enhance text is to use lines and other objects creatively, as shown in Figure 5-27.

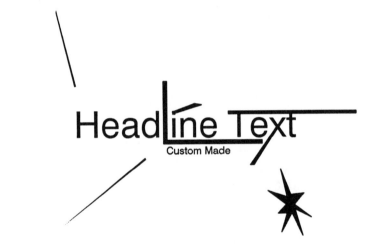

Figure 5-27: You can enhance text by using objects creatively in the Annotator.

USING EXTERNAL ART

Okay, so you're not Picasso. You can still get attractive graphics for your spreadsheets and presentations by using clip-art. Or maybe you *are* a Picasso, and you prefer to use the more advanced capabilities of a professional graphics program, such as Corel Draw. You can import images created in Corel Draw into the Quattro Pro Annotator, just as you can import clip-art.

When using outside artwork, the images must be saved to disk in CGM (Computer Graphics Metafile) format, a common graphics format for data exchange between programs. If you're purchasing clip-art, the illustrations must come in CGM files. When using a graphics program for your own artwork, be sure the program saves images in the CGM format.

NOTE: Quattro Pro comes with several CGM clip-art files that you can use right away. Others come with the ProView PowerPack utilities. This may have come with your copy of Quattro Pro, or you can purchase it separately from Borland.

If you must use images stored in a different format, you can use a reliable graphics conversion utility to convert graphics between CGM, TIFF, EPS and other formats. See the Resources section of this book for more information about conversion utilities.

Assuming your illustration is stored in the CGM format, getting it into Quattro Pro is fairly simple. Just use the Clipboard feature of the Annotator to read the file from its storage location and place it in your current annotation screen.

IMPORTING ART INTO QUATTRO PRO

1. In the Annotator, select the Clipboard tool or press /C.
2. Select the Paste From option in the Properties List.
3. Select the desired file from the list provided. You can view files in a different directory by typing the desired directory path and pressing Enter.
4. Manipulate the image as soon as it appears, while it remains selected.

Figure 5-28: Use the Clipboard to bring clip-art into the Annotator.

When the image is pasted into the Annotator, it's automatically selected as a group. This is important to remember, since your images are probably made up of multiple objects.

Now you can move and size the objects as a single unit. If you have other objects on the screen, it's important to move and size the imported illustration as soon as you paste it from the Clipboard, while it remains selected. Otherwise, it can be difficult to reselect the group of objects again later (some illustrations are very complex). However, if the illustration is the only thing on the screen, then it will be easy enough to select all its objects again later.

When you size an imported illustration, avoid making it too small, which can distort the illustration. If this happens, just delete the illustration and import it again. To retain an object's proportions as you change its size, use the background grid to measure your sizing changes.

If you use a black-and-white text-based system, color illustrations will appear totally black when imported. As soon as the image is pasted into the annotation screen, use the Group Color option to change the object to white. Also, you may need to change the group's pattern to solid. Often, clip-art images contain separate outlines for each object. However, if you can figure out each object's purpose, you can make changes to the illustration once it has been imported. You can even combine two or more illustrations into one.

Figure 5-29: Don't be afraid to make changes to clip-art.

MOVING ON

Quattro Pro's Annotator plays an important part in creating effective presentations. It can be used to annotate graphs or to create illustrations and slides. When using the Annotator, keep a few things in mind:

- Everything in the Annotator is an object, whether it's a graph, a graph title or a legend.
- Using Annotator tools, you can manipulate the objects on the screen and create new objects.
- When annotating a graph, keep the illustrations simple to avoid conflicting with the graph's message.
- You can manipulate objects individually or in groups.

- Annotator text can be formatted with any typeface, size and style available in Quattro Pro—not just the eight spreadsheet fonts.

- Quattro Pro may alter your colors and patterns when you print an Annotator graphic in black and white.

- Import useful illustrations from outside Quattro Pro. Any CGM file can be imported into the Annotator.

You'll find more ideas on applying graphics to your spreadsheets and presentations in the following chapters. If you are printing graphics in black and white, be sure to read Chapter 7, "Printing Reports." Creating slides is covered in Chapters 8 and 9.

PUTTING IT ALL TOGETHER

Designing Effective Pages

6.

The previous chapters have shown you how to use and manipulate Quattro Pro's graphing and graphics features. In this chapter, you'll learn how to translate that information into printed pages. We'll illustrate some design ideas for building tables, databases, financial reports, forms and other spreadsheet projects. Later, in Chapter 11, we go even further with these projects and show you "makeovers," which put these design tips to work.

TABLE ARRANGEMENTS

Most spreadsheet reports are tables of one kind or another. A table, like a straightforward spreadsheet, displays information in columns with headings at the top of each. For the most part, table formats are relatively simple. Here are some basic rules to follow:

- Use only as many lines as you need (horizontal lines are often unnecessary).

- Make sure the data fits comfortably within the columns.

- Make headings prominent.

- Be sure important values are treated in such a way that they stand out.

- Add footnotes if needed.

LINES, BORDERS AND BOXES: EASY DOES IT

It's easy to overdo lines. Resist the temptation to box in an entire page or spreadsheet area, or to use lines down every column and across every row. Another common mistake is boxing in headings. These design pitfalls can make a spreadsheet look like a road map in the printout. The following illustration is a typical spreadsheet "table" arrangement.

National Sales Corp Sales Performance Report			

Western Division

	January	February	March	Total
Seattle	355,115	312,900	315,650	983,665
San Francisco	624,212	590,002	630,012	1,844,226
Los Angeles	557,334	500,505	512,300	1,570,139
San Diego	245,600	200,080	230,987	676,667
Total Western Sales	1,782,261	1,603,487	1,688,949	5,074,697

Central Division

	January	February	March	Total
Dallas	218,556	199,899	235,655	654,120
Chicago	625,899	500,970	600,023	1,726,892
Phoenix	156,500	212,300	225,450	594,250
Detroit	450,500	379,534	400,500	1,230,534
Cleveland	245,000	200,070	200,340	645,410
Total Central Sales	1,477,899	1,292,874	1,426,313	4,197,086

Eastern Division

	January	February	March	Total
New York	689,112	612,234	678,300	1,979,646
Boston	412,400	398,989	400,100	1,211,489
Atlanta	457,020	210,789	300,000	967,809
Pittsburgh	212,788	200,340	198,000	611,128
Total Eastern Sales	1,771,320	1,422,352	1,576,400	4,770,072

Figure 6-1: A typical "boxed-in" spreadsheet.

Now remove the lines around the entire print area or spreadsheet area. Because your printout is already contained on an 8.5 by 11 page, there's no need to contain the data again. In fact, those lines are distracting and make the table look cramped.

Since the horizontal flow of data is usually pretty easy to follow without help, let's also remove the horizontal lines. But we'll leave the horizontal lines under the headings and above the column totals.

A strong horizontal line at the top of a table can be useful for emphasizing and separating headings and totals from the rest of the data. Here's the example with a more appropriate use of lines and borders.

National Sales Corp
Sales Performance Report

Western Division

	January	February	March	Total
Seattle	355,115	312,900	315,650	983,665
San Francisco	624,212	590,002	630,012	1,844,226
Los Angeles	557,334	500,505	512,300	1,570,139
San Diego	245,600	200,080	230,987	676,667
Total Western Sales	1,782,261	1,603,487	1,688,949	5,074,697

Central Division

	January	February	March	Total
Dallas	218,556	199,899	235,655	654,120
Chicago	625,899	500,970	600,023	1,726,892
Phoenix	156,500	212,300	225,450	594,250
Detroit	450,500	379,534	400,500	1,230,534
Cleveland	245,000	200,070	200,340	645,410
Total Central Sales	1,477,899	1,292,874	1,426,313	4,197,086

Eastern Division

	January	February	March	Total
New York	689,112	612,234	678,300	1,979,646
Boston	412,400	398,989	400,100	1,211,489
Atlanta	457,020	210,789	300,000	967,809
Pittsburgh	212,788	200,340	198,000	611,128
Total Eastern Sales	1,771,320	1,422,352	1,576,400	4,770,072

Figure 6-2: A spreadsheet table arrangement with better use of lines and borders.

MAKE TITLES TALK

Table titles should not only be prominent and meaningful; they should also act as headlines that convey the purpose of your presentation, in two to five words. Instead of "Budget for Fiscal 1992," try "Fiscal 1992 Budget Increases by 5%." Then show the data to support that projection. Not all tables will qualify, but check to see if yours would benefit from a more explanatory title.

Titles are usually displayed in a large headline font above the table—typically, centered or flush-left. As mentioned in Chapter 3, "Creating Effective Graphs," centering titles above several columns can be tricky. Try using a typeface different from the face used for the data inside the table. Column headings can be set in a smaller size of this same face or in a bold version of the font used inside the table.

Avoid making column headings significantly wider than the rows of data inside the columns. If you feel you must increase the size of the heading, you may be forced to expand the column width or split the heading into two or more vertical cells, or rows. If you do split it, make the bottom line the longest, and use no more than three vertical cells. If more space is required, either change the heading or expand the column to fit more characters on each line.

Within a table, try to use the same number of lines in all headings. Using three rows for one column heading and only one row for the next creates an unbalanced, confusing layout.

And be sure to leave sufficient blank space around the headings; if a heading is too wide for the column, you could abbreviate it or elevate it above the others.

Biomedical Firms
Investor Analysis

	Western Biomedical	Pacific Biomedical	Atlas Biomedical Research Group	ACME Medical	RAM
Sales	13.0	13.5	4.8	34.5	55.4
Net Profit (loss)	-50.2	12.5	-1.2	8.8	20.3
Return on CSE	-0.6%	2.4%	0.1%	3.1%	3.5%
Stock Price Range	45 to 65	23 to 60	20 to 31	40 to 59	55 to 79
Recent Share Price	56.12	58.6	22.1	58.5	79.0
Total Return to Inv.	-30.1%	1.8%	-0.5%	2.2%	3.0%

Figure 6-3: Headings too wide for the column can be abbreviated or elevated.

Sometimes, the left-side headings will require too much space, forcing you to break them onto two rows each.

Biomedical Firms
Investor Analysis

| | Western Biomedical | Pacific Biomedical | Atlas Biomedical Research Group | | RAM |
			ACME Medical		
Sales	13.0	13.5	4.8	34.5	55.4
Latest Four Quarters in millions					
Net Profit (loss)	-50.2	12.5	-1.2	8.8	20.3
In Millions					
Return on CSE	-0.6%	2.4%	0.1%	3.1%	3.5%
Stock Price Range	45 to 65	23 to 60	20 to 31	40 to 59	55 to 79
Last 12 Months					
Recent Share Price	56.12	58.6	22.1	58.5	79.0
Total Return to Inv.	-30.1%	1.8%	-0.5%	2.2%	3.0%
12 Months					

Figure 6-4: Use two rows for extra-large headings. Often the second row can be smaller than the first.

In this example, the second rows use a small font to minimize the gaps between the values in the table. The values are entered on the first row for each item. For example, the first value in the table, 13.0, is entered on the same row as the Sales heading rather than its subhead.

However, if you move the values down one row, but display them in a fairly large font (a font larger than the row height containing the values, such as 14-point type in a 9-point row), then you can overcome the gaps created by the inserted rows.

If you insert rows above the headings, you can use them to hold footnote numbers set in a small type size.

Biomedical Firms

Investor Analysis

	Western Biomedical	Pacific Biomedical	ABRG	ACME Medical	RAM
Sales [1]	13.0	13.5	4.8	34.5	55.4
Net Profit (loss) [1]	-50.2	12.5	-1.2	8.8	20.3
Return on CSE	-0.6%	2.4%	0.1%	3.1%	3.5%
Stock Price Range [2]	45 to 65	23 to 60	20 to 31	40 to 59	55 to 79
Recent Share Price	56.12	58.6	22.1	58.5	79.0
Total Return to Inv. [2]	-30.1%	1.8%	-0.5%	2.2%	3.0%

1. Figures in Millions
2. Last 12 Months

Figure 6-5: Create footnotes by inserting small rows to contain the footnote numbers.

In this example, horizontal lines were added to keep the reader's eyes on track. However, you could increase the point size of the table's values to minimize the gaps between them. And if you increase the size of the left-side headings, without increasing the row height, you might improve the appearance of your footnote numbers.

Biomedical Firms

Investor Analysis

	Western Biomedical	Pacific Biomedical	ABRG	ACME Medical	RAM
Sales [1]	13.0	13.5	4.8	34.5	55.4
Net Profit (loss)	-50.2	12.5	-1.2	8.8	20.3
Return on CSE	-0.6%	2.4%	0.1%	3.1%	3.5%
Stock Price Range [2]	45 to 65	23 to 60	20 to 31	40 to 59	55 to 79
Recent Share Price	56.12	58.6	22.1	58.5	79.0
Total Return to Inv. [2]	-30.1%	1.8%	-0.5%	2.2%	3.0%

1. Figures in Millions
2. Last 12 Months

Figure 6-6: Use smaller row heights to make footnote numbers look better.

If your table serves as a database in the spreadsheet, your column heading choices will be limited. They can appear only in the row above the first record. You may want to make the database headings invisible by using the Style-Number Format-Hidden command. You may also use the Style-Shade command to shade this row of headings and shrink the row height to make the row appear as a separation line above the data. Then, add a second set of headings in the rows above this line.

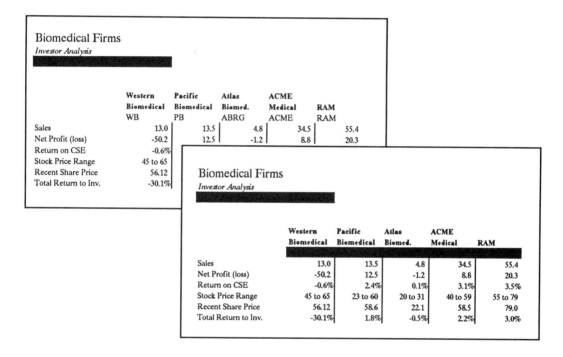

Figure 6-7: Database headings can be hidden and extra headings added above them.

ADD POLISH WITH GRAPHIC DEVICES

Tables don't often require graphics to illustrate their messages. But simple graphic enhancements, such as shading, can give the table a more finished look.

Figure 6-8: *Use shading and other graphic devices to give tables a more finished look.*

In the first example, a shaded block was added to the top and bottom of the table, and the narrow columns on the right and left sides were shaded black. The second example uses shading to create a drop shadow. To create this effect, an extra (narrow) column was added to the left side of the table and incorporated into the table's outline. The width of this column matches the height of the first row in the table, so that the shadow is offset from the left side and top by the same amount. Next, shading was applied to two areas: the row immediately below the table, minus the first column; and the row immediately right of the table, minus the first row.

The height of a shaded block can be manipulated by changing the point size of the font used in the row containing the shade. You can set this point size even if the row contains no actual data. The row's height, as well as the height of the shaded block, will still be adjusted.

Another special graphic element you can use in a spreadsheet is a bullet. Quattro Pro gives you access to seven different bullet types that are useful in comparison tables and forms. (These are also useful for slide shows. See Chapter 8.)

USING BULLETS

1. Move to the cell that is to contain the bullet.
2. Type the apostrophe to begin a text entry.
3. Type \blt n\ where n is a number from 0 to 6.
4. Add any text you like after the bullet.
5. Press Enter.

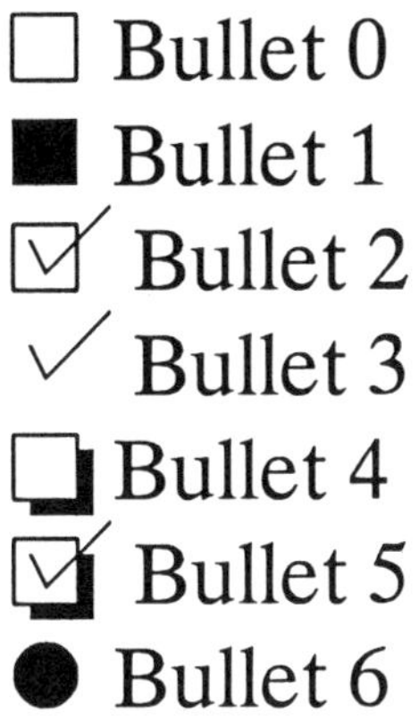

☐ Bullet 0
■ Bullet 1
☑ Bullet 2
✓ Bullet 3
☐ Bullet 4
☑ Bullet 5
● Bullet 6

Figure 6-9: Quattro Pro offers several types of bullets.

To access one of these bullets, type \blt n\ where n is a number from 0 to 6 that determines which bullet is used. Be sure to enter the command as a text label by typing an apostrophe (') first. You can include text with the bullet by adding it to the command. Note that the currently selected typeface doesn't affect the bullet, but the point size does.

FINANCIAL REPORTS: DESIGN'S BOTTOM LINE

Don't underestimate the importance of using good design for your basic financial reports. When you present a balance sheet, income statement and other financial reports to your bank for a loan approval, the quality of your presentation can influence the outcome.

Using graphs, you can emphasize aspects of the business in a professional manner. And the overall appearance of your numbers will say something about you and your company.

However, designing an effective financial report doesn't present a major challenge, since there isn't a lot of room for experimentation and creativity. Nevertheless, there are some basic rules to follow and some generally accepted designs:

* Always make the reports businesslike: choose conservative fonts and stick to two or three fonts, maximum.

* Limit your horizontal lines to major section breaks; avoid unnecessary vertical lines altogether.

* Limit graphics to company logos and simple graphs that present the financial data.

* Avoid decimal places unless values represent thousands or millions of dollars.

* Highlight or use boldface fonts for important columns or values.

* Don't crowd or clutter the page; allow plenty of "breathing room."

GENERALLY ACCEPTED FORMATS

Financial reports should not go far beyond commonly used formats, especially when they're being presented to financial institutions. (Restrictions can be relaxed for internal financial reports when appropriate.) It's customary to include dollar signs with the first and last values in a column and with major totals. Usually, these dollar signs are aligned with the far left edge of the column, whereas the value itself is aligned with the right edge.

This can be done by placing the dollar signs in a small column to the left of the values column. Instead of using the Currency number format on the column of values, use the Comma format with no decimal places (unless the figures are shown in thousands or millions, in which case you can include one decimal place).

National Business Group
Consolidated Balance Sheets

	Fiscal Year End: December 31	1990
Assets	Current Assets:	
	Cash and Equivalents	$ 22.9
	Accounts and Notes Receivable	684.8
	Inventories	767.0
	Other	212.3
	Total Current Assets	1687.0
	Property, Plant & Equipment	3855.1
	Accumulated Depreciation	-877.2
	Property, Plant & Equip. - Net	2977.9
	Land	103.9
	Goodwill	1089.8
	Other	395.1
	Total Assets	$ 6253.7
Liabilities	Current Liabilities:	
	Notes Payable	$ 66.4
	Current Portion LTD	286.0
	Accounts Payable	355.9
	Income Taxes Due	71.1
	Accrued Liabilities	293.2
	Total Current Liabilities	1072.6
	Long Term Debt	2598.0
	Subordinated Debt	671.1
	Other Long-Term Liabilities	78.6
	Deferred Taxes	185.8
	Total Non-Current Liabilities	3533.5
	Stockholders' Equity:	
	Common Stock	556.8
	Retained Earnings	1090.8
	Total Stockholders' Equity	1647.6
	Total Liabilities and Equity	$ 6253.7

Figure 6-10: Use dollar signs on the first and last values in a standard financial report.

Indent items within a financial category by using two different columns for the data. The first column should be narrow (the width of your indent) and the second can be wide enough to hold the longest line of data. When the amount of data entered into the first column exceeds what the width of the column can accommodate, the excess data will continue into the next column. Data entered into the second column will appear indented.

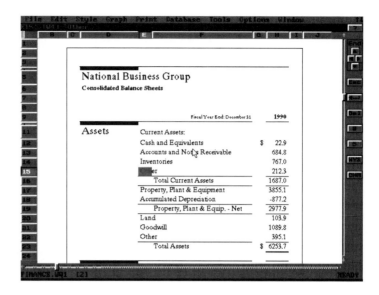

Figure 6-11:Use two columns to indent tables.

You can also set up three columns, to produce a third-level indent; but more than three levels may be distracting and hard to follow.

A report containing several financial statements usually highlights the current figures, as shown in the previous illustration. Also note the dash used in cells that contain zero(s). If your spreadsheet calculates its figures, you can use a formula to do this automatically:

@IF(FORMULA=0,"-",FORMULA)

Replace the word "FORMULA" in both instances with the actual calculation in your cell. Any 0 (zero) produced by this calculation is then converted to the - (hyphen) character.

GRAPHS AND GRAPHIC ELEMENTS SIMPLIFIED

You should include graphs wherever appropriate in your financial reports. Usually they're presented on separate pages. However, simple graphs can be included with your numeric data—if they don't detract from the page design and are still easily readable when reduced to fit onto the page.

National Business Group
Consolidated Balance Sheets

		Fiscal Year End: December 31	1990
Assets	Current Assets:		
	Cash and Equivalents	$	22.9
	Accounts and Notes Receivable		684.8
	Inventories		767.0
	Other		212.3
	Total Current Assets		1687.0
	Property, Plant & Equipment		3855.1
	Accumulated Depreciation		-877.2
	Property, Plant & Equip. - Net		2977.9
	Land		103.9
	Goodwill		1089.8
	Other		395.1
	Total Assets	$	6253.7
Liabilities	Current Liabilities:		
	Notes Payable	$	66.4
	Current Portion LTD		286.0
	Accounts Payable		355.9
	Income Taxes Due		71.1
	Accrued Liabilities		293.2
	Total Current Liabilities		1072.6
	Long Term Debt		2598.0
	Subordinated Debt		671.1
	Other Long-Term Liabilities		78.6
	Deferred Taxes		185.8
	Total Non-Current Liabilities		3533.5
	Stockholders' Equity:		
	Common Stock		556.8
	Retained Earnings		1090.8
	Total Stockholders' Equity		1647.6
	Total Liabilities and Equity	$	6253.7

Change In Stock Price
NBG
DOW
79 81 83 85 87 89

Figure 6-12: Use graphs in your financial reports if they don't distract from the message.

The only other graphic image you should include in a financial report is your company logo. Even this small exception should be handled carefully. To include a logo or company identification graphic, first produce the logo as a Text graph using Quattro Pro's annotation tools. Or you can bring in a predesigned logo using the Clipboard. Be sure the logo completely fills the annotation screen.

Color can be an effective way to make your financial reports stand out. You can print the entire report in dark blue or use a simple combination of two colors. Or you might display your company name or logo in a different color. If graphs are included, you can use additional colors on the graphs. For more about using color, see Chapter 8, "Designing Slides, Overheads and Screen Shows."

Finally, for consistency, use the same elements, in the same way, throughout your financial reports.

FORMS FOLLOW FUNCTION

Because Quattro Pro is so good at performing business calculations, many of the forms you create will be business forms. Although Quattro Pro is not a forms-design program, it can be used to create and process two basic types of business forms: forms that supply information (display forms) and forms that request information. Display information will likely come from your spreadsheet calculations. Forms that request information, including surveys, order forms and coupons, can also serve as data entry forms, since the data derived from them can be entered back into the spreadsheet.

Today, well-designed business forms are part of a company's overall image. Your customers probably see your business forms more often than they see you or your advertisements. Business forms can often be filled out right inside Quattro Pro.

Some forms, such as insurance and real estate documents, don't lend themselves to a wide variety of design options. So we'll focus instead on a few response forms that especially need good design to get the reader's attention.

But always remember that whether you're requesting or displaying data, the purpose of a form is to organize data and make it understandable. Don't let the design stand in the way of this mission. Be sure you've accomplished these basic things:

- The title is visible and bold enough to quickly convey the form's purpose to the reader.

- Totals and important values stand out from other data so your customers can't miss the point (e.g., how much they owe).

- Column headings are descriptive and readable.

- Company name and address are prominently displayed.

- Information is presented clearly and concisely, without excess verbiage.

- Instructions for completing and returning the form are unobtrusive but easy to find and understand.

You may find that your needs outgrow the design capabilities of Quattro Pro. On the other hand, you may be surprised at how far Quattro Pro can take you.

FORM COLUMNS AND HEADINGS

Business forms generally are made up of sections of columnar data. The composition of these sections is similar to the tables described earlier. Other information, such as a customer's name and address, is presented above and below these item listings. Invoices, statements, purchase orders and many other forms use this basic structure.

When creating such a form in Quattro Pro, you should design around the columnar data. Choose column widths that accommodate this data, then fit the rest of the items into this structure. You'll find that data above or below the columns can spill over into other columns. Use blank columns to create space down the sides of the form and between columns, especially if you include a border around your form.

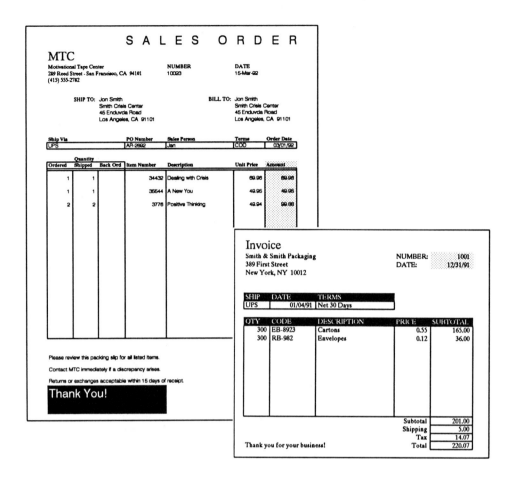

Figure 6-13: Many forms use a basic table-oriented structure.

When you're creating the columnar portions of the form, make sure column headings are bold and visible, but not too large. Use a large font for the form title and perhaps for your company name as well. Use one font for the form's body text and another for filled-in data. This will help the customer distinguish between the two. Courier is a good font to use for filled-in data, since it looks as if it were typed in.

ADDING GRAPHICS TO FORMS

Graphics can make a business form friendlier and lend some identity to your documents. Graphics are more appropriate in response forms than in business forms, so don't be afraid to use them liberally in those formats.

DISK OFFER

Companion Disk

for Quattro Pro Spreadsheet Publishing

On-Disk examples to accompany this book

☐ **Yes!**

Send me the companion diskette for *Spreadsheet Publishing With Quattro Pro.* I have indicated my diskette size below.

Send to: _____

_____

☐ 3.5.....$39.95

☐ 5.25....$39.95

_____

Figure 6-14: Use graphics in your response forms to make them more attractive.

As described earlier, these graphics start out as text graphs. You can then draw the desired image, using Quattro Pro's annotation tools, or you can use the Clipboard to insert a predesigned graphic into the text graph area. The finished text graph is then inserted onto the spreadsheet.

Make sure that the graphic image fills the graph area as much as possible. This makes it easy to predict its final size on the page.

MOVING ON

Turning your hard data into attractive, easy-to-read pages enhances your ability to reach and influence those who read and use your documents. Keep these design principles in mind for all your page formats.

The next step in the creation process is printing the pages you've designed. Chapter 7 focuses on how to use Quattro Pro's features with your printer to get the results you want.

Printing Reports 7

Now that you've learned how to use and manipulate Quattro Pro's graphing, annotating and spreadsheet formatting features, you should be able to create the elements of an effective report. Then it comes down to printing and your output device—and in the way you "lay out" the pages. What's the most effective way to combine graphs on your spreadsheets? How do you use patterns and gray shades effectively? How do you get everything you want onto a single printed page?

That's what this chapter is all about. Here, you'll learn about Quattro Pro's printing capabilities and the effects of various types of printers. You'll also learn about some important design considerations for page layout. Although the chapter deals mostly with black-and-white printing, you'll also see how Quattro Pro handles color printouts.

PRINTING SPREADSHEETS

Quattro Pro gives you several options for printing your spreadsheets. Let's begin with an overview of the printing process and the options available for your printouts. Then, we'll get into the details of these options. The basic process is simple, involving five steps:

SELECTING YOUR PRINTER

1. Choose Options-Hardware-Printers.
2. Choose 1st Printer.
3. Choose Type of Printer.
4. Select the printer's manufacturer in the list provided.
5. Select the printer model in the list provided.
6. Select the desired print mode from the list provided.
7. Press Q twice, then U to update the program.
8. Repeat this process for the 2nd printer if desired.

CHOOSING THE DEFAULT PRINTER

1. Choose Options-Hardware-Printers.
2. Choose Default Printer.
3. Choose either 1st Printer or 2nd Printer.
4. Quit to return to the spreadsheet.

1. Make sure the correct printer is selected. You can select two different printers for use in Quattro Pro (or two modes of the same printer). Then, tell Quattro Pro which of these two printers you would like to use for the printout. This is done with the Options-Hardware-Printers-Default Printer command.

2. Indicate the block of cells you want to print by using the Print-Block command. Details about selecting print blocks are discussed in the next section, "Print Blocks, Margins and Page Breaks."

3. Enhance or modify the printout using the various formatting options available in the Print menu. Many of these options are discussed in this chapter.

4. Choose the desired print destination using the Print-Destination command. This lets you preview the printout on screen, print a draft of your report in your printer's text mode or print a final version of the file. You can also use this command to print your report to disk for use with other programs. Select the Graphics Printer option for a normal printout.

5. Print the report with the Print-Spreadsheet Print command or the Print-Print To Fit command.

That's the basic process. Now let's examine the various printing commands available in Quattro Pro. These are found in the Print menu:

Block—Determines the area in the spreadsheet that will be printed. The block will begin at the left and right margin settings.

Headings—Includes headings across the top and/or down the left side of each page in the printout. These headings are taken from cells in the spreadsheet that you specify. This is excellent for repeating column headings or row labels across multiple pages.

Destination—Determines where the print block will appear. Destinations include the following:

Printer—The printer's draft mode (no graphics, fonts or sideways printing).

File—A text (ASCII) file on disk (no graphics, fonts or sideways printing).

Binary File—A binary file on disk. This file is created for the printer currently active in Quattro Pro, and will probably not print successfully on other printers. The file will contain all data needed to reproduce the report on this printer.

Graphics Printer—The printer's graphics mode (includes graphics, fonts and other features).

Screen Preview—The screen. This shows what the printout will look like on the graphics printer.

Layout—Provides options for customizing the report. This includes setting manual page breaks, changing margins and specifying the page orientation.

Format—Prints the cell's formulas and settings rather than the cell's contents. This is useful for debugging complex spreadsheets.

Copies—Sets the number of copies for the printout.

Adjust Printer—Lets you control the printer from within Quattro Pro.

Spreadsheet Print—Begins printing to the established destination.

Print To Fit—Begins printing to the established destination and reduces the printout to fit onto one page.

Quit—Returns to the spreadsheet.

PRINT BLOCKS, MARGINS AND PAGE BREAKS

You can print only one block of data at a time with Quattro Pro using the Print-Block command. Normally, Quattro Pro prints the block starting at the upper left corner of the page.

DEFINING A PRINT BLOCK

1. Select Print-Block.
2. Type the name or range reference of the desired block. Alternatively, you can "point" to the block by pressing Esc, moving the pointer with the Arrow keys, pressing the Period key and then using the Arrow keys to highlight the block. Finally, press Enter.

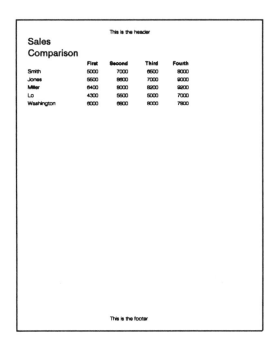

Figure 7-1: *Your selected print block starts out in the upper left corner of the page.*

You can adjust the position of the block on the page by adjusting the page margins with the Print-Layout-Margins command. In particular, you would change the top and left margins since those affect the starting position of the block. The disadvantage to this technique is that any header or headings you print will be adjusted by the margin settings. For example, in Figure 7-2, three-inch top and left margins move the print block into the center of the page, but the header no longer prints at the top of the page.

For details about adding headers, see "Adding Headers and Footers" later in this chapter.

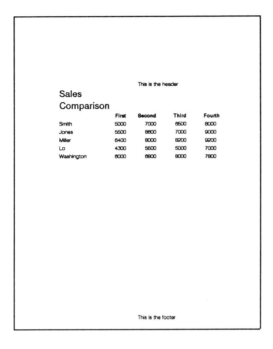

Figure 7-2: Use left and top margin settings to adjust the position of the print block on the page. Note, however, that this will move your header.

Another way to adjust the print block is to highlight extra cells above and to the left of the block itself. These cells will serve as spacing for the printout. Of course, the extra cells should be blank. If you don't have blank cells above and to the left of the print block, consider duplicating the block into a blank area of the spreadsheet using the Edit-Values command. You will then have to adjust the column widths and add any desired lines to the duplicated data. This technique will not displace the headings on the page.

Still another method is to increase the height of the top row of the print block to add extra space to the top of the data. Include an extra blank column on the left side of your print block, then expand this column to add extra space on the left edge.

TIP: If you have already defined a print block on the spreadsheet, and want to change it to a new block, first name the new block with the Edit-Name-Create command. Then, when you change the print block with the Print-Block command, simply type the name of the new block and press Enter.

PRINTING MULTIPLE BLOCKS TOGETHER

You can print two sections of the spreadsheet together by hiding the columns between them. Use the Style-Hide Column-Hide command to temporarily remove any columns between the two areas. If the second block is below the first, you can reduce the row height to virtually eliminate the rows. Use the Style-Block Size-Height command and enter 1 as the height. Then specify the rows you would like to eliminate.

TIP: You can specify the entire spreadsheet as the print block by selecting only one cell with the Print-Block command. Rather than printing this one cell, Quattro Pro will print the entire sheet.

PRINTING LARGE BLOCKS

If the print block you specify is too large to fit onto the page, Quattro Pro will automatically split the data at the right and bottom margin settings you've specified. And since Quattro Pro will not split the data in the middle of a column, the right edge of the data will probably fall short of the right margin setting. Hence, the space on the right side of the page may be greater than the space on the left—even though the margin settings are the same on both sides. The wider your columns, the more dramatic this will be.

NOTE: If your right margin setting is too large for the page, your printouts may appear double-spaced. Reduce the right margin and print again.

Sales Comparison — Jan through May

	Jan	Feb	Mar	Apr	May
Smith	5000	7000	6500	8000	6000
Jones	5500	8800	7000	9000	9000
Miller	6400	8000	8200	9200	9800
Lo	4300	5500	5000	7000	9800
Washington	6000	6800	8000	7800	6650

This is the header / This is the footer

Jun	Jul	Aug	Sept	Oct	Nov
7800	9800	8000	6500	9755	6700
6640	7800	6500	9760	9900	8900
5800	7900	8808	8200	9200	7700
8700	8600	6650	8000	7000	6500
9000	7770	9500	8000	8000	9890

This is the header / This is the footer

Figure 7-3: *If your print block is too large for one page, Quattro Pro splits it at the nearest column.*

REDUCING THE BLOCK TO FIT ON A PAGE

You can make a large block fit onto a single page by using the Print-Print To Fit command. Just specify the block in the normal manner, then print using the Print To Fit option instead of the Spreadsheet Print option. Quattro Pro will automatically reduce the print block to fit on the page within your specified margins.

Note that Quattro Pro will not reduce the image beyond the point of readability. If your block is too large to be reduced legibly, Quattro Pro will fit the block onto as few pages as possible, while keeping a legible font size. Quattro Pro takes your printer's resolution into account when making this assessment.

NOTE: The Print To Fit option is not available if you are printing in the printer's text mode with the destination set to "Printer."

Another way to reduce the printout is by using the Print-Layout-Percent Scaling option. You can enter a reduction percentage of your choice, shrinking (or expanding) the printout from 1 to 1000 percent of normal. This can be handy when you need only a little extra space to make the block fit onto the page. A reduction of, say, 80% might do the trick.

FORCING A PAGE BREAK

You might find that the best method of controlling the way your print block is split between pages is to force the page break at a particular column or row. You can force a columnar break, a row break or both. Note that forced page breaks are relative to the print block. Hence, you should note the column and row within the print block where you want to break the page.

To break the page at a particular column, keep the pointer in row 1 and move to the desired column, then select Style-Insert Break. This places a special marker at the top of the spreadsheet to indicate the break location. Any print block crossing this column will break onto a new page at this point. You can set as many different columnar breaks as you like. Columns to the right of your page breaks will be controlled by Quattro Pro (assuming they contain data and are being printed).

To break the page at a particular row, keep the pointer in column A and move to the desired row. Next, enter the Style-Insert Break command. Enter as many row breaks as you like. All data below your row breaks will be controlled by Quattro Pro unless you enter another break below.

SETTING A COLUMN OR ROW BREAK

1. Keeping the pointer in column A or row 1, move to the column or row where you would like Quattro Pro to break the page.
2. Select the Style-Insert Break command.

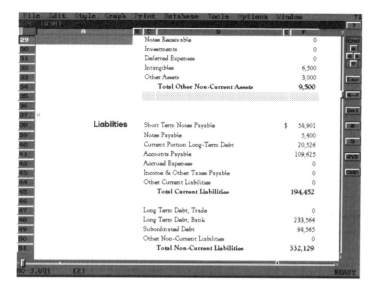

Figure 7-4: Inserting a forced page break places a special marker in the spreadsheet.

If you enter a column and row break, you might as well perform both breaks in one shot. Do this by moving to the cell that intersects the desired column and row and selecting the Style-Insert Break at this point.

Deleting Forced Page Breaks

To remove a forced page break, simply move to the cell containing the marker and select the Edit-Erase command to remove it.

Temporarily Ignoring Your Page Breaks

If you want to print a spreadsheet without the page break settings you've established, you don't have to delete them. You can ignore the page breaks by selecting the command Print-Layout-Page Breaks-No command. Switch this back to the Yes option to print using the breaks again.

SETTING COLUMN AND ROW BREAKS

1. Move to the cell that intersects the column and row where you would like Quattro Pro to break the page.
2. Select the Style-Insert Break command.

PRINTING SIDEWAYS

PRINTING SIDEWAYS

1. Select Print-Layout-Orientation-Landscape.
2. Select the Margins option and set margins to match your new orientation.
3. Press Q to exit the layout options.
4. Select your destination and print block, then print using the Spreadsheet Print option.

If your print blocks are extra wide, you may want to print them sideways onto the page. By using a sideways (landscape) orientation, you can often squeeze your data onto a single page rather than breaking it across two or more pages. Combine sideways printing with reduction (described above) for even more control.

When you print sideways with the Print-Layout-Orientation-Landscape setting, be sure that your margins match the new orientation. Your left and right margins now apply to the long dimension of the page. The page length setting should match the short dimension of the page (which is 8.5 inches for letter-size paper).

If you want to print sideways across several pages, without breaks between the pages, you should use the Print-Layout-Orientation-Banner setting. This tells Quattro Pro to ignore the page breaks and right margin setting, and gives you a continuous printout. This option is available only for dot-matrix printers with continuous-feed paper. Use the banner printing feature with print-scaling capability to print large banners across several pages.

Sales Comparison												
	Jan	Feb	Mar	Apr	May	Jun	Jul	Aug	Sept	Oct	Nov	Dec
Smith	5000	7000	8500	8000	6000	7600	9800	8000	6500	9755	6700	9000
Jones	5500	8800	7000	9000	9000	6640	7800	6500	9780	9900	8900	8000
Miller	6400	8000	8200	9200	9800	5900	7900	8908	8200	9200	7700	8700
Lo	4300	5500	5000	7000	9600	8700	8500	6650	8000	7000	6500	9900
Washington	6000	6800	8000	7900	6650	9000	7770	9500	8000	8000	9890	6700

Figure 7-5: The banner printing option lets you print continuously across several pages.

NOTE: Sideways printing is not available for text-mode printing (i.e., when your destination is set to "Printer").

ADDING HEADERS AND FOOTERS

You can add a one-line header and footer to your printouts by using the Print-Format-Header or Footer command. This is useful for adding page numbers, dates, your name and other identification information to the top or bottom of each page. Quattro Pro places the header just below the top margin and makes it fit within the left and right margins you've set. The footer goes just above the bottom margin.

When typing a header, you can enter any of the following characters for special effects:

@   Enters the current date.

Enters the current page number.

| Separates the header into three sections.

The separation character (vertical bar or Shift-Backslash on some keyboards) lets you divide a header and footer into two or three sections. If you include two vertical bars, the header is divided into three sections: left, center and right. Figure 7-6 shows some examples.

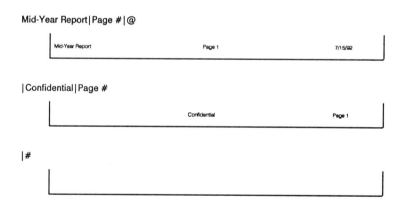

Figure 7-6:   Use special characters in your headers and footers for various effects.

The header and footer are automatically printed in Font 1. So if you want the header and footer to look different, you should format the other text with a font other than Font 1. (See Chapter 4, "Fonts and Printers," for details.)

TIP: You can include bullet characters in your headers and footers by typing \blt n\ where "n" is a number from 0 to 6. (See Chapter 6, "Designing Effective Pages," for details.)

ADDING HEADINGS ON EACH PAGE

If your printout contains numerous columns that continue for several pages, you may want to repeat each column heading on each additional page. This can be done with the Print-Headings-Top Heading command. First, the column headings must appear on the spreadsheet above each column you're printing. When you specify the print block, don't include these headings or they will print twice on the first page.

The Left Heading option is useful when your printout is extra wide and prints across several pages. This is an alternative to the sideways (landscape) printing options listed earlier in this chapter.

Remember that only the headings directly above or below the columns being printed will appear on the printout. Quattro Pro knows to match your headings with your print block. You can include several rows above the data by highlighting several rows when you specify the heading. Likewise, you can specify several columns for the left heading.

NOTE: Any formatting and fonts applied to the cells containing the headings will also appear in the printout.

TIP: To remove the headings from the printout, use the Print-Layout-Reset-Headings command.

ADDING COLUMN OR ROW HEADINGS TO EACH PAGE

1. Select the Print-Headings command.
2. Select Top Heading or Left Heading.
3. Move the pointer to the column or row containing the desired headings (any cell in the column or row will work), then press Enter.

PRINTING GRAPHS

Unless you insert a graph onto the spreadsheet (discussed later), your graphs will be printed on separate pages from the spreadsheet data. In fact, Quattro Pro uses a completely different set of commands for printing graphs. These are found in the Print-Graph Print menu. Following are the commands in this menu:

Destination—Sets the destination for the printout to a File, the Graphics Printer, or the Screen Preview. The File option creates a binary image of the graph specifically for your printer.

Layout—Offers several layout options, including margin settings and page orientation.

Write Graph File—Prints the graph to a file on disk using one of several file formats, including EPS and PCX. This is useful for printing graphs from other programs.

Name—Lets you select one of the graphs currently in the graph list for this spreadsheet.

Quit—Returns to the Print menu.

GRAPH PROPORTIONS—THE COMPLETE STORY

Graphs are normally wider than they are tall. In fact, graphs use a 4:3 width-to-height aspect ratio (similar to most computer screens).

In Chapter 3, "Creating Effective Graphs," and Chapter 5, "Using the Annotator," you saw how you can change a graph's proportions in the Annotator. But this only changes the proportions of the graph itself within the screen; it does not change the proportions of the screen or the graph's background. When you print a graph, Quattro Pro prints the entire screen you see in the Annotator. Although the graph may be tall and narrow, the rest of the screen (such as the background) is still printed in the normal 4:3 aspect ratio.

So you might want to find another way to change a graph's width-to-height ratio. One way is to use the Graph-Graph Print-Layout command with the Height and Width options. A second way is to insert the graph into the spreadsheet using the desired block size, then print the graph from the spreadsheet. This technique is discussed later.

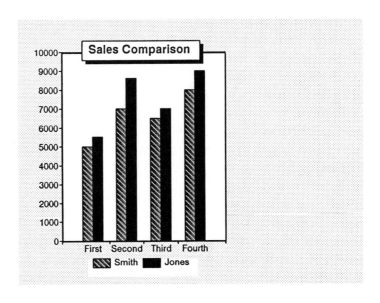

Figure 7-7: Graph screens are normally printed with a 4:3 aspect ratio.

The height and width you select with the Graph-Graph Print-Layout command control the size of the graph on the page. Of course, the measurements you give should fit within the page and its current orientation. You can change the page orientation for the graph with the Graph-Graph Print-Layout-Orientation command.

Make sure you set the 4:3 Aspect command to No or the graph will not fill the height and width you've specified. In other words, when 4:3 Aspect is set to Yes, Quattro Pro forces the graph into the normal aspect ratio—regardless of your height and width settings. This will usually result in blank space around the graph.

NOTE: The page size is determined by your printer setup. Many printers offer a legal-size option, which you can choose by resetting your printer.

One advantage to this technique is that you don't actually change the graph itself—merely the way in which the graph prints. When displaying the graph on-screen (with the Graph-Name-Display command), the normal aspect ratio is used.

TIP: Use the Left Edge and Top Edge settings to control the placement of the graph's upper left corner on the printout. The height and width settings are relative to the upper left corner of the graph.

INSERTING GRAPHS INTO SPREADSHEETS

You can insert a graph into the spreadsheet to combine graphs with spreadsheet data, to change a graph's proportions, or just to view the graph on the sheet. You can insert up to six graphs on the same spreadsheet if desired.

Placing a graph onto the spreadsheet is a good way to view your Graph menu changes as you make them. Otherwise, you must use the Graph-View command to see how your changes affect the graph.

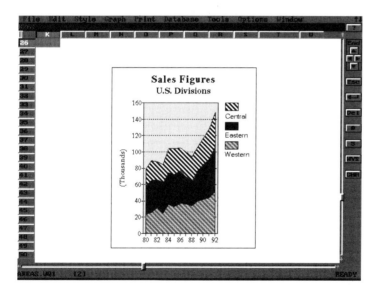

Figure 7-8: With 4:3 Aspect set to No, inserted graphs will fill the entire block you specify on the spreadsheet.

CHANGING A GRAPH'S HEIGHT AND WIDTH FOR PRINTING

1. Select the Graph-Graph Print-Layout command.
2. Select the Height command and enter the desired height for the graph, taking your page orientation into consideration. Maximum height is 10 inches.
3. Select the Width command and enter the desired width for the graph. Maximum width is 8 inches.
4. Select the 4:3 Aspect command and choose No.
5. Press Q to return to the Print menu, then select Go to begin printing.

If 4:3 Aspect is set to Yes, then Quattro Pro will "force" the graph to maintain its normal aspect ratio. If your insert range is not roughly the same proportions (4:3), then extra space will appear in the block.

When you insert a graph, Quattro Pro asks for the block of cells into which the graph will be placed. The size and shape of this block determines the size and shape of the graph. If the 4:3 Aspect command is set to No, then the graph will fit exactly into the block you specify, changing its proportions to match the block.

Hence, if you plan to keep the 4:3 Aspect set to Yes for your inserted graphs, try to highlight a block that has roughly the same proportions.

NOTE: The 4:3 Aspect setting applies to all graphs in your spreadsheet. You cannot change this setting for individual graphs.

TIP: If you change the 4:3 Aspect setting and the graph does not change, press F9 to "redraw" the graph within its block.

TIP: You can reduce a graph by highlighting a small block of cells in which to insert the graph. You can then print the graph by printing the block that contains it.

Inserted graphs can overlap each other on the spreadsheet. Just overlap the block into which they are placed. The order in which you create the graphs determines which ones are "covered" by the others.

INSERTING A GRAPH INTO THE SPREADSHEET

1. Select the Graph-Insert command.
2. Select the name of the graph you want to insert into the spreadsheet.
3. Enter or point to the range where you want the graph inserted.
4. Optionally, select Graph-Graph Print-Layout-4:3 Aspect-No to turn the 4:3 Aspect ratio off.

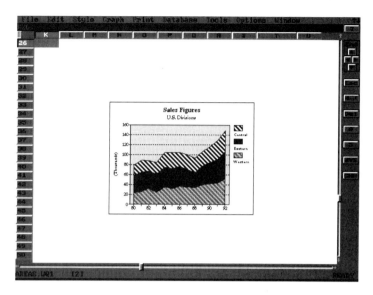

Figure 7-9: With 4:3 Aspect set to Yes, Quattro Pro keeps the basic
shape of the graph and fits it into the designated block
on the spreadsheet.

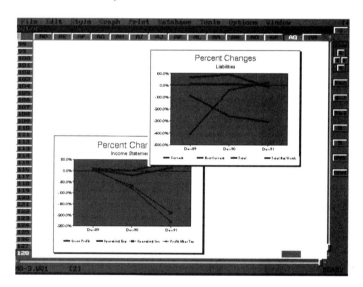

Figure 7-10: You can overlap graphs on the spreadsheet if desired.

You may find that your graphs are transparent when they are
printed. Overlapping graphs may look good on the screen
but cause confusion on the printout.

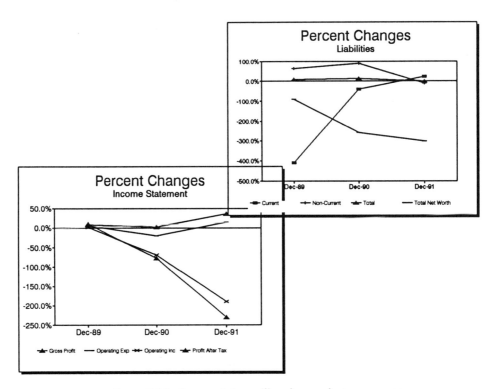

Figure 7-11: Some printers will make graphs transparent.

You can fix this in the Annotator by inserting a plain white (empty) text box behind the graph. In the Annotator, type several spaces (by pressing the space bar) in a white text box. Then resize the box to the desired size and shape. Finally, use the Clipboard to send this box to the bottom of the other objects in the Annotator. This box will make the graph opaque when printed. (See Chapter 5 for details about using the Annotator.)

PRINTING WITH NON-POSTSCRIPT PRINTERS

If you are using a non-PostScript printer, chances are your printouts do not include gray shades in place of colors. You'll find that Quattro Pro handles your graphs and spreadsheets in the following ways:

- Your graph text is always black on a white background (or a transparent background if you've eliminated the border and fill pattern). Hence, reversed text in a graph will simply unreverse to print normally. And, since most colored objects are converted to black, colored text printed over colored objects may appear black on black.

Figure 7-12: Text in your graphs will print black on white if you are using a non-PostScript or noncolor printer.

- Patterns used in text boxes are ignored.

- All nonwhite objects in the Annotator are printed black (unless they have a pattern, in which case they are always printed black on white).

- Graphs are printed transparently on a white background. Objects or text hidden "behind" the graph on the screen will show through the graph on the printout. (Chapter 5 discusses how to use this to your advantage.)

- Patterns are converted to black on white. Even patterns that are simply reversed as white on black will change to black on white when printed—no matter what colors you've used for the foreground and background.

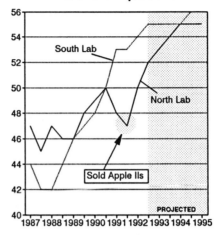

Figure 7-13: On non-PostScript or noncolor printers, graphs appear transparent.

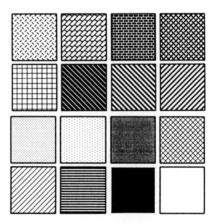

Figure 7-14: Quattro Pro prints all patterns in black and white.

With these printing restrictions, you may think it's impossible to get a solid white opaque box on the printout. Such a box could be placed behind a graph to make it opaque. Actually, you can create a solid white box by using an empty text box. Select the Text tool and click on the Annotator screen to begin typing text. Then just type a bunch of spaces and press Enter. Finally, stretch the text box to the desired size and shape, and manipulate it like a rectangle object. (See Chapter 5 for details about manipulating objects in the Annotator.)

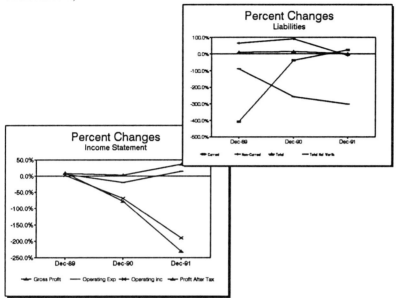

Figure 7-15: An empty white text box produces an opaque white rectangle on the screen for various purposes.

Other techniques can be used to overcome these restrictions. For example, to add patterns to a text box, try removing the text box and using a rectangle object instead. Format the rectangle with the desired pattern and place it behind the text. It will look like a patterned text box.

PRINTING WITH POSTSCRIPT PRINTERS

When you print onto a black-and-white PostScript printer, your screen colors will convert to shades of gray. Most likely, you will get the following shades.

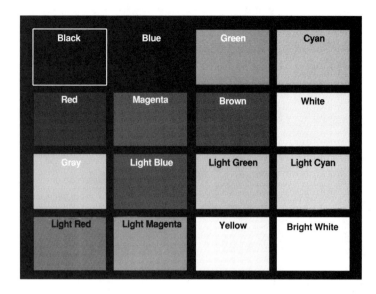

Figure 7-16: PostScript printers convert these colors into these shades of gray.

So when using color in your spreadsheets and graphs, consider how they will look on your black-and-white printer. Often, colors that look terrible together will look great in black and white.

PostScript printers will not apply these gray shades to your patterns. If you use patterns in a PostScript printout, Quattro Pro will simply ignore them and give you shades to match the Color settings used by the objects.

You can use the Options-Hardware-Printers command to reselect your printer with one of the "Patterns" modes. This will give you black-and-white patterns. You cannot get shaded patterns.

Often, distinct shades of gray can be used instead of patterns and colors. Many of the graphs used in this book were printed with gray shades on a PostScript printer.

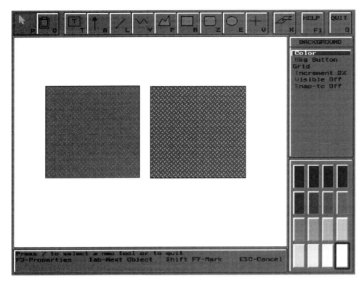

Figure 7-17: These objects will print as patternless gray boxes on the printer.

When printing with gray shades, consider whether text should be white or black. Often, reversing the text to white makes it more readable. But if the gray is very light, bold black text will work best.

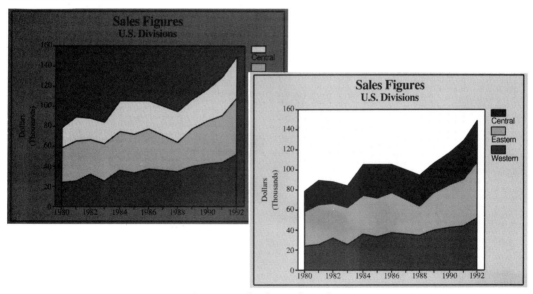

Figure 7-18: Consider how you combine gray shades and text in your graphs. Strive for good contrast.

NOTE: You can eliminate the gray shades on your PostScript printer by reselecting the printer with one of the "Patterns" modes. Details about selecting your printer appear earlier in this chapter.

MOVING ON

Printing is an important part of your spreadsheet publishing process. Your printer largely determines your printing capabilities, but Quattro Pro gives you as much freedom as it can. Consider the following points when printing your spreadsheets and graphs onto a printer:

* PostScript printers convert colors to shades of gray.

* Non-PostScript printers convert colors to black and white, and limit your use of patterns.

* You can print across several pages by using the banner orientation.

* Use the Print To Fit option to keep your print block on a single page.

* Use the Print-Layout-Orientation option to switch from tall (portrait) to wide (landscape) printing.

You should have enough information to make your printed reports look professional. Now, you're ready to learn about nonprinted reports—that is, reports that use different media. Chapter 8 gets you started with designing slide shows and overhead presentations.

Designing Slides, Overheads and Screen Shows

Your first step in making a presentation is deciding which medium you'll use to deliver your message. Your Quattro Pro images can be presented on paper, on slides or overhead transparencies or on the computer screen. Entire books have been devoted to how each of these media communicates in its own particular way. (For further reading on evaluating presentation media, see the Resources section in the back of this book.)

In Chapter 6, "Designing Effective Pages," and Chapter 7, "Printing Reports," you explored print media, including related design tips and how Quattro Pro handles printed reports. This chapter focuses on designing nonprinted media—slides, computer screens and overheads. It also describes slide types, color options and procedures for creating a successful, effective presentation.

SLIDE SHOW TECHNIQUES

Professionally designed slide shows use a number of special techniques, or devices, to help make a point. If you're trying to make a sale or change a customer's buying practices, you'll want to consider some of these techniques for your own shows.

MAKE SEQUENCES

Sequences, or additive slides, are groups of slides that build on each other. These are often augmented by the script to help the audience form the connections and conclusions. There are many ways to create sequenced slides. You can reveal a new item in each new slide, or highlight each item as you discuss it.

Figure 8-1: Additive slides can be handled in various ways.

Sequencing should be used frequently throughout your presentations to keep the message moving along and to keep the audience from losing interest.

USE "CROSSROADS"

You may need to return to the same slide often during a presentation—referring each time to a different item or aspect of the slide. For example, to present your company's management personnel, you may have a slide for each person, but you return to an organization chart when introducing each one. You can use copies of the same slide or slightly altered versions of it. For example, as an introduction you can highlight the person's name in the organization chart.

COLORS AND BACKGROUNDS

Proper use of color is a major part of a good presentation. It's so important that this chapter contains an entire section on it, including color examples. Color should be appealing but not jarring or distracting. Usually, a few colors are sufficient for your entire presentation if used skillfully.

ADD A DASH OF HUMOR

Humor can be used more liberally in slide shows than in printed presentations. (Something about being in a dark room and watching a screen makes people expect to be entertained.) Experts have found that presentations that include humor and personal anecdotes are more likely to make a lasting impression. Generally, humor should be written into the script, but it can be worked into your slides, too.

SIMPLE BUT POWERFUL DESIGNS

When designing slides, consider that each type of slide you create has its own design and formatting concerns. But remember that slides are usually displayed for only a few moments. They should not try to communicate more information than the audience can easily absorb in a short period of time. Make your slides simple and powerful. Concise headlines and phrases, plenty of blank space and good use of color are priorities.

Use no more than five data series on one graph slide, and keep the graph labels short. To test if your slide will be readable, print a copy of it onto paper and place it six feet away. If you can read it, it will make a good slide.

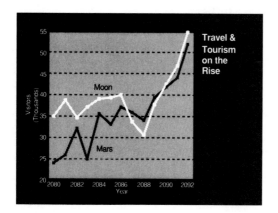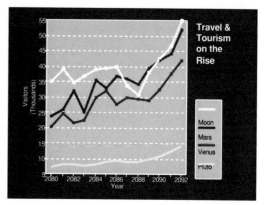

Figure 8-2: Keep data series to a minimum to make graphs easier to read.

CONSTRUCT A STRONG SCRIPT

Slide shows are structured like any oral presentation of similar length. And the slides should be secondary to the script. The script should probably begin with a main point, followed by supporting arguments and examples, and conclude with a re-examination of the main point in light of the new evidence. This outline illustrates the structure:

Introduction
Main Points
   First Point
      Explanation/Support/Arguments
        Graphs
        Tables
        Illustrations
        Lists
      Summation of Point

Second Point
>   Explanation/Support/Arguments
>   Graphs
>   Tables
>   Illustrations
>   Lists
>   Summation of Point
Third Point
>   etc . . .
Unification
Conclusion

Instructional and orientational presentations often follow a different pattern. Rather than making a point, these presentations are designed as progressive lesson tours, to teach or inform. A concluding summary is usually not required in these presentations—except, perhaps, to suggest the next step, or ideas for further study.

For these presentations, it's helpful to sketch out story boards on paper and refer to them as you create your slides.

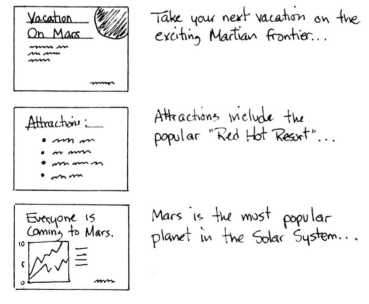

Figure 8-3: Story boards help you organize your show.

TITLES TELL THE STORY

If you include headline slides between main segments of a presentation, consider the purpose of each headline and how long it will remain on the screen. Is it a simple transition slide or a slide that introduces a new topic?

Figure 8-4: Title slides can be simple transition markers.

Transition slides can be understated and simple. But a topic introduction slide may remain on the screen while you discuss the topic. You can give these slides more complexity and more pizazz, since the audience will have plenty of time to view and understand them. But, as with any presentation design, make form subservient to function.

Figure 8-5: Topic introduction slides can be exciting and colorful.

Energize Your Headlines

Depending on specific needs, some headlines consist of only one or two short words, while others may be newspaper-type phrases. However, some basic rules apply to all headlines, long or short.

- Use gerunds. Generally, gerunds project action and excitement better than their noun equivalents. They're more likely to draw the audience into the topic. For example, use "Insulating Your Home" rather than "Home Insulation." Use "Cutting Costs" instead of "Cost-Cutting."

- Use active verbs. Active verbs are alive and moving, whereas passive verbs are less direct and less active. Use "Management Wants a Change" rather than "A Change Is Wanted by Management."

- Use commands. Commands are not offensive in headlines or instructions. Use "Begin Selling" rather than "Selling Begins." Use "Take Another Look" instead of "This Deserves Another Look."

- Avoid dead phrases. Dead phrases just take up precious space in your headlines. Convert "Cost-Cutting Measures" to "Cutting Costs." Turn "50 Feet in Size" into "50 Feet." Change "The Time-Keeping Module" to "The Time Keeper."

- Use parallel structures. Use the same form of the verb in every slide and within single slides with several lines.

- Use abbreviations consistently.

Change these headlines:	to these:
How to Make Contacts	Making Contacts
Start Selling	Starting to Sell
The Sale-Closer	Closing

Punctuation: Bend the Rules

Headline slides are somewhat like ad copy in that you can take some liberties with punctuation, provided the message is clear to the viewer. Sometimes punctuation adds to the message; other times, it's best left out.

Figure 8-6: Punctuation emphasizes a message.

Omit ending punctuation on listed items, even when they're complete sentences (although there's usually not enough room on a slide for complete sentences anyway).

Graphics: Complement, Don't Clutter

Graphic images for headline slides should be kept simple. Creative use of basic shapes and colors add interest without distracting. If you want to try more complex graphics, be sure they complement rather than interfere with the headline. Usually, the more detail in the graphic, the more distracting it can be. And remember that type can be your most effective graphic.

Figure 8-7: Graphic images can enhance your headline slides.

Text: Design for Easy Reading

An effective design simply places text on a solid or graduated background. In this case, be sure the text fills the frame and that it's bold enough to be read. On the other hand, don't overfill the frame; leave comfortable margins on the sides. Making the slide's bottom margin slightly larger than the top lends stability to the composition.

Figure 8-8: Leave a bit more room at the bottom of your headline slides to make them more stable.

Generally, headlines should be centered or placed flush-left on the slide, although adding graphics can sometimes make flush-right or other unusual alignment schemes work well.

Consistency: Repeat Design Devices

Slides should be designed around a common scheme. Choose an appropriate font, style, color and graphics scheme, and stick with it for all your headline slides. Consistently repeating a familiar design and format helps the audience focus attention on your message, not on the slide design.

If you use a shadow effect for text or objects, be sure the shadow is offset by the same amount on each slide. This is a subtle detail but one that will make your presentations more professional.

SLIDES THAT LIST

Slide shows almost always feature list slides. These are useful for summarizing and introducing topics to be covered. Most of the suggestions offered for headlines apply equally to lists—particularly in regard to filling the frame, writing the copy and using graphics. But there are some special considerations when you're creating lists.

Set Off the Items

Your lists should always include an informative headline above the listed items or topics. Make the headline stand apart from the topics by changing its location, font, style or color. Using all caps can be effective in some cases.

 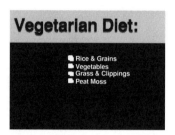

Figure 8-9: Lists should include headings that stand out.

As shown in Figure 8-9, listed items usually need some sort of bullet or check box beside them. The check box is useful to identify current topics when you use multiple versions of the same list (building on the same topic). But other building techniques can work equally well.

Normally, you should not further divide a listing on a particular slide. The slide show organization should present the subtopics on different slides. Save the expanded summary outline for your handouts.

Add Consistent Graphics

Lists are fairly easy to embellish with lines and shading. A simple line or underscore can add just the right touch. Remember to keep the graphics consistent for all lists in the presentation.

MAKE TABLES SIMPLE

Using tables in slides is similar to using them in spreadsheets. In fact, the same rules you learned in Chapter 6, "Designing Effective Pages," apply to tables in slides. However, your slides must be easier to read. Omit footnotes and display only a few items in each table.

You probably don't need vertical lines between columns, since the table contains so few items. You can use contrasting colors for the columns. Also, be sure to give the table a title.

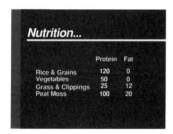

Figure 8-10: Tables need a title and should have only a few columns.

If you use multi-line text boxes for each column, the lines will naturally have equal spacing between them when you press Ctrl-Enter to break the lines. Otherwise, you can use the Annotator's grid to help align the columns and rows (available in Version 3.0 only).

USE BASIC GRAPH DESIGNS

Graphs are discussed at length in Chapter 3, "Creating Effective Graphs," including design tips for the various graph types. Most of these tips apply equally to slides. Like tables, graphs used in slides should be much simpler than graphs on paper. This is because the slide cannot be studied as closely. Here are some ways to simplify a graph:

* Keep values on the Y-axis scale to a minimum.

* Use abbreviations in X-axis labels.

* Use a minimum of data series and categories.

* Use colors without patterns for data series.

- Make labels larger than normal for easy readability.
- Turn the overall 3D effect off, unless you are using a 3D graph.

Except for identifying data series, keep graph annotation to a minimum. Your oral presentation should adequately explain the graph's messages. Save the annotation for your handouts.

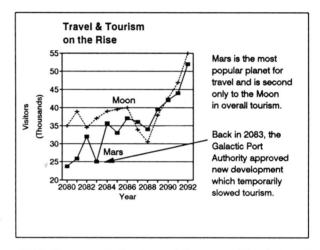

Figure 8-11: Keep annotation to a minimum on slides, but use it liberally on your handouts.

Because they can be more difficult to read, use 3D graphs only when 2D graphs cannot adequately display the data.

ILLUSTRATE WITH PICTOGRAPHS

You can build a pictograph in Quattro Pro's Annotator. Copy an image over and over, then stack the images to create the graph. These usually take the form of bar graphs.

Figure 8-12: Copy graphic objects to build simple pictographs.

Since pictographs have no direct link to spreadsheet data, you should use them only when specific values aren't important.

PERT AND FLOW CHARTS: PROGRESS AND PROCESS

PERT charts reveal a critical path among a series of project stages. While various parts of a project may fall behind schedule without adversely affecting the general deadline, those stages on the critical path cannot fall behind. PERT charts make excellent progress summations for projects.

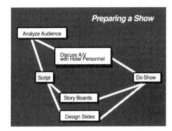

Figure 8-13: A PERT chart can be created with rectangles or text boxes.

Flow charts are similar in design, but serve a different purpose. They show the logical process used in a decision. Much is communicated by the shapes of the boxes used in the chart. An oval represents the starting point; rectangles represent inputs; diamonds represent decision points or branches.

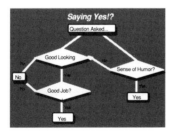

Figure 8-14: Flow charts show a procedure.

You can create PERT and flow charts in Quattro Pro's Annotator using simple objects. Some clip-art packages offer other flow-charting symbols (see the Resources section in the back of this book). You should use the Clipboard to send all connecting lines behind other objects, so that you don't have to take the time to make precise connections. To add shadows to each symbol in the chart, you can place a copy of it (shaded in gray or a contrasting color) beneath the main symbol. You can highlight the critical path of a PERT chart or the current path of a flow chart by using red for the connection lines.

Avoid crowding the slide when making PERT and flow charts. Try to keep symbols in these charts to a maximum of eight— even if you have to break up a larger chart into smaller units. (You can print the entire chart for your handouts.)

A more complex PERT or flow chart can serve as a return point for more detailed slides. In this case, you can simplify the text inside the symbols and highlight each section of the chart as you discuss it. When you return to the overall chart, highlight the next section.

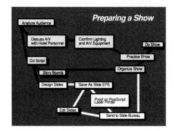 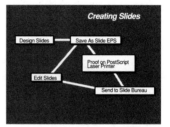

Figure 8-15: Complicated flow or PERT charts can be broken into sections.

GANTT CHARTS: SCHEDULES

A Gantt chart is a project schedule shown in a timeline style. Blocks of color show where certain stages of a project begin and end, and how much buffer is included in each. The top of the chart shows the dates.

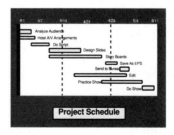

Figure 8-16: Gantt charts are excellent for showing schedules.

ORGANIZATION CHARTS
AND TREE DIAGRAMS: HIERARCHY

Organization charts and tree diagrams convert text outlines (lists of primary and secondary items) into graphic symbols. Headings of the same level are shown as boxes located on the same level of the chart. In a business organization, box locations correlate with authority or responsibility levels. The menu structure of a program like Quattro Pro can also be shown this way.

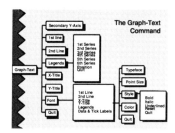

Figure 8-17: Tree diagrams are a graphic representation of items on different levels, such as a Quattro Pro menu.

Like PERT and flow charts, these charts can get rather large for a slide. It may be necessary to divide them into smaller units. You may also be able to group some individuals into departments or show lower-level items in a list rather than in boxes.

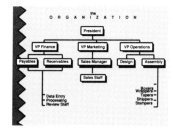

Figure 8-18: Consolidate some levels of an organization chart.

Be sure to keep boxes on the same levels by using the Annotator's grid tool. Also, avoid including too much text inside the boxes. Cover the details in the presentation itself.

MAKE COLORFUL MAPS FROM CLIP-ART

Maps are useful for slide presentations. You can begin with a map from a clip-art package, then modify it as needed. Most modifications can be accomplished in Quattro Pro's Annotator. One idea is to use different colors for various regions in the map. These are easy to understand at a glance.

Figure 8-19: Colors emphasize regions of a map.

Also, you can pull some regions away from others, just as you'd "explode" a pie chart to isolate one piece.

Figure 8-20: "Explode" regions of a map to emphasize their importance.

To show regional saturation, you can add graphic symbols to the map. The number of symbols reflects the saturation. This lets you compare two or more items on the same map. Or you can just use dots.

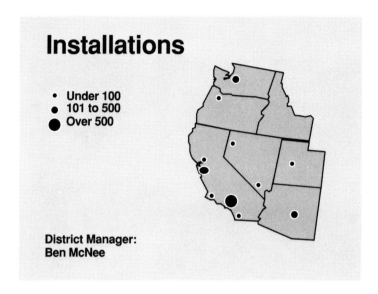

Figure 8-21: Add data points to maps to show saturation.

ILLUSTRATIONS

The type and quantity of illustrations you use depend on the presentation itself; and how much time and effort you can give to produce them.

Some material may require technical illustrations, such as a product diagram. Generally, you'll need a professional-level graphics program to create that kind of image. Save the image in CGM format, then you can bring it into Quattro Pro and keep it with your other slides. If your graphics package can save images for color slide output, you might use it to print the image.

You may also want to use mechanical methods for showing illustrations. You can use color slide film in a 35mm camera to capture all kinds of flat artwork, portraits, buildings and so on.

PHOTOS AND COMPOSITE IMAGES

Many service bureaus can make a composite image from a photograph and a Quattro Pro slide. This can be useful for superimposing an employee's photo on his or her sales graph, or showing your company building behind an organization chart.

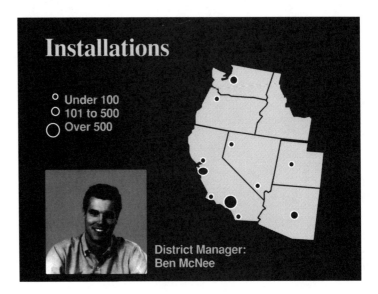

Figure 8-22: You can combine photographs with your Quattro Pro slides.

To create such images, you need to supply the service bureau with your Quattro Pro EPS or Slide EPS file, a slide of the second image, and instructions for combining them. Often, you can design your Quattro Pro slides with "windows" for photographs.

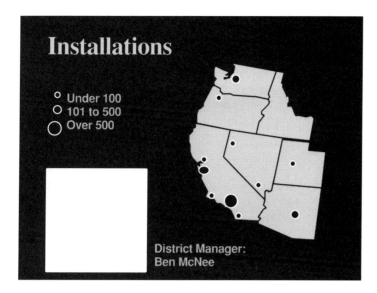

Figure 8-23: *To mix photographs with your slides, allow "windows"*
for the photos.

The process usually consists of scanning the photograph and merging it with your EPS file through specialized software. This can be costly but effective.

EFFECTIVE OVERHEAD PRESENTATIONS

Overhead presentations have elements of both slide and printed presentations. You can use them for small groups where a slide show would be overkill. But they're also effective for larger audiences. These presentations use fewer images than slide shows, and each one remains on the screen longer. For this reason, each overhead transparency can communicate more information than a slide. Also, such slide-show devices as progressive lists and headlines are not used in overhead presentations.

Two devices that work well in overhead presentations are presenter interaction with the transparencies and printed handouts that reinforce the presentation script and graphics.

INTERACTING WITH THE AUDIENCE

You can interact with each transparency if you like. For example, you can write on the transparency with a highlighter or grease pencil while it's on the projector. This is more effective than pointing to the screen. You can also hide certain areas (usually the bottom) of a transparency with a piece of cardboard, until you're ready to reveal that part of your information.

Returning to a previous transparency is easy and can be useful when answering questions from the audience. In fact, you can modify your presentation as you go along, leaving out portions or adding portions, according to the response or "vibrations" you get from the audience. This would be difficult to do in a slide show.

USING HANDOUTS

Your handout materials can be direct duplicates of the overhead transparencies (in black and white, usually). Handouts for slide shows, on the other hand, should usually be condensed and the slides annotated.

DESIGNING OVERHEAD TRANSPARENCIES

Overhead transparencies can come from your spreadsheet printouts or your slides. Therefore, if your printouts and slides are well designed, your overheads will also be well designed.

Since overhead transparencies often remain on the screen for several minutes while you talk, they can contain more data than slides. Your audience will have time to study the image. If you want to selectively reveal portions of an overhead as you talk, design the overheads around this need.

SCREEN SHOWS: A DYNAMIC MEDIUM

Screen shows are a lot like slide shows, but are given from your computer and involve interaction. For the purposes of this discussion, screen shows do not include projecting the computer screen onto the wall. That is simply a variation of a slide show. Instead, a screen show is an interactive presentation given on the computer to one person. By pressing keys or using the mouse, the audience can change the presentation. Quattro Pro offers several devices for screen shows.

TRANSITION EFFECTS

You can include transition effects between slides, including dissolves, fades and spirals, that make a show more interesting. By mixing effects in the same show, you can keep the viewer guessing.

SOUND

Sound effects are useful during transitions or when particular actions are taken. Sounds can indicate when the viewer has entered the wrong information or used the mouse in the wrong part of the screen.

TIMING

Each screen in a screen show can be timed or untimed. Untimed screens can be viewed as long as desired; the viewer moves on by pressing a key. Timed screens allow a controlled amount of viewing time. You can mix timed and untimed screens in the same show.

OVERLAP

This effect lets you move from one screen to another and overlap them. With this technique, you can display a screen, then display new information without the appearance of switching slides. It appears as though you've added information to the first screen.

BUTTONS

Buttons are portions of the screen that respond to mouse clicks. They can be used to make slide transitions, branch the show to a different segment, stop the show, return to previous screens and print copies of the screens.

DESIGNING SCREENS

Most of the rules for designing slides apply equally to screen shows. However, there are several differences. Primarily, interactive screen shows let the viewer examine the screen for an extended period of time. The viewer can pause the presentation to study a screen—even push a button to bring up more information on the screen. This makes it possible to include much more information than you could present on a slide. In addition, the viewer is closer to the screen and therefore able to read more detail.

USING COLOR

Color can make or break a presentation—especially a slide show. Your main concern should be choosing colors that do and say what you want them to. Another concern is choosing compatible colors. Sometimes these colors should contrast with each other; other times, they should complement each other.

COLOR TALKS

When creating your slides and color reports, keep in mind the fact that color can communicate subtle messages. It's also important to select colors that work well together visually. A bad color combination can distract your audience, though they may not know exactly why they're distracted. Some colors clash, others blend.

Let's start by looking at Quattro Pro's Color palette.

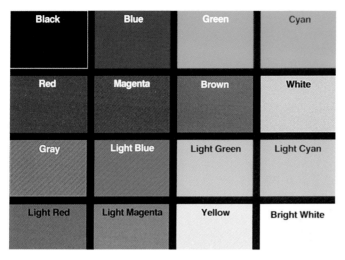

Black	Blue	Green	Cyan
Red	Magenta	Brown	White
Gray	Light Blue	Light Green	Light Cyan
Light Red	Light Magenta	Yellow	Bright White

Figure 8-24: Quattro Pro's Color palette offers 16 different colors.

Dependable Blues and Grays

Medium to dark values of blue and gray are associated with trust and dependability. You'll find these colors used by banks and large organizations such as IBM. Presentations use blue backgrounds frequently to instill trust in the speaker.

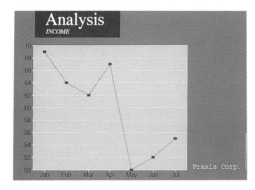
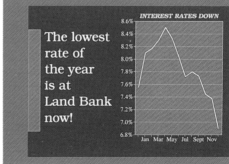

Figure 8-25: Blue and gray inspire trust.

Active Red, Yellow, Orange

Combinations of red, yellow and orange are festive and exciting. They're often used by fast-food establishments to communicate "fun." They're also thought to suggest speed and activity, which can make diners eat their meals quickly and leave. If this is true, these colors do not promote good digestion (or is it the food?).

Figure 8-26: Red and yellow combine for a festive message.

Individually, these colors can have different meanings. For example, red is not a positive color in an accounting context, yet it's associated with health and strength in a medical context.

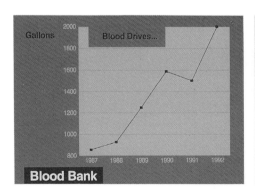
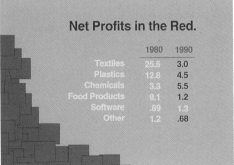

Figure 8-27: Red alone can be healthy or unhealthy, depending on the context.

Yellow can seem pale and weak unless it's contrasted sharply with dark blue or black.

Figure 8-28: Combine yellow with blue or black for best contrast.

Comfortable Yellow, Brown and Gold

Combinations of yellow, brown and gold seem to communicate warmth and friendliness. These earth tones are used by many food packagers and real estate companies.

Figure 8-29: Yellow with brown makes a friendly impression.

Elegant Black and Gray

Black and gray used together look like black and silver—a combination that has rich, aristocratic connotations. To get this appearance, use plenty of black. Otherwise, you might end up with a clinical look.

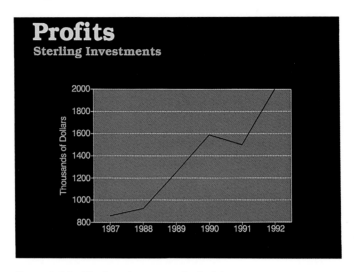

Figure 8-30: Black and gray can look rich.

Affluent Green and Dark Green

Green is the money color—if you use a certain shade. Otherwise, it can evoke associations with the environment and nature. Greens are often used by brokerage and investment firms. Dark green is sometimes used for luxury cars to communicate "old money."

Figure 8-31: Green is the money color.

Contrasting and Complementary Colors

It's important to combine colors skillfully in your presentations. Some colors should not be used together, for various reasons. Some combinations clash, others cause eye fatigue or contrast problems. Here are some color combinations to avoid:

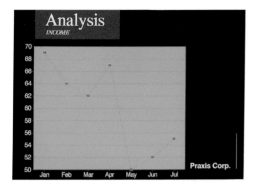

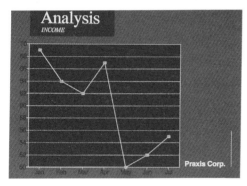

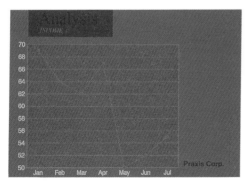

Figure 8-32: Avoid these color combinations if possible.

Here are some that work well together.

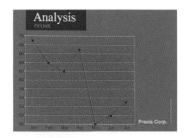

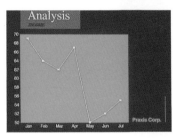
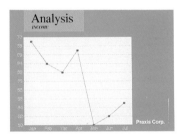

Figure 8-33: Use these color combinations for best results.

Remember that the eye will naturally be drawn to the brightest part of a slide. So use brightness to emphasize certain slide elements. As a rule, place brighter objects and text onto darker backgrounds.

COLORING GRAPHS

Avoiding bad color combinations applies to adjacent data series as well as background/foreground combinations on your graphs.

You can often separate bad combinations in a bar graph. The lines in line graphs require so little color that they might not present a problem. Just make sure the background works well with all the colors.

In color graphs, you should avoid using heavy, dramatic fill patterns. These will detract from the graph and its colors. Lighter fill patterns can be used effectively with colors, or just remove patterns entirely.

Figure 8-34: Avoid bad combinations among graph data series.

Besides the background for the entire graph, remember that your data series are plotted on a special background. Often, this plot-area background can be the same color as the graph background—but it doesn't have to be if this makes it difficult to read the data.

If you use a color for the plot area, choose one that works well with the chart's background. Often, a lighter or darker version of the background color is effective. When in doubt, use white or gray.

BACKGROUND COLOR

Your backgrounds will set the tone of your presentation. First and foremost, the background should use a color that's appropriate and compatible with other colors on the slide. You may want to start with the background color and choose colors for the other elements to fit the background. Since the eye is drawn to the brightest thing on the slide, type should be lighter than the background. Blue, black and gray backgrounds offer the most freedom in choosing text colors.

Mix a few colors on the same slide to highlight certain items; but don't overdo it.

Figure 8-35: Use color wisely to highlight items in a list.

You may want something more than a solid background color. Examine the sample backgrounds that Quattro Pro offers. Some of these appear as clip-art with the .CGM extension; others appear as spreadsheet files labeled BKG1.WQ1, BKG2.WQ1, BKG3.WQ1 and so on. All are located on the ProView PowerPack diskettes and must be installed separately. Other pre-designed backgrounds are available from various sources. Many can be found on the *Spreadsheet Publishing With Quattro Pro Companion Diskette*. (See the Resources section in the back of the book for others.)

You can also try your hand at making your own backgrounds. Using Quattro Pro's annotating tools, you can produce some interesting effects by adding simple graphics, such as lines and shapes, to a solid background. The key is to keep the background subtle. Don't use bright colors or distracting shapes. And don't crowd the background. Often, the most professional-looking backgrounds are the simplest.

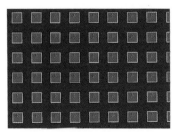

Figure 8-36: You can use Quattro Pro's Annotator to create some interesting backgrounds. (More are available on the companion disk.)

MOVING ON

Each type of presentation has its advantages and drawbacks. An effective presentation makes the most of its medium with good design, good use of color and good scripting. With this in mind, you're ready to start creating slides, overhead transparencies and screen shows. The next chapter will show you how. It explains the Quattro Pro commands and options used to print slides and overheads and to prepare on-screen shows.

Creating Slides, Overheads and Screen Shows

Now that you've delved into the various aspects of designing a presentation, you're ready to actually produce the presentation. In this chapter, you'll learn how to create nonprinted media with Quattro Pro. First, we'll look at Quattro Pro's slide-generation features. Since slides can be created with Quattro Pro's Annotator, you may want to refer back to Chapter 3, "Creating Effective Graphs," and Chapter 5, "Using the Annotator," for details about the Annotator's tools and drawing techniques.

Also in this chapter, you'll learn the basics of creating screen shows with Quattro Pro. This includes grouping screens together for a show, adding transition and sound effects, and incorporating audience interaction with buttons.

CREATING SLIDES AND OVERHEADS IN QUATTRO PRO

In general, slides and overheads should be created with Quattro Pro's Annotator. To use the Annotator, you must create and display a graph, then use the Graph-Annotate command to move the graph into the Annotator where you can embellish it. (This procedure was discussed in Chapter 5, "Using the Annotator.") But you won't have a graph in every slide or overhead transparency in your presentation. Many

CREATING SLIDES FROM GRAPHS

1. Create and name the graph in the usual manner (see Chapter 3).
2. Display the graph with the Graph-Name-Display command.
3. Press the Slash (/) key while the graph is in view.
4. Annotate the graph as desired.
5. Quit the Annotator.
6. Use the Print-Graph Print-Write Graph File command.
7. Select Slide EPS.
8. Select the Go command.

CREATING SLIDES WITHOUT GRAPHS

1. Select the Graph-Graph Type command.
2. Select the Text type from the list.
3. Select the Annotate command.
4. Create the slide using the Annotator's tools.
5. Quit the Annotator.
6. Use the Print-Graph Print-Write Graph File command.
7. Select Slide EPS.
8. Select the Go command.
9. Be sure to name the graph for permanent storage on the spreadsheet.

slides will contain only illustrations or text, such as headlines or lists of items. You can use the Annotator for these slides and overheads as well, but you'll use the special Text graph type as the starting graph.

When you select the Text graph type, you're selecting a blank graph screen. Once you move it to the Annotator, you can draw or type anything you want on this blank screen. You can name the screen, using the Graph-Name-Create command, as if it were a graph, then use the Graph-Name-Display command to view it again. So it operates like a graph, but it isn't a graph. (Be sure to save the spreadsheet containing this screen [graph].)

CURRENT GRAPH

The graph you're working on is called the "current" graph. For example, when you exit the Annotator, the screen you created is the current graph. If you display a graph with the Graph-Name-Display command, it becomes the new current graph, replacing the graph that was previously current. This is true any time you display or annotate a graph. Therefore, you should always name your graph as soon as you finish creating and annotating it.

When you enter the Annotator, Quattro Pro always gives you the current graph, which is great when you're frequently entering and exiting the Annotator to work on the same graph. However, if you want to create a new slide from scratch, you'll have to clear the current graph (after you save it) using the Graph-Customize Series-Reset-Graph command before you enter the Annotator.

If you're creating a group of similar slides, such as an additive list, you can use the current graph as a "template" for all the slides. When you create and name the first slide, it becomes the current graph (slide). Then, you can build on this slide for the next one, which becomes the new current graph. Then build on this one again, and so on. In fact, any slide you have previously created and named can be used as a starting point for new slides. Just be sure to give each new slide a different name when using the Graph-Name-Create command.

SAVING AND PRINTING SLIDE FILES

After you create and name all your slides and graphs (and save the spreadsheet on which they appear), you're ready to turn them into slides or overhead transparencies. First, you must save each graph as an EPS or Slide EPS file on disk, using the Print-Graph Print-Write Graph File command. The result is a special Encapsulated PostScript (EPS) file that contains the PostScript instructions necessary to print your slide in color on a 35mm film-imaging device. These EPS files can then be sent to a service bureau that performs this service (some of these services are listed in the Resources section in the back of the book). Slides will cost from $5 to $15 each.

The EPS file describes your image to a PostScript device, such as a slide printer or other PostScript printer. Your local service bureau will use the program they prefer—perhaps from a PC or Macintosh—rather than Quattro Pro, to print the files. Often, film-imaging devices require special software packages to print these files. The EPS standard makes this possible, so you shouldn't be concerned about it.

If possible, save your files in the Slide EPS format. This is similar to EPS, but automatically prints the slide with the proper orientation and aspect ratio for 35mm slides. A standard EPS file will use the orientation and other layout settings in the Graph-Graph Print-Layout command. Depending on your settings, the slide may contain the image in the tall (portrait) orientation or with improper margins. Figure 9-1 shows what can happen.

Figure 9-1: *Using EPS and Slide EPS files can produce major differences in your slides.*

CLEARING THE CURRENT GRAPH SETTINGS

1. Be sure you've saved the current graph using the Graph-Name-Create command.
2. Select the Graph-Customize Series-Reset command.
3. Choose the Graph option.
4. Quit to return to the spreadsheet.

BUILDING ON PREVIOUS SLIDES/GRAPHS

1. Return to the desired slide using the Graph-Name-Display command. (This graph must have been saved previously.)
2. Bring this slide into the Annotator by pressing the Slash key (/).
3. Modify the slide as desired.
4. Exit the Annotator by pressing /Q or clicking on the Quit button.
5. Use the Graph-Name-Create command to give this graph a unique name.

1. Choose the Print-Graph Print command.
2. Select the Name command.
3. Choose the desired graph from the list provided. These are your existing named graphs.
4. Choose the Write Graph File command.
5. Select EPS or Slide EPS from the list of formats provided.
6. Press Backspace and enter a name for the file, including the entire directory path. For example, enter C:\SLIDES\Title to save the slide under the name Title in the SLIDES directory of the C: drive. Type A:\Title to save the slide on the floppy disk in the A: drive.
7. Select the Go command to write the file.
8. Select Quit to return to the spreadsheet.

Before you send the EPS files for color slide output, you may want to proof them on a PostScript printer. Since the EPS files will print identically onto any PostScript printer, you can use the same files you use for the color slides. Ideally, your service bureau can make proofs with a color PostScript printer, which will show you exactly how the slides will look in color. Black-and-white proofs will suffice for catching major problems, such as font incompatibility and orientation. If you print graphs or slides in black and white for proofing, refer to Chapter 7, "Printing Reports," for black-and-white printing information.

Since your service bureau probably won't be using Quattro Pro, they (or you, if it's a self-serve bureau) will have to print the EPS files from another program. Ideally, they'll have a PC connected to the PostScript printer and a program (Page-Maker, Corel Draw, Word, WordPerfect or Ventura Publisher, etc.) that can print EPS files. If this doesn't work, ask if you can install Quattro Pro onto their disk drive temporarily. Then, print the screens directly from Quattro Pro using the Print-Graph Print-Go command. (Be sure to set the destination and current file name first, and select the proper printer from Quattro Pro's printer list.)

If the bureau has only Macintosh computers connected to the PostScript printers, you'll have to convert the file to Macintosh format before printing. Ask the technicians if they can do this for you.

FONT SUBSTITUTION

If you print Quattro Pro's EPS files to a PostScript device, you may run into font substitution problems. Sticking with Quattro Pro's Swiss, Dutch and Courier fonts can minimize these problems, since these fonts match the Times, Helvetica and Courier PostScript fonts. The difference between the screen display and printer output should be negligible. (For more information on using PostScript fonts, see Chapter 4, "Fonts and Printers.")

CREATING
OVERHEAD TRANSPARENCIES

Some service bureaus can print large color overhead transparencies from your Slide EPS files. These will be high-quality color transparencies. If your bureau provides this service, you should provide the same type of file you would for a 35mm slide. If your service bureau cannot produce large transparencies for about $40 apiece, have them print a 35mm slide, and take it to a color photographic lab that can transfer it to a large transparency.

If you don't want to spend $40 apiece for your color overhead transparencies, there are other ways to produce overheads. Try making one or two color transparencies that you can use as backgrounds for all your others. Print the rest in black and white and combine them with a background during the show. If color is not required, you can create transparencies from a high-quality printout using a photocopier with transparency film. Some laser printers even let you feed transparency film directly. If designed well, black-and-white transparencies can be quite effective. Another advantage to this technique is that you can create transparencies from your spreadsheets as well as from your graphs (you can print a spreadsheet onto transparency film as easily as you can print a graph or slide onto film). This lets you compose larger and more complex images, such as showing two graphs at the same time. Basically, anything you can print onto paper can be used as an overhead transparency in this manner.

PRINTING EPS FILES FROM VENTURA PUBLISHER

1. With a blank page on the screen, select the Load Text/Picture command from the File menu.
2. Click on the Line Art option at the top of the dialog box.
3. Click on PostScript option.
4. Click on the Several option near the bottom of the dialog box.
5. Click OK.
6. Insert your floppy disk into the A drive and type the directory path A:*.* into the space marked Directory. Press Enter when finished.
7. Click on any or all of the files in the list that you want to insert, then click OK.
8. Use the File-To Print command to print the graphics.

PRINTING EPS FILES FROM PAGEMAKER

1. With a blank document on the screen, select the File-Place command.
2. Insert your floppy disk (containing the files) into the A drive.
3. Type A:*.* and press Enter.
4. Choose the file from the list provided.
5. Click the mouse to place the image onto the page.
6. Choose File-Print to print.

PRINTING EPS FILES FROM WORDPERFECT

1. With a blank document on the screen, press Alt-F9.
2. Press F for Figure.
3. Press C to Create.
4. Press F for Filename.
5. Insert the floppy disk into the A drive and type the file name at the prompt. Type A:Filename and press Enter.
6. Press Enter.
7. Press F7 to return to the document.
8. Press Shift-F7 to begin printing.
9. Press F for Full Document.

PRINTING EPS FILES FROM MICROSOFT WORD

1. With a blank document on the screen, press Esc to activate the menus.
2. Press L for Library.
3. Press L for Link.
4. Press G for Graphics.
5. Insert your floppy disk (containing the files) into the A drive.
6. Type A:\ and press F1.
7. Select the desired file from the list provided.
8. Press Enter twice, then repeat the procedure for the next file.
9. Press Esc-P P to print.

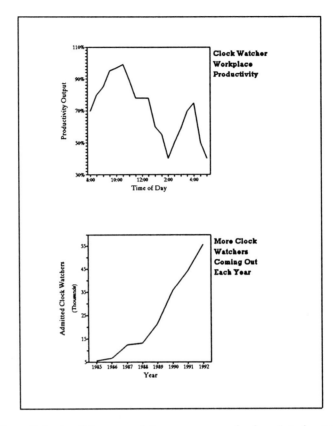

Figure 9-2: Anything you print on paper can also be printed onto overhead transparency film.

If you have a color printer (or have access to one at a service bureau), and your copy shop can make color transparencies from its output, try one to see if you like the result. Sometimes color transparencies look muddy and faded. Sharp, clean black and white is better than washed-out color.

If you require only small color highlights on your transparencies, you can use markers to color them by hand (water-based markers may not work effectively). Or locate some transparent color Zipatone™ from your local art supply store. This is adhesive color film that can be cut and applied to clear transparencies—giving them basic but rich colors.

CREATING SCREEN SHOWS

You can display a sequence of screens directly from Quattro Pro as a type of on-screen slide show. The computer screen can then be projected for a large audience much like a slide show, or it can be viewed directly from the computer screen by one or more people. When creating screen shows to be viewed individually, you may want to include buttons in the slides for viewer interaction. This lets the viewer move forward or backward between slides, skip to various parts of the presentation, or ask for more information about some aspect of the show.

The basic steps for creating a screen show are simple. Just open the spreadsheet that contains the graphs (slides) for the show. Then, type all the graph names in a column of the spreadsheet. Use the next four columns for effects described under "Building a Slide Show Table." Finally, use the Graph-Name-Slide command and specify the range of cells containing graph names and effects. The show will begin as soon as you press Enter.

BUILDING A SLIDE SHOW TABLE

The slide show table contains the names of the slides and the effects you want to add to each. It requires from one to five columns, depending on the effects you want to add. Figure 9-3 on the following page shows a typical slide show table.

USING THE LIST GRAPH NAMES MACRO

1. Install the ProView PowerPack software onto your system.
2. With your spreadsheet in view, select the File-Open command to open the file called LIB_MU1.WQ1, which is located in the QPRO directory.
3. Switch back to your spreadsheet after the new file is opened. To switch back, press Alt with the number of your spreadsheet window.
4. Press Alt-M to activate the special macro.
5. Select List Graph Files from the menu.
6. Press C to continue after reading the message that appears.
7. Select the All option from the menu that appears.
8. Specify a column of cells to contain the graph names. Move to the top cell in the column and press Enter. The macro will enter the graph names beginning at this cell.

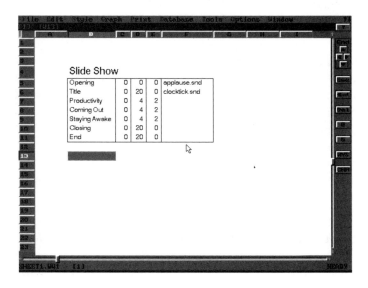

Figure 9-3: A slide show table contains the names of the slides and the transition effects.

Following is a summary of each column in the table:

Column 1: Graph Name

Enter the desired graph names, in order, down the first column. These should match the names listed in the Graph-Name-Display command. Remember that the order of the names determines the order of the slides.

Rather than type each name, try using the "List Graph Names" macro utility provided in the ProView PowerPack. This macro automatically enters the graph names for you. However, do not use this utility if you have more than 15 slides and you are using a 286-based (slow) computer; it's much too slow. To use this utility, you must first install the ProView PowerPack disks onto your system. This adds many graphics and spreadsheet files to the QPRO directory. Then, from within your spreadsheet, open the spreadsheet called LIB_MU1.WQ1 and activate the macro from your spreadsheet with the Alt-M command. See the sidebar steps for complete instructions.

Column 2: Duration

Enter the number of seconds that the slide is to remain in view. Enter 0 to make the slide remain in view until the viewer presses a key or a mouse button. Using the 0 value for all your slides is a good idea when you are projecting the screen to a large audience; it lets you control the duration of each slide as you would control a slide projector. If you're creating a self-running show to be viewed on the screen, consider using the 0 time value for the first and last slides in the show so the viewer can begin the show by pressing a key. (The first slide may contain a message such as "Press Enter to begin the show.") Self-running shows are useful when there is no audience interaction with the show, for example in unsupervised demonstrations.

You can enter values between 0 and 1 to move quickly between slides. This can be used to create crude animation effects. Just create a number of "frames" that combine to show motion. You should use duration values of .1 for these slides—and keep them simple for the animation to look its best. For example, you can make an arrow move across the screen to point to some part of a graph. You may require four slides for this effect—each with the arrow farther along.

Column 3: Transition

Enter the number of the desired transition effect in the third column. Transition effects are numbered 0 through 24 and control the way a slide initially appears on the screen—not the way it goes away. A transition effect entered for the first slide determines how the opening slide comes onto the screen and not the transition between the first and second slides. Effects include:

    0   Instant cut; draws each object on the screen

    1   Instant cut; draws the entire screen at once

    2   Momentary black screen before presenting image

    3   Wipe right

    4   Wipe left

    5   Wipe down

    6   Wipe up

    7   Barn door closing in

8 Barn door opening out

9 Barn door closing top to bottom

10 Barn door opening top to bottom

11 Iris close

12 Iris open

13 Scroll up

14 Scroll down

15 Stripes right

16 Stripes right then left

17 Spiral out

18 Dissolve 1

19 Dissolve 2

20 Dissolve 3

21 Dissolve 4

22 Dissolve 5

23 Dissolve 6

24 Dissolve 7

Use effect 2 to simulate a slide projector changing slides. Dissolves 1 through 7 get faster and larger. You may find dissolves 1 and 2 to be too slow for your transitions.

If you make any of these values negative for the transition effect, Quattro Pro will leave the previous slide on the screen as it adds the new one using the effect. You can use this to create the effect of adding information to an existing slide—without changing slides. For example, suppose you create these two slides.

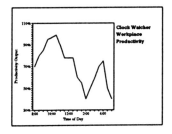 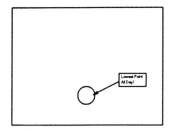

Figure 9-4: Make two slides to create the overlapping effect.

If the second slide follows the first in the list and uses the transition effect –3, the circle will appear to be "drawn" onto the first slide and result in the following.

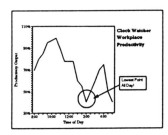

Figure 9-5: Use a negative transition effect number to make the two slides overlap on the screen.

When creating overlapping slides, remember that the second slide should not be a duplicate of the first slide with new information added. Instead, the second slide should contain only the information being added—and it should be in the proper position on the screen. A good way to create an overlap slide is to start with the first slide, add the desired data in the correct position, then delete all the other elements, leaving only the new data. Save this slide under a unique name.

Avoid using too many different effects in the same show, as the effects tend to become a show all by themselves. Use a mixture of wipes and dissolves, and avoid the barn doors and stripes. These flashy effects are more appropriate for casual and less sophisticated shows.

Column 4: Trans Speed

Enter a number from 0 to 16 in column four to indicate the speed of the transition effect. Numbers stand for 70ths of a second, so 16 is the slowest.

Column 5: Sound Effect

Enter the name of the desired sound effect in column five. The sound effects that come with Quattro Pro and the Pro-View PowerPack include the following:

APPLAUSE.SND

FANFARE.SND

CANNONS.SND

THANKS.SND

DRUMS.SND

WOW.SND

These should be located in the QPRO directory. If Quattro Pro cannot locate the specified effect, it will ignore the request. Note that the sound effect occurs as the image is coming onto the screen. You can leave this column blank to omit the effects.

VIEWING THE SHOW

While you are viewing a screen show, you can press the Backspace key to go backward and view a previous slide. Continue to press Backspace to go backward through the slides. Press any other key to move forward again.

If the slides are timed, pressing Backspace will cause the show to go backward through the timed slides. Press any key (except Backspace) to move forward again. If you press Enter during a timed presentation, Quattro Pro will move to the next slide, disregarding the remaining time on the current slide. This is useful for moving quickly through a timed show. If you want to pause during a timed show, press Enter and hold it down. When you release the key, Quattro Pro moves to the next slide. If you press the Backspace key and hold it, Quattro Pro moves to the previous slide when you release the key.

MOVING ON

With Quattro Pro, you have numerous possibilities for your slide and overhead presentations. After creating slides in the Annotator, you can save them as EPS files that can be printed by a service bureau. Or you can display the images on the computer screen and project the show for your audience. Screen shows can also be created as self-running shows that involve interaction. Even if you don't use screen shows, you might find them useful for constructing your slide presentations while the slides are being created at the bureau.

The next section of this book is about design do's and don'ts. You'll see some actual examples of good and bad spreadsheet design and a summary of design rules for future reference.

DESIGN IN ACTION

Design
Do's and Don'ts

10

Throughout this book, you've learned how good design can enhance your presentations and why poor design works against you. In other words, design profoundly affects your message. Although experienced graphic artists can reap results from indulging in iconoclastic experimentation, there are basic devices and techniques that benefit everyone. Conversely, designers should be wary of the pitfalls as well.

It's often easier to understand and apply design do's and don'ts when you see them illustrated. The examples in this book provide a handy visual reference to guide you in your work.

LESS IS MORE

Avoid information overload. Graphs, slides, printed reports all suffer when too much information is coming across at once. Don't put too much data in one graph; use two or a series. Avoid overannotation, especially in slides. Save the explanatory information for your oral comments and handouts. Allow plenty of breathing room on the page or slide. Use only as much text as you need. In short . . . keep it simple.

DON'T FENCE THEM IN

Your presentations are already "contained" within the page or slide boundaries inherent in the medium. So you usually don't need extra borders and boxes around data. Too many lines or frames create clutter and overcrowding.

CALM YOUR COLORS

Avoid placing incompatible colors together, and choose an appropriate color for your slide background. Make all your slides match in their color schemes, and limit colors to three or four that work well together. The eye naturally goes to the brightest thing on the slide, so use bright colors only on important data.

Remember that colors speak louder than patterns and shades, so be equally careful using patterns or shades with colors. Dotted patterns *can* be used to create darker versions of a color.

TAME YOUR TYPE

Fonts, like color, can enhance a presentation. But too many fonts can create chaos. Choose two or three typefaces that work well together, and use them in various sizes and styles for variety. Use contrasting rather than similar typefaces to make your headlines stand out. Sans-serif for headlines and serif for body text combine well.

We'll Beat Any Price!

	Full	Queen	King
Simmons	$349.95	$489.95	$549.95
Serta	$369.95	$499.95	$569.95

We'll Beat Any Price!

	Full	Queen	King
Simmons	$349.95	$489.95	$549.95
Serta	$369.95	$499.95	$569.95

Figure 10-1: When combining typefaces, use one for the headlines and another for the body. Avoid combining similar-looking faces.

For spreadsheets, different sizes and styles of one face can provide enough variety. You can also use boldface and italic to highlight particular information.

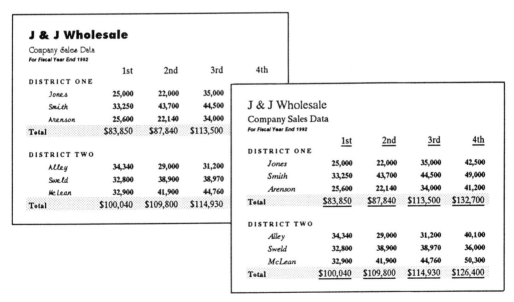

Figure 10-2: Use font styles rather than faces for variety.

THINK BIG

Especially in designing reports, keep the entire page layout in mind. Remember that white space helps make a page easier to read. Use white space in large blocks around the data. Design headers and footers to blend well with all other page elements.

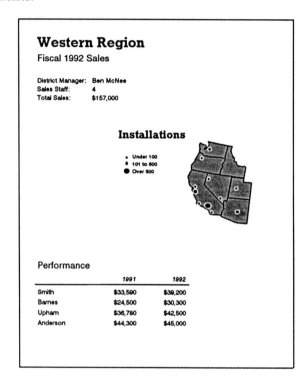

Figure 10-3: White space around the data adds breathing room.

CURB THE CUTE

By all means, use graphics to enhance your pages and slides. But avoid silly or trite images. Simple icons and shapes are appropriate graphic enhancements; but "cute" drawings to illustrate a headline are grossly out of place.

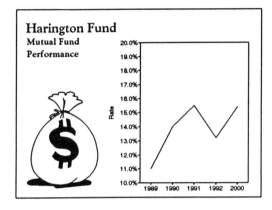
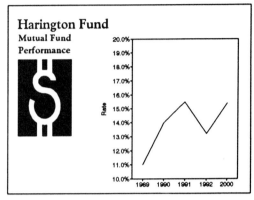

Figure 10-4: Simple is superior.

Often, the best graphic enhancements are blocks of color and shading inserted in strategic locations.

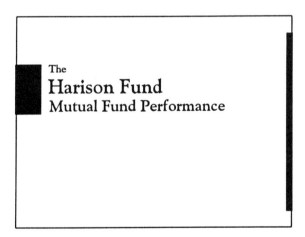

Figure 10-5: Color and shading can be the most effective graphic enhancements.

CASE-SENSITIVITY

Text set in all uppercase letters is difficult to read. Combinations of uppercase and lowercase letters work best, especially for headlines and annotation. Boldface type or larger point sizes are better for providing emphasis than all caps.

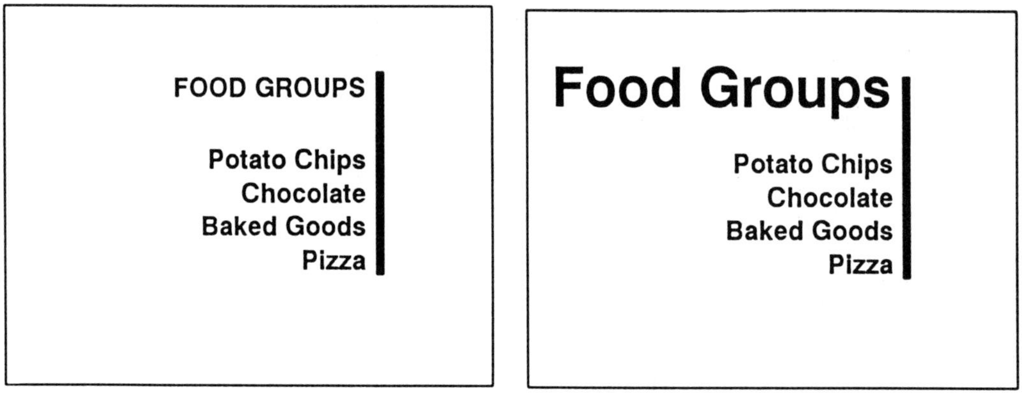

Figure 10-6: Avoid all-uppercase headlines; use boldface or larger type instead.

THEY'LL GET YOUR NUMBER

Numbers and dates must be designed for readability. In many cases, this means avoiding decimal places and unnecessary symbols, such as dollar signs. In a displayed column of values, dollar signs and decimal places can just get in the way.

Date formats that spell out month names are usually comprehended quicker than formats using numbers. Use custom formats, if necessary.

TABLE TALK

READ BETWEEN THE LINES

Use horizontal and vertical lines to make a table more readable and to separate groups of values. But be sure there's
plenty of space on each side of the line. You can insert extra
columns and rows to create more space.

BOLD IS BETTER

The columns in your table may not be wide enough to
include a large heading at the top. The heading will likely
have to be set in the same type size as the contents of the
column. Try using a boldface version of the same font to
make the heading stand out. Or combine bold and italic type.

Transactions

Date	*Number*	*Description*	*Amount*
03/05/92	1001	James & Co.	120.44
03/21/92	1002	Lowell Printing	29.95
04/01/92	1003	RGE	210.34
04/15/92		Deposit	1033.56
04/23/92	1004	Mellin Corp.	12.59

*Figure 10-7: Use boldface and/or italic for column headings
on tables.*

GREAT GRAPHS

KEEP IT SIMPLE

Avoid overloading a graph with too many data series and plot points—especially in a slide. Often, you can use two or more graphs to chart more data items. Line graphs, particularly, look confusing with too many data series.

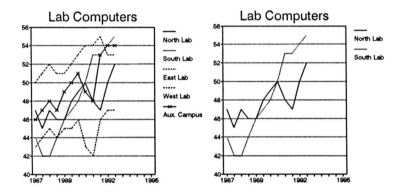

Figure 10-8: Keep data series to a minimum.

SHAPE TO SUIT

You can change a graph's overall proportions using a number of techniques. Many graphs benefit from being tall and narrow. This orientation can also serve to emphasize the fluctuation in the plot points. Changing a graph's proportions in the Annotator creates extra space for annotations.

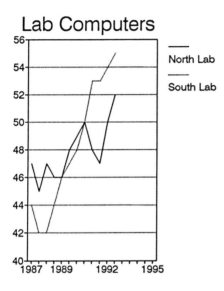

Figure 10-9: Use taller graphs to aid in annotation and emphasize data fluctuation.

SUIT TO FIT

You can often make graphs more attractive by avoiding the default text positions you're limited to with the Graph-Text command. Instead, use the Annotator to add custom text boxes to your graph. You can then move the text to any location you like. This is especially useful for main headings and legends.

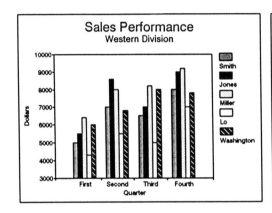 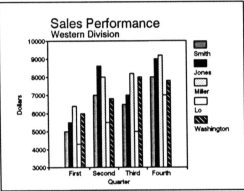

Figure 10-10: Use Annotator text instead of standard headings.

COMMUNICATE

Remember to use the graph type that best communicates the message your data should deliver. Line graphs emphasize fluctuation in data over time. Bar graphs compare items to one another. Stacked graphs show how parts make up a whole over time. Pie graphs are excellent for companywide data. Consider whether your data would benefit from a 3D graph, or if the precise measurements of a 2D graph would be more useful.

AVOID GRIDLOCK

Grid lines can help your graph, but they can also be distracting if overdone. Consider changing your Y-axis scale to control placement of the grid lines. Consider using a subtle color for the grid lines so they don't stand out too much.

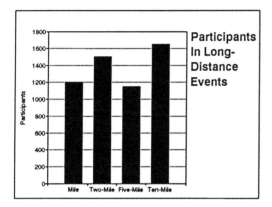
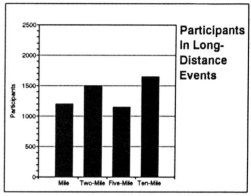

Figure 10-11: Control grid lines by changing the Y-axis scale.

RELIEVE CONGESTION

X-axis labels can easily become overcrowded. You can solve the problem by splitting them onto two lines with the Graph-X Axis-Alternate Ticks Command, or by erasing every other label in the X-axis data series. Other solutions include using smaller fonts and abbreviating.

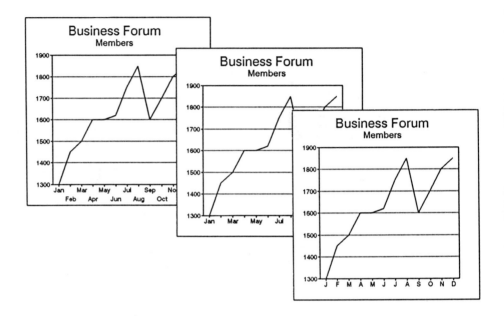

Figure 10-12: Rx for overcrowded X-axis labels.

Overcrowding can be a problem with pie labels as well. One strategy for dealing with the problem is to rearrange the pie slices. You can also omit the values that accompany the labels. Or you can use a legend instead of labels.

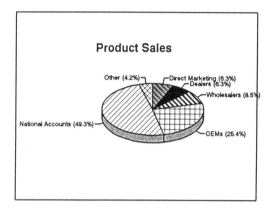 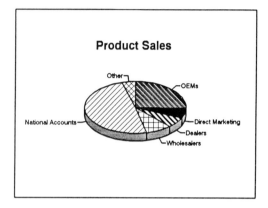

Figure 10-13: Eliminate cramped pie labels.

SLICK SLIDES

SELECT A SCHEME

Design a color and graphic theme for your slides and stick to it throughout your slide show. Most of your slides should repeat common elements. Design consistency will make your audience more comfortable and help to integrate the presentation.

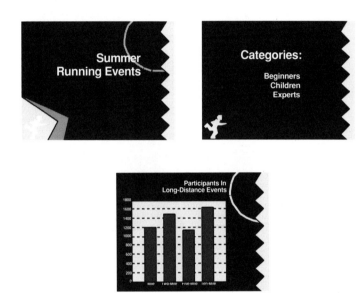

Figure 10-14: Use a color and graphic scheme throughout your slide show.

BEAUTIFY WITH BACKGROUNDS

Add simple graphic backgrounds to your slides for a professional touch. You can create these backgrounds in Quattro Pro's Annotator, or select from predesigned backgrounds. Make sure the selected background uses the desired color scheme and works well with your particular slides. Avoid backgrounds with heavy parallel lines.

MOVING ON

As the old adage says, seeing is believing. Armed with the advice and warnings in this chapter, the next chapter offers a collection of spreadsheet publishing makeovers and design samples that exemplify good design at work.

Makeovers and More

The best way to become a good designer (of anything) is to keep trying. It may seem trite, but practice eventually makes perfect. It also helps to become more observant of others' work. The more you notice, the more discriminating you become in designing your own published pages and presentations.

Each time you happen upon a document that's hard to read or understand, try to analyze where the problems are, where the designer went wrong—and apply your design knowledge.

In this chapter, we'll look at before-and-after examples of graphs, tables, forms, financial reports and slides. In each illustration, you'll be able to recognize the design flaws we focused on in Chapter 10, "Design Do's and Don'ts." In the makeovers, you'll see the results of using Quattro Pro and add-in enhancements along with the principles of good design described and stressed throughout this book.

And keep these examples handy while you work. You may want to refer back to them as a set of checks and balances for your spreadsheet publishing projects.

GRAPHS

ORIGINAL

When a graph has only a few plot points and the change between points is slight, you should look for ways to make the message clear. But a big red arrow is not the way! A combination of effects makes this ho-hum graph say something important.

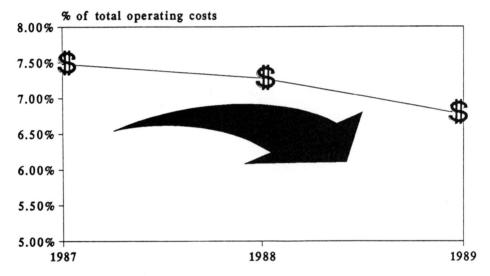

Flight Attendant Costs At United Over the Past 3 Years Have Been Declining As A Percentage of Total Operating Costs

Source: AFA calculations using data from DOT and The Airline Monitor

An explanatory headline is a good thing, but don't overdo it. Keep headlines to a maximum of two lines.

Beware of using trite graphics for series markers or other enhancements; they can make your work look unprofessional.

Keep decimal places to a minimum. You can see that only one decimal place is required here.

MAKEOVER

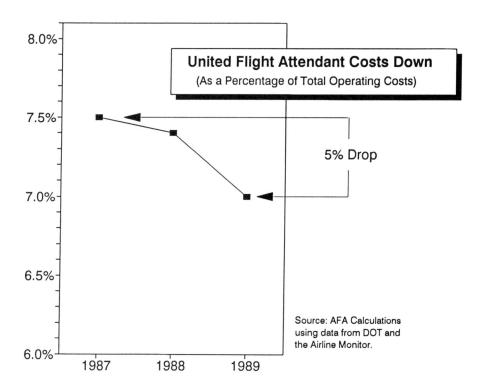

A vertical orientation helps emphasize the downward slope of the line, and provides space for some creative elements on the side. This graph was made taller and narrower in the Annotator by dragging the right edge to the left with the mouse.

The drop is further emphasized with the callout, "5% Drop," and the arrows, all created with the Annotator.

Vertical axis values and tick marks also emphasize the drop in the line. Increasing the low value of the scale by only 1% makes a large difference in the graph's perspective and the slope of the line.

The title is reduced to essential information and placed prominently on the graph. A simple drop shadow sets the title apart. The two title lines are separate text entries placed onto a white rectangle that prints in a light gray shade on a PostScript printer. Finally, the graph itself was moved to the bottom.

GRAPHS

ORIGINAL

A financial newsletter should go for simple, professional-looking effects, not cute graphics that get in the way of the message.

Small data points look taller than they are long when you display them in 3D. This effect also makes the graph more crowded. With so many plot points, simplicity is essential.

Dollar signs don't need to be repeated over and over. Readers will know that values represent dollars.

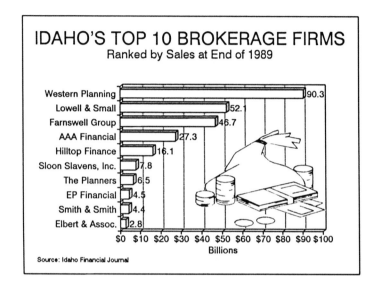

MAKEOVER

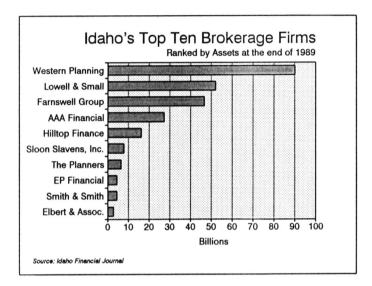

Mixing uppercase and lowercase letters makes the headline more readable and allows room for spelling out the number ten, which gives the headline more dignity.

Shading makes the graph stand out on the page. This is achieved by printing on a PostScript printer.

TABLES

ORIGINAL

Dot leaders make the table easier to read, but all those dots are a strain on the eyes. There are better ways to accomplish the same thing.

IDAHO POTATO GROWTH: 2nd QUARTER 1990

Southern Idaho

	Baking	No Eyes	Boiling	Full Eyes
Bakerstown	23%	71%	3%	3%
Millennium City	13%	77%	7%	3%
City of Production	45%	36%	19%	0%
Tradeville	13%	84%	3%	0%
Crown	29%	57%	13%	10%
Glenville	10%	90%	0%	0%
Metro Area	18%	66%	8%	8%
Lemon County	22%	69%	7%	2%
Oxburg	17%	70%	10%	3%
Paxton	28%	55%	10%	7%
Lakeside	53%	44%	3%	0%
Bernardston	3%	90%	7%	0%
Diablo	37%	57%	6%	0%
Barberville	30%	67%	3%	0%
Clarkston	52%	35%	10%	3%
Marysville	10%	63%	7%	20%
Million Maples	27%	73%	0%	0%
Downland	27%	70%	3%	0%
Van Knees	23%	54%	13%	10%
Wooded Mtn.	13%	80%	7%	0%
TOTAL	24%	65%	7%	4%

Source: Spuds Over America

Northern Idaho

	Baking	No Eyes	Boiling	Full Eyes
Zinfandel	19%	81%	0%	0%
Scaly City	30%	50%	20%	0%
Freemon	34%	63%	3%	0%
Fresca	29%	61%	10%	0%
Strawville	10%	90%	0%	0%
Mercedes	43%	47%	10%	0%
Mudston	43%	50%	7%	0%
Colby County	40%	50%	10%	0%
Pineland	43%	50%	7%	0%
Peaceville	21%	72%	7%	0%
Pimento	44%	44%	10%	2%
Francis Town	18%	65%	6%	11%
Josephville	19%	55%	14%	12%
Matson	24%	66%	7%	3%
DaVinci	16%	55%	3%	26%
Raysville	20%	50%	13%	17%
Cruxton	21%	72%	7%	0%
Roseburg	17%	73%	7%	3%
Stackton	27%	70%	3%	0%
Vickstown	27%	70%	3%	0%
Oak Creek	28%	52%	10%	10%
TOTAL	27%	60%	8%	5%

A column of percentages is acceptable, but when every value in the table is a percentage, the individual % symbols should be removed.

Reader cues are poorly designed. Column headings lack sufficient contrast and separation from list items.

Idaho Potato Growth
Second Quarter 1990

Southern Idaho
Numbers in percentages

	Baking	No Eyes	Boiling	Full Eyes
Bakerstown	23	71	3	3
Millennium City	13	77	7	3
City of Production	45	36	19	0
Tradeville	13	84	3	0
Crown	20	57	13	10
Glenville	10	90	0	0
Metro Area	18	66	8	8
Lemon County	22	69	7	2
Oxburg	17	70	10	3
Paxton	28	55	10	7
Lakeside	53	44	3	0
Bernardston	3	90	7	0
Diablo	37	57	6	0
Barberville	30	67	3	0
Clarkston	52	35	10	3
Marysville	10	63	7	20
Million Maples	27	73	0	0
Downland	27	70	3	0
Van Knees	23	54	13	10
Wooded Mtn.	13	80	7	0
Total	**24**	**65**	**7**	**4**

Source: Spuds Over America

Northern Idaho
Numbers in percentages

	Baking	No Eyes	Boiling	Full Eyes
Zinfandel	19	81	0	0
Scaly City	30	50	20	0
Freemon	34	63	3	0
Fresca	29	61	10	0
Strawville	10	90	0	0
Mercedes	43	47	10	0
Mudston	43	50	7	0
Colby County	40	50	10	0
Pineland	43	50	7	0
Peaceville	21	72	7	0
Pimento	44	44	10	2
Francis Town	18	65	6	11
Josephville	19	55	14	12
Matson	24	66	7	3
Da Vinci	16	55	3	26
Raysville	20	50	13	17
Cruxton	21	72	7	0
Roseburg	17	73	7	3
Stackton	27	70	3	0
Vickstown	27	70	3	0
Oak Creek	28	52	10	10
Total	**27**	**60**	**8**	**5**

Totals are set off from the rest of the table with a black-shaded bar, which balances the shaded bar at the top.

Table titles are set flush-left for easy reading.

Percent symbols have been removed. A notation placed prominently under the heading makes them unnecessary.

Setting the main title in Hammersmith, a Bitstream typeface, distinguishes it from the rest of the text set in Swiss.

Shaded bars give the reader horizontal direction and continuity, without separator lines or dots. If you have a LaserJet printer, you can adjust the shading percentage with the Options-Hardware-Printers-Fonts-LaserJet Fonts-Shading Level command.

FORMS

ORIGINAL

This form lacks good order and organization. Too many boxes and dividing lines create an obstacle course instead of a logical progression for the reader. The form has no bordering white space except the small margin around the edges, making it hard to scan the form for information.

Different-sized boxes are a result of the organization problem.

The Macintosh and IBM check boxes interfere with the layout scheme that separates prices (right) from information (left).

COPIES TO GO
1000 Every St.
Anytown, US

Charge ❑
Cash ❑

Name _____

Phone# _____ Contact _____

Date In _____ Date Due _____ Taken By _____

SELF SERVICE			☐ **Macintosh**	☐ **IBM**
Start	End	Total Time	Hourly Rate	Total Amount
			$12.00	

Laser prints _____ @ _____ ¢ →
Misc: →

LINOTRONIC 300			☐ **Macintosh**	☐ **IBM**
Start	End	Total Time	Hourly Rate	Total Amount
			$22.00	

Misc: →

❑ RC Paper ❑ Film

(8½ x 11) _____ @ $ _____ →

(8½ x 14) _____ @ $ _____ →

(11 x 17) _____ @ $ _____ →

Rush Charge _____ % of $ _____ →

Special Instructions:

Subtotal _____
Tax _____
Total $ _____

MAKEOVER

Organizing the form into neat sections makes it easier to locate the data. Extra white space also helps make the form easy to read. White space is added by inserting extra rows and columns into the form, then modifying their heights and widths.

COPIES TO GO
1000 Every St.
Anytown, US
(212) 555-1234

NAME & ADDRESS

INSTRUCTIONS

SELF-SERVICE

☐ Macintosh ☐ IBM
Start Time
End Time
Total Time   @   10.00
Laser Prints   @   0.60
Misc:

LINOTRONIC 300

☐ Macintosh ☐ IBM
☐ RC Paper   ☐ Film
Start Time
End Time
Total Time   @   20.00
8 1/2 by 11   @ $
8 1/2 by 14   @ $
11 by 17   @ $
Rush Charge   of $
Misc:

TOTALS

☐ Cash ☐ Charge
Date In   Subtotal
Date Due   Tax
Taken By   Total

Vertical alignment and shading of entry boxes make it easy to find and compare information items and prices. These are simply blocks of cells on the spreadsheet.

Prices align uniformly along the right side.

Check boxes were created with the "\blt 0\ Macintosh \blt 0\IBM" bullet entry.

The logo can be pasted in by hand or drawn with a graphics program and moved into Quattro Pro's Annotator via the Clipboard feature.

The headline uses 18-point Broadway from Bitstream. The body type is Bitstream's Baskerville.

FINANCIAL REPORTS: Cover Sheet

ORIGINAL

Report cover sheets can benefit from Quattro Pro's Annotator tools. This cover sheet is too bland. An interesting graphic motif used on the cover and throughout the report would add interest and make the report look more professional.

The simple centered approach isn't bad, but it doesn't exactly make the words jump off the page either.

Emphasis is misplaced here. The company and officer names should be more prominent than the "Confidential" message.

Investor Profile
Travis & Smith

CONFIDENTIAL

Alan Smythe, President & CEO
Thomas G. Harding, Vice President
Edward A. Greenbaum, Secretary

Prepared
May 15, 1991
by Branning & Assoc.
Certified Public Accountants

MAKEOVER

Confidential

Travis & Smith Investor Profile

Prepared for internal use
by Branning & Assoc.
Certified Public Accountants

May 15, 1991
(Without the benefit of audit)

Alan Smythe
President & Chief Executive Officer

Thomas G. Harding
Vice President

Edward A. Greenbaum
Secretary

This graphic image was produced entirely in the Annotator with the black-and-white printout in mind. Therefore, only patterns—not colors—were considered. However, this would make an excellent color printout.

After combining the objects within the box, white rectangles are placed adjacent to the box on all four sides, to cover the parts of the objects that extend outside the box. The image was then inserted into the spreadsheet and the rest of the page designed around it.

Futura Extra Bold gives the main headings some punch while still being businesslike. The extra-bold type projects a feeling of power that's appropriate for financial reports. It also combines well with Swiss and Swiss Bold.

Row heights were adjusted to provide breathing room between the names.

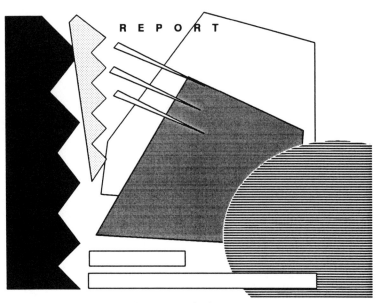

Figure 11-1: Objects used to create the image.

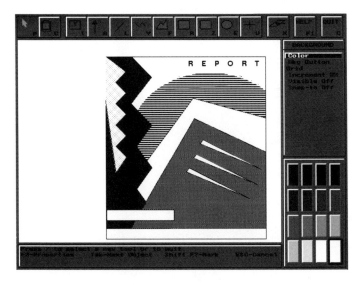

Figure 11-2: The completed image inside the Annotator.

If this report were given as a slide show, much of the detail could be left to the oral presentation. The slides would contain only the essential information. Each officer would be presented on a separate slide.

FINANCIAL REPORTS: Balance Sheet

ORIGINAL

Although this balance sheet looks acceptable, it doesn't stand out. Combine a few broken rules with dull, lifeless design, and the report is a loser. Fonts and a simple graphic theme will be put to use here.

Dollar signs and decimal values are not needed for every value on this form.

Totals don't stand out. Actually, nothing on this report stands out, including the company name.

BALANCE SHEET
Pacific Production, Inc.

Prepared for period ending: 12/31/90	by: Alan Engle, CPA

ASSETS

Cash & Cash Equivalent	$56,893.34
Gross Receivables	$108,479.12
Less Allowance for Bad Debt	$5,423.96
Net Receivables	$103,055.16
Inventory	$23,899.98
Supplies	$5,023.00
Marketable Securities	$0.00
Other Current Assets	$3,890.49
Total Current Assets	$192,761.97
Land	$50,000.00
Buildings	$0.00
Machinery and Equipment	$208,670.98
Furniture and Fixtures	$5,489.00
Leasehold Improvements	$0.00
Vehicles	$25,000.00
Other Fixed Assets	$0.00
Plant & Equipment	$389,000.00
Less Accumulated Depreciation	$6,490.34
Net Fixed Assets	$382,509.66
Notes Receivable	$0.00
Investments	$0.00
Deferred Expenses	$0.00
Intangibles	$6,500.00
Other Assets	$3,000.00
Total Other Non-Current Assets	$9,500.00
TOTAL ASSETS	$584,771.63

LIABILITIES

Short-Term Notes Payable	$58,900.55
Notes Payable	$5,400.00
Current Portion Long-Term Debt	$20,525.99
Accounts Payable	$109,625.23
Accrued Expenses	$0.00
Income & Other Taxes Payable	$0.00
Other Current Liabilities	$0.00

MAKEOVER

Pacific Productions, Inc.
Balance Sheet
For period ending 12/31/90
by: Alan Engle, CPA

Assets		
Cash & Cash Equivalent	$	56,893
Gross Receivables		108,479
Less Allowance for Bad Debt		5,424
Net Receivables		103,055
Inventory		23,900
Supplies		5,023
Marketable Securities		0
Other Current Assets		3,890
Total Current Assets		**192,762**
Land		50,000
Buildings		0
Machinery and Equipment		208,671
Furniture and Fixtures		5,489
Leasehold Improvements		0
Vehicles		25,000
Other Fixed Assets		0
Plant & Equipment		389,000
Less Accumulated Depreciation		6,490
Net Fixed Assets		**382,510**
Notes Receivable		0
Investments		0
Deferred Expenses		0
Intangibles		6,500
Other Assets		3,000
Total Other Non-Current Assets		**9,500**
TOTAL ASSETS	**$**	**584,772**

A combination of Swiss and Goudy Old Style type gives the page more eye appeal and distinguishes it from other financial reports.

Main headings are separated from the body to make them stand out and to break up the page. Important totals are highlighted with a simple gray shade, while less important totals are set in boldface. These simple refinements make the page more interesting.

Simple graphic elements will be used consistently for all the reports in this presentation, and will serve to make the company name more memorable. In this case, the company name is more prominent than the report title.

ORIGINAL

If possible, the balance sheet should be kept to a single page. If that's not possible, then the pages should have some uniformity. Page 2 should not look like it ended up in the wrong document.

The unrelieved monotony of Page 1 continues on the second page.

The all-important bottom line is given no emphasis to set it off.

Total Current Liabilities	$194,451.77
Long-Term Debt, Trade	$0.00
Long-Term Debt, Bank	$233,564.00
Subordinated Debt	$98,565.30
Other Non-Current Liabilities	$0.00
Total Non-Current Liabilities	$332,129.30
Less: Treasury Stock	$0.00
Common Stock	$0.00
Paid In Capital	$0.00
Retained Earnings	$27,300.00
Other Equity	$0.00
Interim Profit & Loss	$30,890.56
Total Equity	$58,190.56
TOTAL LIABILITIES & NET WORTH	$584,771.63

MAKEOVER

Liabilities		
Short-Term Notes Payable	$	58,901
Notes Payable		5,400
Current Portion Long-Term Debt		20,526
Accounts Payable		109,625
Accrued Expenses		0
Income & Other Taxes Payable		0
Other Current Liabilities		0
Total Current Liabilities		**194,452**
Long-Term Debt, Trade		0
Long-Term Debt, Bank		233,564
Subordinated Debt		98,565
Other Non-Current Liabilities		0
Total Non-Current Liabilities		**332,129**
Equity		
Less: Treasury Stock		0
Common Stock		0
Paid In Capital		0
Retained Earnings		27,300
Other Equity		0
Interim Profit & Loss		30,891
Total Equity		**58,191**
TOTAL LIABILITIES & NET WORTH	**$**	**584,772**

Dollar signs placed only on first and last lines are sufficient.

Separation and distinguishing type styles organize and prioritize the information.

FINANCIAL REPORTS

ORIGINAL

Too many lines and boxes "imprison" the data in this report. As part of the total financial report, it should tie in with the Balance Sheet, but it seems to have nothing in common.

DOLLAR & PERCENT CHANGES

	Date:	12/31/89		12/31/90		12/31/91	
	Changes:	$$$$	%%%	$$$$	%%%	$$$$	%%%
ASSETS:							
Total Current Assets		100	7.9%	82	6.6%	78	5.5%
Accounts Receivable		20	7.6%	38	11.6%	(38)	-9.8%
Inventory		179	22.5%	90	9.4%	100	13.5%
Net Fixed Assets		(300)	-30.0%	10	2.6%	(55)	-10.0%
Other Non-Current Assets		(48)	-99.0%	91	89.0%	164	125.0%
Total Assets		(250)	-12.5%	181	10.1%	189	7.9%
LIABILITIES & NET WORTH:							
Total Current Liabilities		(60)	-410.0%	(504)	-39.4%	171	22.3%
Notes Payable		(180)	-19.5%	(460)	-55.0%	36	12.4%
Accounts Payable		145	44.8%	15	3.6%	80	17.5%
Current Portion LTD		(32)	-49.0%	9	35.8%	(4)	-14.2%
Total Non-Current Liabilities		225	63.4%	772	90.7%	(126)	-10.7%
Long Term Debt		(38)	-33.9%	389	523.0%	(28)	-5.9%
Subordinated Debt		250	108.0%	368	66.2%	(101)	-12.1%
Total Liabilities		167	10.0%	259	12.9%	32	1.1%
Total Net Worth		(412)	-90.2%	(80)	-258.0%	155	-302.3%
Retained Earnings		(412)	-91.2%	(80)	-200.4%	155	-229.7%
INCOME STATEMENT:							
Net Sales		(20)	-0.6%	589	24.7%	459	12.3%
Cost of Good Sold		(111)	-5.1%	552	35.1%	22	1.6%
Gross Profit		84	7.7%	30	2.1%	422	36.4%
Operating Expenses		88	5.5%	(290)	-20.0%	169	14.2%
Operating Income		(2)	1.3%	278	-69.1%	255	-189.6%
Net Profit Before Tax		(32)	9.4%	212	-75.4%	224	-229.9%
Net Profit After Tax		(34)	9.3%	225	-77.5%	228	-229.9%

Vertical lines are too close to the data. An extra column is needed for spacing.

The monotonous columns of numbers in small type invite the reader to ignore them.

MAKEOVER

Pacific Production, Inc.
Dollar & Percent Changes
Three-Year Composit

		Dec 89		Dec 90		Dec 91	
		$	%	$	%	$	%
Assets	Total Current Assets	100	7.9%	82	6.6%	78	5.5%
	Accounts Receivable	20	7.6%	38	11.6%	(38)	-9.8%
	Inventory	179	22.5%	90	9.4%	100	13.5%
	Net Fixed Assets	(300)	-30.0%	10	2.6%	(55)	-10.0%
	Other Non-Current Assets	(48)	-99.0%	91	89.0%	164	125.0%
	Total Assets	(250)	-12.5%	181	10.1%	189	7.9%
Liabilities	Total Current Liabilities	(60)	-410.0%	(504)	-39.4%	171	22.3%
& Net Worth	Notes Payable	(180)	-19.5%	(460)	-55.0%	36	12.4%
	Accounts Payable	145	44.8%	15	3.6%	80	17.5%
	Current Portion LTD	(32)	-49.0%	9	35.8%	(4)	-14.2%
	Total Non-Current Liabilities	225	63.4%	772	90.7%	(126)	-10.7%
	Long Term Debt	(38)	-33.9%	389	523.0%	(28)	-5.9%
	Subordinated Debt	250	108.0%	368	66.2%	(101)	-12.1%
	Total Liabilities	167	10.0%	259	12.9%	32	1.1%
	Total Net Worth	(412)	-90.2%	(80)	-258.0%	155	-302.3%
	Retained Earnings	(412)	-91.2%	(80)	-200.4%	155	-229.7%
Income Statement	Net Sales	(20)	-0.6%	589	24.7%	459	12.3%
	Cost of Good Sold	(111)	-5.1%	552	35.1%	22	1.6%
	Gross Profit	84	7.7%	30	2.1%	422	36.4%
	Operating Expenses	88	5.5%	(290)	-20.0%	169	14.2%
	Operating Income	(2)	1.3%	278	-69.1%	255	-189.6%
	Net Profit Before Tax	(32)	9.4%	212	-75.4%	224	-229.9%
	Net Profit After Tax	(34)	9.3%	225	-77.5%	228	-229.9%

The identity graphic ties this report with the other pages in the financial package. It also keeps the company name in front of the reader.

Other graphic devices, such as the headings and shades, are in keeping with the presentation's overall design scheme.

Dates are much easier to read in this format.

A small blank column eases the tension on the right side of each section.

The landscape orientation allows a more natural layout for this data.

Removing the border gives you freedom to emphasize important information in this report.

SLIDES

ORIGINAL

If you create a bar graph in Quattro Pro without doing much customization, this is pretty much what you'd get. This composition suffers from crowding, weak headings and general clutter.

The 3D effect is unnecessary in this graph.

X-axis and Y-axis titles are not required with such a simple message.

Refrain from using patterns in slides. Instead, rely on colors to communicate. Even in black and white, this example is improved by eliminating the pattern.

The boxed-in heading is too small and weak.

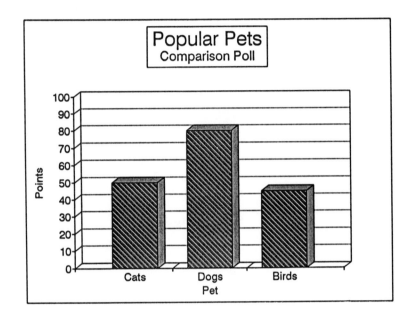

MAKEOVER

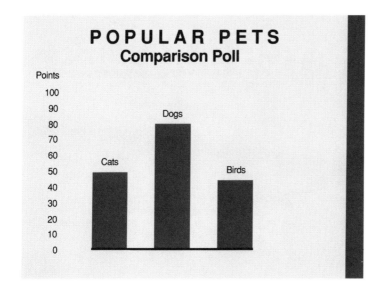

POPULAR PETS
Comparison Poll

A line is added manually to create a baseline.

The headline is enlarged and set in bold type for a stronger effect.

A simple graphic element adds interest and balance to the composition.

Most of the lines, borders and boxes were removed in this version of the graph, including the grid lines. The graph is so simple that these elements are not required. The grid lines are given the same color as the background—which makes them invisible.

SLIDES

ORIGINAL

This slide is trying too hard to get your attention. While it may communicate the message, it looks amateurish.

All-uppercase letters make for slow reading.

The title crowds the slide by not leaving enough blank space on all sides.

Shouting the company name is overkill. There are better ways to make the name stand out.

MAKEOVER

The company name is spoken softly here, but it's still quite prominent on the slide.

The right graphics help to communicate the message.

Leaving space on all sides and mixing uppercase and lowercase letters relieves the pressure and leads the eye to the text.

A sentence headline communicates the message instantly.

An eye-catching background gets more attention than large uppercase type.

GRAPHS

ORIGINAL

Here's an example of using a graph type that's inappropriate for the data. Comparing a change in values over time is best handled by a line graph. In addition to changing the graph type, the makeover simplifies and streamlines the design.

X-axis labels are cramped. These should be alternated or abbreviated.

The headline could use some punch. A different font or a bolder version would do the trick.

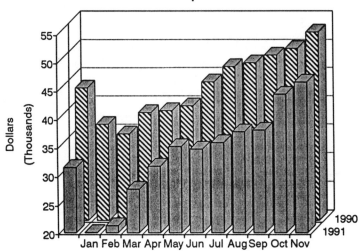

MAKEOVER

A custom Y-axis scale makes the lines fit comfortably in the chart. On the Y-axis line, tick marks between increment points show intermediate values.

Simple annotation is used instead of a legend.

A subtle background adds interest and a contemporary look to the slide. The graph was resized slightly to allow more room for the background element.

Months along the X-axis are reduced to initial caps— a solution that works well with month names.

The bold italic type strengthens the headline. Placing it flush with the right edge of the chart draws attention to it.

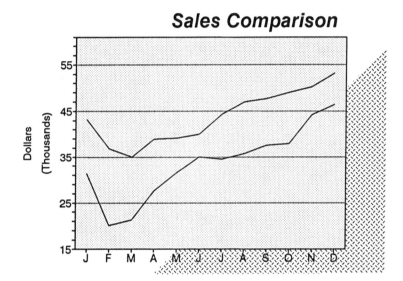

Sales Comparison

PARTING THOUGHTS

Improving your spreadsheets and graphs does not require a great deal of design expertise—just an awareness of design pitfalls. By applying the basic advice offered in this chapter, you can dramatically enhance your presentations.

Go ahead and copy the designs and formats offered in Chapter 10. Also, refer back to the makeovers in this chapter and study the design elements that add to the overall appearance of the documents. (Remember that many of the examples in this book are included as templates on the accompanying diskette.) Pretty soon, well-designed spreadsheets and graphs will flow from your computer.

Quattro Pro in tandem with some basic design knowledge gives you all the tools you need to be a prolific spreadsheet publisher.

Resources

••••

••••

For additional information and tools that will enhance your Quattro Pro presentations, here's a list of resources, some of which were used in preparing this book. The field of spreadsheet publishing is rich with resources, so you'll probably be able to add to this list immediately.

BOOKS

Envisioning Information, Edward Tufte. 1990. Graphics Press. P.O. Box 430, Cheshire, CT 06410. (203)272-9187.

A general design book for information display. Not specifically related to computer graphics, this book is still a good reference for design and information display.

Looking Good in Print, Second Edition, Roger C. Parker. 1990. Ventana Press. P.O. Box 2468, Chapel Hill, NC 27515. (919)942-0220.

The definitive guide to desktop publishing design. This book shows you how to create attractive, persuasive desktop-published pages. Much of the information and illustration pertains equally to spreadsheet publishing. Includes makeovers and resources.

••••

The Presentation Design Book, edited by Margaret Y. Rabb. 1990. Ventana Press. P.O. Box 2468, Chapel Hill, NC 27515. (919)942-0220.

A good generic book about designing, producing and setting up presentation media. Text and examples on how to create effective slides, overheads and screen shows are clear and well-thought-out. The chapter on color is particularly interesting. This book is not software-specific; some of the examples will not apply to Quattro Pro.

Quattro Pro in Business, Christopher Van Buren & Mark Shmagin. 1991. Howard W. Sams. P.O. Box 90, Carmel, IN 46032. (317)573-2500.

Not a design book but an intermediate-to-advanced guide to Quattro Pro for business applications. (Just a plug from the author.)

Visual Display of Quantitative Information, Edward Tufte. 1983. Graphics Press. P.O. Box 430, Cheshire, CT 06410. (203)272-9187.

A guide to displaying numeric information graphically. Gives additional information and techniques for presenting numeric reports and graphs. (Because this isn't a software-related book, some of its examples are not applicable to Quattro Pro.)

Using Quattro Pro 3.0, Stephen Cobb. 1991. Osborne/ McGraw-Hill. 2600 Tenth St., Berkeley, CA 94710. (800)227-0900.

This is the "official" Borland book on Quattro Pro 3.0; it carries the Borland seal of approval. The entire Version 3.0 program and numerous illustrations are included.

NEWSLETTERS/PUBLICATIONS

Christopher Van Buren's Software Newsletter. P.O. Box 117144, Burlingame, CA 94010.

A compilation of tips and tricks for various software packages, including many relating to Quattro Pro. Also contains commentaries, information about new computer books and miscellaneous flotsam. Free sample.

Inside Quattro Pro. The Cobb Group, P.O. Box 35160, Louisville, KY 40232-9719. (502)491-1900.

A monthly newsletter dedicated to Quattro Pro. Some beginner information, but mostly intermediate and advanced. Somewhat dry, but always informative. Much on macros. An occasional article on spreadsheet publishing. Answers reader questions. Documents complex Quattro Pro operations. Subscriptions are $59 for 12 issues.

TEMPLATES/MACROS/PROGRAMS

Borland International, Inc.
1800 Green Hills Rd.
Scotts Valley, CA 95067-0001
(408)438-5300 or 438-8400
ProView PowerPack

This package is designed specifically for spreadsheet publishing tasks. It includes two extra typefaces (good for headlines), several sample slides with backgrounds, numerous clip-art files from MGI, some useful macros and a color booklet on designing slides. This package is included in Quattro Pro 3.0 if you purchase it straight off the shelf. If you upgrade, the ProView PowerPack is not included, but you can purchase it for $59. This package is mentioned often in this book.

CompuServe
P.O. Box 20212
Columbus, OH 43220
(800)848-8990

Borland's application forum on CompuServe is a useful tool for getting questions answered and general networking with other Quattro Pro users. Forum topics include Quattro Pro (general), Quattro Pro Printing and Quattro Pro Macros. Many useful files are available in the forum's library section.

SERVICE BUREAUS

Brilliant Image
Seven Penn Plaza
New York, NY 10001
(212)736-9661

These are the folks who advertise in the Quattro Pro package, so they're familiar with Quattro Pro EPS and Slide EPS files. The first $100 of slide services are free, so use them to experiment and become familiar with the process. Make your mistakes on their tab.

Colossal Graphics
437 Emerson St.
Palo Alto, CA 94301
(415)328-2264

This bureau will take your EPS file and print it in color at a whopping 24 by 36 inches. Actually, they can print the thing out the size of a billboard if you want. If you need large color graphics for flip charts, trade-show booths or other presentations, this service may save you a bundle. A single poster-sized printout is about $70—not bad.

Impact Graphics
751 Laurel St., #120
San Carlos, CA 94070
(415)941-9913

This company produced many of the color slides in this book. Although they were unfamiliar with Quattro Pro when I started, they have the hang of it now. If you live in the Pacific Northwest and like working with firms in your area, consider this company.

Laser Express
7826 Convoy Court
San Diego, CA 92111
(619)694-0204

Laser Express, San Diego's premier service bureau, offers full Macintosh and PC service. They can handle just about anything, including Quattro Pro EPS files, for which they charge about $12 per slide (call for a price list). They can also handle your special needs. Establish an account, then send files on disk.

McLain Imaging
2043 Westcliff Dr., #108
Newport Beach, CA 92660
(800)457-4020

This service is quite experienced at Quattro Pro EPS and Slide EPS files. They charge $8 per slide and accept files through the mail, over CompuServe E-mail (75066,1257), or over their own BBS system.

FONTS

Bitstream Inc.
215 First St.
Cambridge, MA 02142
(617)497-6222

If you can afford it, stick with Bitstream fonts for your non-PostScript printer and Quattro Pro. You can also find Bitstream fonts to match your PostScript printer's built-in fonts. Imitations are available if you're interested in saving money, but you can't go wrong with Bitstream.

GRAPHICS

Islandview/MGI
6502 Dickens Place
Richmond, VA 23230
(804)673-5601

PicturePak™ clip-art images by Islandview/MGI come in CGM format on disk and can be used directly with Quattro Pro. Many MGI images are included with Quattro Pro and more come with the ProView PowerPack disks. A few more can be found on this book's companion disk. If you use clip art, write to MGI for a catalog.

Index

Clip-art 164–167, 228–229
  CGM files 141, 165, 168
  importing 165
Clipboard tool 140, 150–151,
    155–156, 165
  See also Annotator.
Color 3–6, 14–15, 234–242
  background 14–15, 148–149,
      158, 215, 241–242
  changing 14
  changing in Annotator 16,
      148–149
  combining 16
  foreground 149, 158
Columns
  width 7, 25–28, 114, 174,
      185, 193

D

Data series
  See Graphs.
Databases 171, 177
Dates
  entering 24-25
  formatting 7, 40–42
  serial numbers 24
Design 19–20, 171–187,
    213–243
  pitfalls 21, 172, 261–275, 302
Desktop 14, 16
Display modes 10–13
  CHR 13
  screen preview 7, 114
  switching 13
  text 12
  WYSIWYG 8, 10–11

Drawing 8, 137–139, 141–144,
    150, 159, 245, 264
Drop shadows 9, 159–161, 178,
    279
  See also Annotator.

E

Editing 8
EGA 5, 10–11, 15–17, 113
EPS files
  See slides.

F

Fast Graph command 50–51
Fill patterns
  See Patterns.
Fonts 7–8, 18–19, 105–136
  adding 120
  applying to spreadsheets 112–
      113
  bitmapped 110–111, 117
  Bitstream 7, 32, 116–117,
      120–122, 128–133
  boldface 122, 180
  building 117–119
  built-in 6–7, 105, 115, 126–
      128, 130–133, 136
  cartridge 18, 126, 133
  changing 112–113
  choosing 120
  Courier 116, 119, 127, 129,
      131, 133, 136, 186, 248
  default 112, 114, 122

titles 54, 156, 168
type 47, 51–53, 57, 65–104,
      139, 223, 246, 270, 300
X-axis 49–50, 52–54, 61–62,
      65, 71, 75, 77–78, 84,
      91, 223, 272, 296, 300–
      301
Y-axis 8, 47, 49–50, 52, 54,
      57, 60–61, 75, 77, 91, 96–
      97, 223, 271, 296, 301
Gray shades 17, 55, 189, 206,
    210–212, 279, 291
Grids
    See Annotator.

H

Handouts 20, 222, 224, 226,
    231–232, 261
Headings 14, 20, 26, 35, 50–51,
    122, 125, 135, 163, 171–177,
    185–186, 190, 192–193, 200,
    222, 267, 270, 282–283, 287,
    291, 295–296
Headlines 4, 9, 107, 125, 173,
    215, 218–222, 231, 246,
    262–264, 266, 278, 281, 285,
    297, 299–301

I

Icons 141, 264
Illustrations 94, 113, 138–141,
    152, 156, 165–166, 168, 229,
    246
    See also Clip-art.
    See also Graphics.

Interaction 4–6, 8, 231, 233,
    245, 251, 253, 257
Italic
    See Fonts.

L

LaserJet
    See Printers.
Leading
    See Line spacing.
Legends 54, 62–64
Letterspacing 110
Lines 7–8, 42–45, 144
    style 56–57, 67, 71, 79, 108,
      140
Line spacing 9, 30
Lists 221–222
Logos 138, 141, 180, 183–184,
    285

M

Macros 8–10, 251–252
Menus 14–16, 138, 190,
    200–201, 203, 227
Modes 10–14
    Draft 118, 121, 128, 133
    Final 118, 121, 128, 133
    See also Display modes.
    See also Printing, modes.
Monitor
    black-and-white 5, 15, 17
    color 5, 16
Monospaced 32

V

VGA 5, 10, 15–17

W

White space 3, 5, 7, 20, 264, 284–285
WYSIWYG
  See Display modes.

X

X-axis
See Graphs.
X-axis labels 52

Y

Y-axis
  See Graphs.

Z

Zoom 9, 134

the
Ventana Press

Desktop Design Series

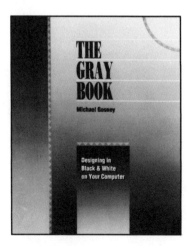

Newsletters from the Desktop
$23.95
306 pages, Illustrated
ISBN: 0-940087-40-5

Now the millions of desktop publishers who produce newsletters can learn how to improve the design of their publications.

The Makeover Book: 101 Design Solutions for Desktop Publishing
$17.95
282 pages, Illustrated
ISBN: 0-940087-20-0

"Before-and-after" desktop publishing examples demonstrate how basic design revisions can dramatically improve a document.

Type from the Desktop
$23.95
290 pages, Illustrated
ISBN: 0-940087-45-6

Learn the basics of designing with type from a desktop publisher's perspective.

Looking Good in Print, Second Edition
$23.95
410 pages, Illustrated
ISBN: 0-940087-32-4

With over 100,000 in print, **Looking Good in Print** is looking even better. More makeovers, a new section on designing newsletters and a wealth of new design tips and techniques to broaden the design skills of the ever-growing number of desktop publishers.

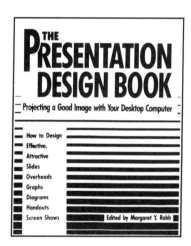

The Presentation Design Book
$24.95
258 pages, Illustrated
ISBN: 0-940087-37-5

How to design effective, attractive slides, overheads, graphs, diagrams, handouts and screen shows with your desktop computer.

The Gray Book
$22.95
224 pages, Illustrated
ISBN: 0-940087-50-2

This "idea gallery" is filled with tips, techniques and visual cues for creating the most interesting black, white and gray graphic effects from laser printers, scanners and high-resolution output devices.

Harvard Graphics Design Companion
$21.95
300 pages, Illustrated
ISBN: 0-940087-78-2

An instructive companion guide to the dozens of Harvard Graphics tutorials, this book explores the graphic design capabilities of the software.

TO ORDER additional copies of *Spreadsheet Publishing With Quattro Pro* or other Ventana Press books, please fill out this order form and return it to us for quick shipment.

	Quantity	Price		Total
Spreadsheet Publishing With Quattro Pro	_____	× $21.95	=	$_____
Looking Good in Print	_____	× $23.95	=	$_____
The Gray Book	_____	× $22.95	=	$_____
Type From the Desktop	_____	× $23.95	=	$_____
The Makeover Book	_____	× $17.95	=	$_____
The Presentation Design Book	_____	× $24.95	=	$_____
Staying With DOS	_____	× $22.95	=	$_____
Newsletters From the Desktop	_____	× $23.95	=	$_____
Harvard Graphics Design Companion	_____	× $21.95	=	$_____

Shipping: Please add $4.10/first book for standard UPS, $1.35/book thereafter; $7.50/book UPS "two-day air," $2.25/book thereafter. For Canada, add $8.10/book.   = $_____

Send C.O.D. (add $3.75 to shipping charges)   = $_____

North Carolina residents add 5% sales tax   = $_____

                                        Total = $_____

Name _____

Company _____

Address (No P.O. Box)_____

City _____ State _____ Zip_____

Daytime Phone _____

_____ Payment enclosed (check or money order; no cash please)

_____VISA _____ MC   Acc't # _____ - _____ - _____ - _____

Expiration date _____ Signature_____

Please mail or fax to:

Ventana Press, P.O. Box 2468, Chapel Hill, NC 27515

919/942-0220, FAX: 919/942-1140

TO ORDER additional copies of *Spreadsheet Publishing With Quattro Pro* or other Ventana Press books, please fill out this order form and return it to us for quick shipment.

	Quantity	Price		Total
Spreadsheet Publishing With Quattro Pro	_____	× $21.95	=	$_____
Looking Good in Print	_____	× $23.95	=	$_____
The Gray Book	_____	× $22.95	=	$_____
Type From the Desktop	_____	× $23.95	=	$_____
The Makeover Book	_____	× $17.95	=	$_____
The Presentation Design Book	_____	× $24.95	=	$_____
Staying With DOS	_____	× $22.95	=	$_____
Newsletters From the Desktop	_____	× $23.95	=	$_____
Harvard Graphics Design Companion	_____	× $21.95	=	$_____

Shipping: Please add $4.10/first book for standard UPS, $1.35/book thereafter; $7.50/book UPS "two-day air," $2.25/book thereafter. For Canada, add $8.10/book.   = $_____

Send C.O.D. (add $3.75 to shipping charges)   = $_____

North Carolina residents add 5% sales tax   = $_____

                                                                 Total   = $_____

Name _____

Company _____

Address (No P.O. Box)_____

City _____ State _____ Zip_____

Daytime Phone _____

_____ Payment enclosed (check or money order; no cash please)

____VISA   ____ MC   Acc't # _____ - _____ - _____ - _____

Expiration date _____   Signature _____

Please mail or fax to:

Ventana Press, P.O. Box 2468, Chapel Hill, NC 27515

919/942-0220, FAX: 919/942-1140

QUATTRO YOUR PRODUCTIVITY

Why re-invent the pie chart? The *Spreadsheet Publishing With Quattro Pro Companion Diskette* offers you numerous files and utilities that can dramatically enhance your spreadsheet publishing projects, including

* PicturePak™ clip-art by Islandview/MGI
* Predesigned spreadsheet and slide templates
* Macros for screen shows
* Font-downloading tool

The disk also contains slide backgrounds to add pizazz to your slide presentations, fonts and many time-saving features. All disks are IBM-compatible.

To order, please complete the coupon below and return to

Ventana Press
P.O. Box 2468
Chapel Hill, NC 27515
(919)942-0220

For faster service, fax us: (800)877-7955

Yes, please send _____ copy/copies of the *Spreadsheet Publishing With Quattro Pro Companion Diskette* at $39.95 per diskette. Add $3.60/diskette for normal UPS shipping. Add $6.00/diskette for UPS "two-day air." NC residents add 5% sales tax. Prompt shipment guaranteed.

Please check one: ___5¼" ___3½" (Disks are IBM-compatible only.)

Name _____

Company _____

Address (no P.O. Box) _____

City_____State_____ Zip_____

Daytime telephone _____

____ Payment enclosed (check or money order; no cash please)

____ Charge my VISA/MC Acc't # _____

Exp. Date_____Interbank # _____

Signature _____

Ventana Press, P.O. Box 2468, Chapel Hill, NC 27515 • (919)942-0220